DREAM TEAM

DREAM TEAM

BY

MICHAEL LETENDRE

INTRODUCTION

Mike Letendre is easily the premiere sportswriter in Bristol and one of the best in Connecticut. As for Bristol, he might be considered the Grantland Rice of Bristol sports, or in the present era, the Bob Ryan or Rick Reilly of local sports coverage. Miss an important high school or legion game, there really has been only one place to look for a complete reporting of the even-Mike. He tells what happened, relates the emotions, and provides context for the ups and downs. Not only that, over the years, he has developed relationships with Bristol coaches and players, and they all know he will be honest and fair in what he reports.

Mike has been writing about scholastic sports in Bristol since 1998. He started by freelancing for the *Bristol Today*, the *Plainville Observer*, the *Bristol Press*, and then the *Bristol Observer* before starting *The Bristol Edition* in 2020. A multi-taker, Mike not only covers a football, basketball, or baseball game, but he also compiles all the statistical data that is included in each article. Besides covering local high school sports events, Mike has served as the players' coordinator for the Bristol American Legion baseball team from 2005-2007 and covered the sport in print since 1999, starting with the Bristol Today.

In 2017, he won the 2017 Connecticut American Legion Baseball Media Award for his coverage of Post 2 in the Bristol Observer and earned a citation from the legion program for his work in 2016. He also did a weekday scholastic sports minute for Bristol Beat Radio in 2017 and has performed as a sideline football reporter for Nutmeg TV over the years. Mike worked in the Sports Information Department at New Hampshire College and established one at Notre Dame College (Manchester, New Hampshire) in 1998.

Mike graduated from Bristol Eastern High School in the class of 1994 and earned his degree in Sports Management from New Hampshire College in 1998. Mike and his wife, Danielle were married in 2006 and have a son, Asa, who is five years old. Mike's father, Herve Letendre, frequently handles the photography aspect of Mike's coverage, as the love of sports is a family affair for the Letendres.

The thing about all of this is that Mike's reporting is not his full-time job. He has been an employee of the Crowley Auto Group since 1999 and has managed the Crowley Kia Parts department since 2002.

We at The Bristol Edition have been honored to have Mike publish his articles in our on-line community newspaper for the past three years. In another time, when print journalism was thriving in the United States, I truly believe Mike Letendre would have been scooped up by some major sports news organization like the Associated Press, the *Boston Globe*, or the *Washington Post*. Instead, we are so lucky to have him in Bristol.

This book covering the accomplishments of the Bristol Central boys' basketball team, shows the passion Mike brings to every assignment. Enjoy as you sit down to relive a glorious season.

Jack Krampitz,

President, Bristol Sports Hall of Fame

Contributing editor, The Bristol Edition

<u>SECTIONS</u>

The one chance to knock off the boys basketball team from Bristol Central...

Wilbur Cross had a chance, the *only* real chance, to hang a loss on the Bristol Central boys basketball team over the 2021-22 campaign. The upset bid, which occurred in New Haven, far away from the Mum City, saw the Rams battle "Cross" on the Governors' home court, the Floyd Little Athletic Center. The game turned chaotic. The pressure was intense. Central trailed early but regained the lead late in the first quarter, eventually extending the lead to 10.

But any margin for error closed rapidly. Central's 7-foot-2 dynamo Donovan Clingan needed a blow and came out of the game for just over a minute at the end of the first quarter and beginning of the second. In that short time, Cross was in the lead again.

Eventually, the Governors grabbed a 29-20 lead off a Jarel Delgado three-pointer to the delight of the home crowd. The Governors led 35-29 at the half, but Bristol Central was about to surge ahead as a sizzling 18-0 run saw Stephen Alseph, Damion Glasper, Carson Rivoira, Victor Rosa, and Clingan all net hoops.

Quickly the visiting aggressors were in charge at 47-37 with 1:10 left in the third quarter. The game appeared to be in hand. But the Governors then scored 14 of the next 18 points, and a lay-up from Camar'ee Williams knotted the contest at 51-51 with 4:46 left in regulation.

A late scrum saw Cross draw a technical foul, and Glasper canned two free throws. With Central retaining possession of the ball, Clingan dropped in a crucial lay-up giving the Rams a 55-51 lead with 2:26 left in the fourth. That technical foul had proved critical in returning the lead to the Rams.

But Cross struck back with five straight points as Delgado banged in another 3. After Williams blocked an Alseph lay-up attempt, the home team lead 56-55 with 1:20 showing on the clock and the ball in the Governors' possession. Rosa then made a quick steal off a loose ball and fed a charging Clingan for a basket. Central was back on top, 57-56 and immediately called a time-out to set up its vaunted defense.

After a couple of misses by the Governors, the Rams had the ball with its one-point lead in hand, playing keep-away. For BC fans the clock never seemed to move. With 22.76 seconds left, Glasper was fouled and coolly nailed both foul shots. With 14 seconds to play and Cross trailing 59-56, Elijah Jean Guillaume was fouled, after taking a jumper from the foul line. He was awarded two free throws.

Only the first was good..

But Williams nabbed the offensive rebound, quickly laid it back in off contact, and with ten seconds remaining in regulation, the game was tied up at 59-59.

Getting the inbounds pass, Alseph attempted to navigate traffic in a very crowded center-court of Cross defenders, but the ball was tipped away. Incredibly, Cross had possession of the ball!

Was there time left? Could the Governors pull off a miracle in front of their own home crowd? Would this magical run by the Bristol Central boys basketball team end on the road in New Haven? Only seconds remained and Delgado made his attempt. His 30-footer at the buzzer hit halfway off the backboard as the clock showed triple zeros and a 59-59 tally on the scoreboard.

Overtime…and Wilbur Cross never scored again, finally overcome by the Rams' defense over the fifth and final frame. In the end Central's 71-59 victory was the Rams' 29th in a row as the beat continued on for the Bristol Central boys basketball program.

***

After two interrupted seasons that did not include an official CIAC state championship round, the boys basketball team at Bristol Central had been chomping at the bit for the 2021-22 campaign to commence.

Any team with a 7-foot-2 giant would want a *full* season worth of games, especially since a trip to Mohegan Sun was well overdue.

And after an abbreviated "Playoff Experience" that the CIAC put together to end the pandemic-abbreviated 2021 season (seeing Central go 15-0 and scoop up the CCC Tournament Championship), what was the only thing left for the Rams to accomplish? How about a CIAC Division II championship?

That meant a slate of grueling games, another postseason jaunt through the CCC's and a shot at the state's best during championship weekend in March.

The team would be tested by the top squads in all the state—even one from outside Connecticut–and head coach Tim Barrette couldn't wait to get the season started.

Central just didn't want to go back to the Floyd Little Gymnasium again. But as fate would have it another epic challenge took place in that very same venue on March 15.

And it was no retreat, no surrender and *another* overtime showdown. The road to a championship is never easy.

EARLY STAGES

Bristol Central's 2022 State Champions—Starting Line-up

The Skinny: 28-0 overall, 43 straight wins, CIAC Division II champions, CCC Tournament champions, CCC South champions, Bristol Central Holiday Classic champions.

Donovan Clingan (center)—30.1 points, 18.4 rebounds, 6.2 blocks-per-game.

Highlights/Honors—Scored 2,268 career points (seventh all-time on the CIAC's scoring list). Had five triple-doubles, shot 72 percent from two-point territory and was 10-of-30 from the three-point stripe. Career record also include 1,518 rebounds and 540 blocks which were both Bristol Central records. He was a two-time Gatorade Connecticut State Player of the Year, McDonald's All-American finalist and earned All CCC South honors four straight years.

Damion Glasper (guard)—11.0 points, 3.1 rebounds, 3.0 assists-per-game.

Highlights/Honors—CCC South All Conference pick, drained a team-leading 35 three-pointers, carried a 90 assist/48 turnover ratio and averaged just under one steal a game. Hit over 72 percent of his free throws (47-of-65) and scored over 300 points to end his scholastic career. He was a primetime scorer who fit into a secondary scoring role seamlessly, deserving credit for accepting that tough assignment.

Carson Rivoira (forward)—7.8 points, 7.1 rebounds, 2.7 assists-per-game.

Highlights/Honors—CCC South All Conference pick, became a decent three-point shooting threat—splashing in 12-of-44 attempts (27.3-percent). Hit 93-of-189 field goals (49.2 percent) and carried a remarkable 2.7-to-1 assist-to-turnover ratio (76 assists/28 steals). He loaded the stat sheet with 34 steals, giving him a positive steals-to-turnovers ratio. Out of his 200 rebounds, 79 of those came off the offensive glass.

Victor Rosa (guard)—4.8 points, 2.3 rebounds, 3.8 assists-per-game.

Highlights/Honors—Dished out 107 assists to only 49 turnovers. Hit 12-of-45 three-pointers and was critical in Central's 1-3-1 defensive press. The hustler grabbed 32 steals and shot 38-percent overall from the field. He was the only starter that did not make the CCC South All-Conference team, a mind-numbing omission. He does have more football accolades than the law should legally allow. He rushed for 2,728 yards and scored 41 touchdowns. At quarterback as a senior, he threw for 849 yards. He was honored as the 2021 Max Preps and Gatorade Connecticut State Player of the Year. Rosa earned First Team All-State selection in his final scholastic season and was named Academic All-Conference honors three times.

Steven Alseph (guard)—6.3 points, 4.0 rebounds, 4.5 assists-per-game.

Highlights/Honors—The CCC South All Conference selection was the perfect addition to Central's championship team. He was clutch on defense, posting 2.3 steals-per-game and always seemed to hit a critical three-point bomb along the way. Transferred in from the recently-closed Sacred Heart in Waterbury, and over the years the squads Alseph played on didn't lose very much…

***

The Championship Run (or two) that wasn't

The Bristol Central boys basketball team earned a state championship banner to hang on one of the crowded walls of the Marsh Gymnasium after going an impressive 28-0 in 2021-22, bulldozing its way through all competition.

But the roots of that title were planted long before that, and after the Rams lost in the second round of the CCC Tournament in 2020, Central more than liked its chances in the CIAC Division II playoff mix.

The Rams had an imposing 7-foot giant by the name of Donovan Clingan—a sophomore that opponents simply could not handle.

The program had built a good team with Clingan as the nucleus, including junior forward Sean Wininger, senior guards Austin Brown and Shane Ouellette, sharp-shooting sophomore Damion Glasper, junior forward

D'Ante Ross, big sophomore forward Mike Lorenzetti, sophomore speedster Victor Rosa, and a bench that included sophomore Carson Rivoira.

Maybe that unit wasn't as polished as its 2021-22 successors, but there was a path in postseason play that could have led to, at the very least, a state title game.

And Central was thinking that big because of that super center in the middle.

The Rams were fresh off a 17-5 campaign, going 1-1 in CCC Tournament play and were ranked No. 4 in Division II play.

Bunnell, the last team Bristol Eastern had squared off against in the postseason back in 2016, was the opponent in first round play, and the team from Stratford was in for a long first-round encounter.

But the March 10 game never happened.

In fact, scholastic sports quickly came to a grinding halt due to the pandemic.

It was a disappointing end for that group of juniors and seniors who never got to compete for a state championship.

Everything was set for a real shot at a CIAC Division II title run.

In the end, there was nothing…

***

The Division II Tournament picture in 2020 saw No. 1 Prince Tech (20-0) followed by Naugatuck (19-1) and Innovation (17-3).

Those were the three top seeds in Division II play—all earning a bye into the second round.

Central was the highest seed, and Bunnell (8-12) would have been a good opener—the kind of team you want to start a deep tournament run against.

Getting a first game was better than sitting home and not playing.

For the Rams, if the squad had advanced over Bunnell, a second-round date with either No. 13 Xavier (13-7) or Brien McMahon (9-9) loomed.

That showdown would have taken place from Central's home court; advancement by the locals would have led to a quarterfinal battle with the likes of No. 5 Holy Cross (15-5) or No. 12 Amistad (13-7).

If Central could have run the table, a semifinal contest against Prince would have occurred on March 18—again, if the bracket went according to plan (which it never does. Ask No. 26 Plainville, the CIAC Division IV winner in 2006).

No. 2 Naugatuck against No. 4 Bristol Central would have been a sweet battle from the Uncasville Arena that year.

But it was all for naught as Central said farewell to the senior duo of Brown and Ouellette—two athletes who at least should have been allowed to finish the season.

Every student athlete in Connecticut, however, was in the same boat.

Then the spring sports seasons came and went without any campaigns for the kids.

And the following fall and winter, it got even worse—more seasons without the possibility of a championship.

Clingan and crew should have been able to build a dynasty at Bristol Central—much like Hartford Public did back in the mid 1990's.

But that championship campaign wasn't in the cards until the big man's senior season over at 480 Wolcott Street.

***

The 2021 'Playoff Experience' and the Uncrowned champions from Bristol Central

Bristol Central senior Dom Amara deserved a chance to play a championship game from the Mohegan Sun Arena.

Or at least let Amara knock someone down on the court in Uncasville (Uncle Tim Barrette was an expert at that exact feat during his playing days at Bristol Eastern).

But instead, the 2020-21 campaign was delayed due to COVID, and games were not played in December or January.

It was the start of one of the strangest seasons on record.

The CIAC eventually green-lit high school sports, but due to restrictions on travel, playing a full-fledged postseason would not be allowed.

That meant no title opportunity for a talented junior class at BCHS.

On top of that, the senior core of Eli Rodriguez, D'Ante Ross, Sean Wininger and Amara were all out of luck in terms of playing for a title.

Again, it wasn't fair and turned into a lousy life lesson the kids in this state—and all over America for that matter—didn't need to learn this early.

A big incentive for doing well in class has always been the ability to play sports—showing off on the field or court.

That's the privilege student athletes have enjoyed over the years.

In the CCC, the traditional teams were divided into regions. Central was slated into 'Region B' along with Avon, Southington, Plainville, Lewis Mills, Farmington, New Britain, and crosstown rival Bristol Eastern.

Central rolled through the regular season at 12-0, although a couple of opponents gave Central a real run for the money.

The season opened on February 10 as the Rams welcomed Avon and shooting sensation Jack Hall to Bristol. The Rams had a big lead after three quarters but had to hold on for dear life in the end, coming away with a 78-76 win.

Masks were part of the uniform as the pandemic came and went and came again during the 21-22 season. Keeping everyone healthy was a priority.

Four double-figure victories followed, including a 66-51 victory at Bristol Eastern on February 12. But to end the month Central was slated to play Plainville.

And Barrette and company never shoot well from the Ivan Wood Gymnasium there.

After sinking Lewis Mills (59-37) the previous day, the Rams traveled to play the Blue Devils on February 27.

As predicted, Central's shots wouldn't fall and Plainville pushed the squad to the brink.

But the visitors left the Wood Gym 64-61 winners—improving to 6-0 overall.

To open March, Central sank Farmington (55-41) and Southington (55-31) on the road and in the Plainville rematch on March 8, the Blue Devils were down big, trimmed the deficit to 15 but dropped a one-sided 74-41 decision in the end.

Wins at Lewis Mills, followed by New Britain and then Central ended the regular season with a 50-26 home win against Eastern.

Central was on a 12-game winning streak as the "Postseason Experience" was about to commence.

Every team in the CCC was invited to play in the four-tier set-up. Even 0-11 Bulkeley was allotted a postseason berth.

By virtue of its perfect ledger, Central earned a spot in the championship bracket as the fourth ranked team.

The field was loaded as No. 1 Northwest Catholic, No. 2 Maloney, and No. 3 East Catholic—along with Central –all entered undefeated at 12-0, while No. 5 Windsor carried just the one loss.

Windsor, Northwest, and East Catholic ranked in the top-five in the GameTimeCT poll, and they stood in the path the Rams had to take in order to win the CCC's championship bracket.

It was a week-long challenge for No. 4 Bristol Central as the program opened play on Monday, March 22 against Windsor in what turned into an epic challenge.

But it wasn't like that at first.

Central started the game on fire as Wininger (10 rebounds) helped limit the Warriors to one shot over first half play.

Of course, Windsor made its run—closing the deficit to two—but in the end, the Rams came away 73-59 winners, the first ever victory against that elite program.

And then things got really interesting as the first of two schools of choice were on the docket.

Central visited Northwest Catholic on Wednesday, March 24.

Clingan opened the game draining two three-pointers and Rodriguez dropped in 17 big points as the Rams racked up a 71-60 victory in West Hartford.

That made 14 consecutive wins for the Bristol program, and it set up a championship date against top-rated East Catholic—a 55-38 victor over East Hartford.

Friday, March 26, was the date and, keep in mind, the Eagles weren't just the top team in the CCC but the No. 1 ranked program in Connecticut.

But East Catholic hardly looked that way early on, and the squad, though playing from its own home court in Manchester, was down big.

The Rams led 29-16 at the half and nabbed a 21-point edge towards the end of the third period.

But the fourth period belonged to the Eagles as the squad regained the edge at 58-56 with just under 1:45 to play in regulation.

The Rams tied it up late as overtime commenced in Central's biggest game of the past few years.

Central trailed late but, off a missed free throw by East Catholic's James Jones, Clingan grabbed the rebound as the Rams were trailing by a point (68-67) with 14 seconds to play.

Glasper drove the length of the court and found Rosa on the opposite side. Rosa faked a 3-pointer and jammed the ball into Clingan for a quick lay-with just six seconds to play—leading to Central's remarkable 69-68 win for the CCC Tournament Championship.

It would be Central's first CCC Tournament Title since the 2003 campaign.

And what about Clingan, the man who tallied the game-winning shot? He stamped his final game as a junior with 33 points, 26 rebounds, five assists, seven blocks, and five assists.

Clingan scored 108 points and had 79 rebounds over that three-game stretch against the elite programs of the CCC. That equated to averages of 36.0 points and 26.3 rebounds-per-game. Clingan's numbers over tournament play were video-game-like. Averaging a 30-20 over postseason play is simply incredible to comprehend.

Luke Strole scored 20 points—18 of which came over second half play and overtime—while Brody Limric added 19 for East Catholic.

The end result of the contest was the CCC Tournament Championship, the top-ranking in the state, and all the momentum in the world for next season—assuming the pandemic was kept in check.

By all accounts, Bristol Central was the best team in the state and, perhaps, the uncrowned CIAC Division II champions. Just to win that CCC Championship, Central had taken a buzzsaw to the first, second, and fourth ranked teams.

As Clingan said in the postgame interview after Central defeated East Catholic, "To be the best, you've got to beat the best." There was no doubting that.

Once Central won in overtime, Central had even more hardware. But the ultimate prize for the gymnasium at Bristol Central was missing—a 2021-22 Division II state championship banner.

"When we won that CCC Tournament title, [Donovan] said to me 'one more to go,'" in terms of a state title. "It's been our goal from the beginning. We know we have the opportunity, but we also know a lot of things have to go our way to be there in the finals come March (2022)."

***

Again, the No. 1 ranking in the state and that undefeated campaign were impressive, but Amara, Rodriguez, Ross and Sean Wininger *all* deserved a better fate.

You make your own fate unless the pandemic determines otherwise. It would be a long layoff until November of 2021. But once the Rams hit that gymnasium as a group for the first official practice, it was game time!

History Lesson

Central needed a little time to get to state tournament play after Bristol high School was divided into Bristol Central and Bristol Eastern in 1959. But within three seasons, head coach Bill McCooey had his Rams in the 1962 postseason.

That squad lost just twice during the regular season with super sophomore George Benoit firing up shots—the first player from either one of the new schools to eventually tally 1,000 scholastic points.

Benoit was joined by Howie Busse, Bernie Cohen, Art Whitehead, Ray Gagnon, Kev Phelan and Bill Benecick—making for a strong team.

The Rams finished the 1961-62 campaign at 17-2, falling to Eastern twice as the Lancers earned the CCIL Championship. No. 3 Central ended up losing its first ever playoff game in the CIAC's 40th annual tournament, dropping a 67-43 decision to No. 11 Hartford Public on February 23, 1962.

The game took place at the gymnasium at CCSU in front of 1,500 fans and advanced the Owls to the quarterfinal round. And Public's Eddie Griffin had a monster game. He nearly posted a triple double as he collected 15 points, 20 rebounds and nine assists.

Central trailed 28-18 after one period of play and managed to shoot just 25 percent from the field over the losing effort (16-of-65) and was outrebounded, 58-27. Busse nabbed 12 points and nine rebounds while Benoit scored 12 for Central. Gagnon added six, and Whitehead five. After that campaign, McCooey's squad won at least 10 games for three consecutive years.

The following year, at 10-10, the Rams did not qualify for state tournament play. In 1963 merely a .500 record didn't lead to playoff qualification. However, the Rams went 12-9 in 1963-64, and Benoit had a tremendous postseason run.

But first, on February 14, 1964, Central defeated Eastern 71-63—punching its state tournament ticket. On February 22, the Rams traveled to Greenwich and came away with a huge 62-49 victory over West Haven in a Class A Playdown.

Benoit was sensational as he dropped in a game-high 31 points. Jeff Beaucar added 18 while Pat Gilhuly notched nine to pace Central.

And then on February 26, Benoit played in his final scholastic game as Central fell to No. 5 Maloney 70-40 at Conard High School—the third time the Spartans defeated the Rams that season.

No. 28 Central led 9-1 out of the gate and off one final first-half field goal from Gilhuly, the Rams led 22-20 at the break. But the Spartans took off in the third, leading 39-24 through three and never looked back.

Benoit scored 10 points in his last scholastic contest, averaging 20.5 ppg in state tournament play. And then, it would be quite some time before Central won another postseason contest.

An early season game in Southington. A lot of basketball still lay ahead, but even in December, expectations were growing at Central.

2021-22 Preseason talk

All the Bristol Central boys wanted was a chance to play for a state title in 2022.

"That's all you can hope: that we actually have an opportunity to play in that state tournament," said Tim Barrette before the season. "These guys have put in the time and effort. It's been a long four year run for these guys. And that four-year run, I hope, can culminate in competing for a state title."

Then the question became who was going to challenge Bristol Central in the playoffs that season in Division II play?

It wasn't a forgone conclusion that the Rams were going to win the title, or go undefeated along the way, but who was going to stop this group five-seniors strong?

The obvious answer was Northwest Catholic, losers only once to Wilbur Cross in 2021-22 and boasting a 19-1 record in regular season play. They were 25-3 overall.

That squad had the size and skill to give Central fits, but that alone doesn't work over a 32-minute game—not when competing against five seniors who were locked into what they were doing.

What about Conard from West Hartford?

The Chieftains were a tremendous outfit with size up-front and skill in the backcourt.

Sophomore Riley Fox did it all on the floor, scored a school record 51 points earlier in the season, and was already drawing NCAA Division I offers.

But Fox and company, who could just outshoot most of its opponents, could solve the riddle of Northwest Catholic.

The Lions spun the Chieftains 62-35 in the semifinals of the Division II showcase event from Enfield High School on March 15.

No. 4 Wilton (17-3 regular season) was a tremendous program and was one missed free away from possibly ending Central's season on the flip side of the Division II semis. And what a physical confrontation that showdown was became between Central and Wilton.

Failed charge attempts on Clingan, over-the-top antics that just seemed to make Central's giant mad, and an aggressive approach were the only chance Wilton had against the Rams.

However, the ending was the same as the other 27 Central had that year.

Holy Cross (16-4) and Crosby (15-5) were each bounced out of the quarterfinals, and No. 6 Prince Tech (15-5) didn't make it out of the second round—falling to Middletown by a 71-52 score.

Frankly, every team that took the court against Central that season was talented, but when they hit the court, every opposing forward and center was dwarfed by Clingan.

Central had talent at all five positions, using its high-low offense to quickly put points on the board and when the Rams went to its 1-3-1 defensive zone to start third period play, trying to avoid Rosa's speed up top was easier said than done.

***

With a 7-foot-2 center in tow, who really wanted to play Bristol Central in 2022?More teams than one might think. With Barrette promising Clingan the most competitive schedule possible at all the big venues, the coach kept his word.

And all the big teams were added to the Rams' schedule. The Robert Saulsbury Invitational saw Central square off against Wilbur Cross in New Haven. The tournament was held at the Floyd Little Athletic Center, possibly one of the best scholastic venues in New England.

The Hoophall Classic from Blake Arena in Springfield, Massachusetts, would pit Central against a top-ranked opponent from Springfield (Springfield Central)— giving the Rams a chance to play across the Connecticut border.

But due to COVID, that trip to Springfield in 2021 was cancelled. he season before Barrette had mentioned that Notre Dame-West Haven and Ridgefield were possible opponents for the Rams. If Central could have played 22 regular season games, these were among the squads on the menu.

No photo better illustrates the story of Rams basketball 21-22 than this of Donovan Clingan towering over...everyone.

An Aside: Should schools of choice in Connecticut be competing in CIAC's Division I?

Many observers thought that Northwest, a school of choice, should have been playing for a Division I title instead. Most observers feel that, the way the bracket ended up, the Lions would have taken that tournament championship. Instead, the Division I title bout saw No. 8 East Catholic's Eagles defeat Notre Dame of West Haven 50-49.

Northwest had defeated the Eagles twice that season, hanging a 54-51 road loss on them and then repeated the feat on neutral ground during the CCC Tournament. The Lions had won at Windsor (81-80) on January 6 and had beaten Conard twice. That battled-tested team had all the makings of a Division I champion.

Northwest had an excellent shooter in Matt Curtis and plenty of size with an imposing freshman center, the 6-foot-9 Badara Diakite. In brief they had enough size, length and talent to win the title except in a tournament, with Bristol Central looming in the distance.

Was the path any easier in Division II play with Bristol Central—and its 7-foot-2 center in the way? That 20-point victory over Northwest in the finals speaks volumes of Central's tremendous program that season. The Lions, averaging 78.3 points-per-game in tournament play and coming off 101-63 demolishing of Crosby, scored only 36 that night.

Several Central opponents had accumulated one or more 100-point games. But through what some like to call basketball karma but is really just skill, those teams that ran up the score over an overwhelmed opponent all got their just due in the end.

In an early season game against Enfield, the visitors begin to set up against the Rams' zone defense.

Before Alseph

Tim Barrette was extremely confident in his returning cast of starters, featuring Victor Rosa, Carson Rivoira, Damion Glasper and Donovan Clingan. The coach was preparing a regular season schedule that was going to not only challenge the team but also get as many eyes as possible on their 7-foot-2 center.

That was the logic with the returning four.

But to begin the summer Sacred Heart in Waterbury had closed, meaning several talented players—some living in Waterbury, some not—were looking for new schools. And that's when Steve Alseph enrolled at Bristol Central, and suddenly the Rams had their fifth starter.

"They know what each other does well on the floor," said Barrette. "They know where each player is going to be [on the floor]. Including Steve [Alseph] coming into the line-up, who started at Sacred Heart, all five of these guys have one hundred and sixty starts under their belts combined. It's the most experienced team I've ever had, definitely by far. And they played together since they were freshman at the varsity level."

Now all those big games became even bigger…

***

Clingan officially signs with UConn

The auditorium at Bristol Central high school was abuzz with excitement on Wednesday, November 10, 2021, as a certain 7-foot center from the boys basketball team made his collegiate decision official.

On National Signing Day, Donovan Clingan put his name on the dotted line, committing to the University of Connecticut to play for the men's basketball program the following year.

It was one of the most anticipated signings ever in the Mum City.

"If you told me freshman year that I'd be here today, I'd look at you like you're crazy," said Clingan. "After a lot of hard work and determination, I am here [to sign with UConn]."

He thanked his father along with his grandmother and coaches at Central and beyond, for pushing him to be the best player and person he could be,

And he knew his mother was looking down on him as well, extremely proud of the young man he'd become and the choices he'd made.

Clingan thanked the entire school community at Bristol Central from the students, teachers, and staff, along with UConn coach Dan Hurley for the chance to become a member of the Huskies' program.

"I'd like to thank Coach Hurley and the rest of the UConn staff and family for believing in me and giving me such a great opportunity to play at a great school," said Clingan.

"This is not the end. It's just the beginning, and I have to keep working."

It had been an amazing ride for Clingan, the entire Central boys basketball program, and longtime coach Tim Barrette over the last three scholastic seasons.

And that Wednesday in November was yet another special day to celebrate all those remarkable achievements. Coach Barrette summarized it best:

"The way you have handled these accolades, the pressures and the spotlight amaze me every single day," said Barrette. "Donovan, you've never put your personal success in front of your team's, remained humble throughout the entire process and kept working hard both before and after your decision was made to attend the University of Connecticut."

He said UConn was going to get a good player but even a better person, adding, "thank you for letting me be part of this ride."

And there were plenty of people who wanted to let Clingan know how special the decision was to the city of Bristol.

One of them was Athletic Director Chris Cassin. "On behalf of the Bristol board of Education," he said, "I'd like to congratulate Donovan on signing his letter of intent to the University of Connecticut. You should feel great about the decision you've made today and extremely proud of yourself. It was your hard work and your dedication in the classroom and on the basketball court that has brought us here today."

He finished his speech with two simple words: "Go Huskies."

Central senior Carson Rivoira had been playing basketball with Clingan since kindergarten and had seen everything that made the big man and model teammate outstanding and fun.

"Since I've known him, he's not only been a great basketball player but someone everyone wants to be around," said Rivoira. "He's always smiling, laughing and in a great mood. And although he may seem big, you'll not find anyone else that is more like a kid."

The administrative team at Central, including principal Pete Wininger, assistant principal Ryan Broderick and Geoff Sinatro, was personally thanked by Barrette for all the support the trio had given Clingan over the years.

"No other student in the school has a relationship that Donovan shares with Wininger, Broderick, and Sinatro," said Barrette. "From fishing trips to morning workouts, I thank you all for what you have done for this young man."

Wininger, a former coach of the boys basketball program at Central, had seen some of the best athletes compete for the squad.

He'd known Clingan for years from games at the Boys and Girls Club travel program in town, and Donovan was always known as "the big kid."

And while that big kid had made the BCHS boys hoop program one of the best in the state, the young man wasn't only about basketball.

"Even now as a young adult, he's still a big kid," said Wininger. "He enjoys a lot of things outside of basketball and I think it's important to make note of the fact he is probably one of the happiest people I've ever been around. I don't see Donovan have a bad day, and if something goes wrong on the court, you'll see it in his eyes, you'll see it in his mannerisms, but he'll turn it into something else."

"He's a unique individual. He has the heart of a lion and the heart of a teddy bear at the same time."

But that teddy bear will also dunk on any player not wearing the maroon colors of Bristol Central.

Barrette called Clingan a pillar of the school and that wasn't just due to his 7-foot-1 frame.

And when it could have been easy to leave Central, knowing other prep schools and programs were itching to grab him, he stuck it out in Bristol all four years, an admirable decision.

"I can't thank you enough for the trust you have in this team, our school and our coaching staff," said Barrette. "I'm going to miss the goofy looks I get when I ask you a question in AP Environmental class, and you have no idea how to answer."

Barrette called Clingan a hero to his son ("dunking like Donovan"), bringing a smile to his coach's face when he saw the two interact.

"I'm so proud of this young man with the decision he's about to make, the same pride I felt when I hugged you after we captured the CCC tournament last year versus East Catholic," said Barrette.

After that win Donovan said, "One more to go, coach."

And before hitting the court at Gampel Pavilion, Clingan and crew would be looking for the ultimate prize last season at Bristol Central—a state title.

And Rivoira knew that all the hard work Clingan put in every day should lead the Rams to that title game in March.

"He's always in the gym working on his game and he works extremely hard in practice to make himself a better player and his team a more complete team," said Rivoira. "We're very lucky to have Donovan here at Bristol Central and we're looking forward to a memorable senior season with him leading the way."

"UConn is very lucky getting such a great player and an even better person." And that fact about getting a chance to suit up for the Huskies wasn't lost on Clingan.

"I'm excited to play in front of the best fans in college basketball," said Clingan. "I can't wait to see what the next four years have [in store for me]."

"Thank you and go Huskies."

Clingan signs with UConn, from the university website.

STORRS, Conn.—The UConn men's basketball program has received signed National Letters of Intent from Donovan Clingan and Alex Karaban, UConn coach Dan Hurley announced officially on November 10.

"We are very excited to announce the addition of Donovan to the UConn basketball family," Hurley said in an official UConn Athletic Communications on November 10, 2021. "With his size, his ability to pass, and his shooting touch around the basket and on the perimeter, he should have an immediate impact on our frontcourt at both ends of the court.

"Donovan's work ethic and team-first attitude fits in perfectly with the championship culture we are establishing. He has had an outstanding scholastic career under Coach (Tim) Barrette at Bristol Central and on the AAU circuit under Coach (Joe) Chatman with Team Spartans."

The T-shirt says it all. Clingan is headed for Storrs and Big East basketball!

The start of a championship run …

Here's part of the Bristol Central boys basketball preview in the *TBE* that year:

Head Coach: Tim Barrette (15th season).

Overall Record: In 14 seasons at Central Barrette carries an all-time record of 172-140. During that time Barrette's squads have won five CCC South Division crowns.

Last Season's Record: 15-0 overall (CCC Tournament Champs) but could not vie for a CIAC Division II state title due to the pandemic.

Subtractions: Sean Wininger (forward), D'Ante Ross (forward/ guard), Elijah Rodriguez (guard), Dominic Amara (forward), Roberto Negron-Cruz (sr, guard), Tre Jones (forward).

Starters: Donovan Clingan (sr, center), Damion Glasper (sr, guard), Victor Rosa (sr, guard), Carson Rivoira (sr, forward), Steven Alseph (sr, transfer from the closed Sacred Heart, guard).

Key Subs: Aaron Brown (sr), Tre Blair (jr, guard), Julius Powell (jr, center), Jayeson VanBeveren (jr, forward), and Mason Stokes (jr, guard).

Strengths: Long, athletic, experienced, tall, and talented starting five.

Weaknesses: Lack of varsity experience on the bench

Why Central will be successful: The program has five potential NCAA Division I athletes in its starting line-up. What other program in the state can boast that kind of talent?

Relevant Fact: Donovan Clingan is the eighth all-time leading scorer in Bristol boys scholastic history. A full slate of games this season is going to put the big man at the top of the Mum City's scoring list by the completion of the year.

The fact that became clear was Central had the best starting five in the state with all those athletes that came from multiple backgrounds.

Of course, Clingan signed on with UConn and will continue his basketball career.

But the other four should be continuing onto the colligate level, in one form or another, if that's the path they choose.

Rosa is already locked into UConn and will boost its football program, and Rivoira is taking his soccer talents down South.

Glasper and Alseph could be playing hoop somewhere next season, and that's a tribute to the caliber of athletes Barrette employed in his starting line-up.

But getting Alseph was a huge deal for Central.

"I think that's where a lot of people are going to be surprised," said Barrette of Alseph. "Steve plays the game the right way. He plays extremely hard. He's a very, very good defender—on the ball defender. One thing I will say, he did a great job in the preseason getting everyone involved. He doesn't look for his own [offense] that often. He came to this team, and he's tried to get all the other guys involved in the preseason."

***

The Bench

The bench was a bit of a question mark for the program, but that group gave a little here and a little there when called upon.

There weren't going many minutes available for the reserves, but that crew did yeoman work when called upon.

In some games it was a quick stint in the second quarter when someone needed a rest or got into foul trouble.

In other instances, the game was quickly over early in the second half, allowing the chances for extended minutes.

"My depth is unproven," said Barrette before the season. "After my starting five, those guys really have zero experience. So I go from five starters with all that experience to a group of guys that have not played at the varsity level. Obviously, there are things that will happen like COVID and sickness and injury and foul trouble that they're going to have to play. One of the things that make me a little nervous is that we have a lot of big venues. It's one thing to play on a Tuesday night at Berlin, but it's another thing to step in the lineup at Mohegan Sun versus East Catholic."

Over the season, the grouping of Aaron Brown, Blair, Powell, VanBeveren, and Stokes all provided something along the way.

Those in-game contributions also seemed timely for the Rams.

****

There was no other senior in the state of Connecticut with a rèsumé like the one Clingan provided. He didn't have an equal on the court in 2021-22, not at 7 ft. 2 in. and 260 pounds.

He had entered the season with all the accolades an outstanding scholastic player should have; he just wanted a state championship on his way to Storrs. As a junior he had pumped in 27.3 points, pulled down 17.2 rebounds, and had 3.1 assists, 5.8 blocks, and 1.2 steals per game.

Coming into season play he had collected 1,421 points 1,002 rebounds, eventually becoming the city's all-time leading scorer scholastically in both boys and girls play. In the CCC Tournament alone as a junior, Clingan averaged 33.7 points and 26.3 rebounds per game, incredible statistics against challenging programs in hostile venues. That was just a quick sampling of what his senior campaign was going to look like.

"His body has improved," said Barrette of Clingan. "He's in good shape. He's put the time in the weight room. He's stronger, he's bigger, and he really can shoot the ball from outside. I think you'll see an increased amount of activity outside the paint, which some people are hoping for because he's so dominant inside. At the same time, we're hoping to showcase his skill set away from the hoop a little more as well."

Clingan dropped in 10 three-pointers that season, showing more of an outside game than ever. And his skill set was tailor made for the collegiate level. Big men like him don't just plop down in the middle of the paint anymore, calling for the ball. Clingan will help drag forwards and centers away from the hoop in the Big East.

The University of Connecticut, Syracuse, Providence, Yale, UMASS, Iowa, Michigan, Michigan State, Ohio State, Notre Dame, Georgetown, Maryland, Virginia Tech, South Carolina, Iona, Rutgers, Wake Forest and Boston College were programs hungry to add Clingan to their program. But the big man stayed home, and we'll all be able to watch his game grow in Storrs over the next four years or so.

There probably won't be a rebound off Clingan's free throw.

***

Before the pandemic Tim Barrette was looking to stack Central's schedule. Then when Covid was at its worst and travel out of the state to play scholastic sports was not allowed, Central's schedule shrunk to just 12 games at the CIAC's "playoff experience." But as the 2021-22 campaign arrived, Barrette did stack his schedule, keeping a promise he made to Donovan Clingan. Central was probably out of gas money after just two games and trips to Hartford and Uncasville.

"One of the things I talked about with Donovan and his family is if he stayed [at Central], I told him I'd go out there and try to get the best possible schedule that I could,' said Barrette. "Hearing from a lot of college coaches, most people have not [played at] all those venues in one season that we are going to be able to play at. Those venues included Mohegan Sun Arena (twice), Trinity College (Hartford), Springfield College (Blake Arena), Floyd Little Athletic Center (Hillhouse), and the XL Center (the former Hartford Civic Center).

"My guys deserve to have people see them play," said Barrette. "The big venues allow us to have more people because these guys deserve to have people watch them." The XL Center backed out of its game due to COVID restrictions, but since Central was slated as the home team, the contest was played at home, And that wasn't a bad change of venue.

***

Despite a full schedule, the boys team supported Rams girls' basketball throughout the season.

THE GAMES BEGIN TO COUNT

Week 1—Game 1

Game 1—Bristol Central versus Southington (Saturday, Dec. 18)—GHPA High School Sixth Annual Basketball Classic, "The 6th Spirit of Doc Hurley" Tournament (from the Ferris Athletic Center, Trinity College)

The Score: Bristol Central 55, Southington 29

The good teams can hang with a powerhouse for a quarter, perhaps a half.

But in the end, they all fell like a house of cards.

Central played 21 different teams over 2021-22 and five of those squads lost to the Rams *twice*.

And Southington was probably happy that it had to play Central just once that season…

***

The Knights gave the Rams a bit of a run over first half play as Southington started the season against the state's top-rated squad.

Central led by two points early in the third period, but Southington was about to fall flat.

The Rams' outscored the Knights 29-7 over the final 16 minutes of the showdown to make the game a blowout.

"One thing about [Southington coach's] John [Cessario] teams, they run that offense like Novocain," said Central coach Tim Barrette. "It takes a little while to work, but they run their cuts hard, they screen well; they do all those things well. We hung in there with that pace, and then we got out early. We went to our zone in the fourth quarter, and we turned the game around with our ball-pressure."

In fact, the Knights notched just five points over the final 14:25 as Central started the season with a huge win.

Donovan Clingan (24 points, 14 rebounds and five blocked shots) won the Spirit of the Doc Player of the Game Award but had plenty of help.

Damion Glasper quietly slipped in 16 points while Carson Rivoira added nine.

And when Victor Rosa (three points) came up hurt, and Alseph got into foul trouble, the bench came through in a big way.

Tre Blair, Mason Stokes, and Aaron Brown played well to help Central stay ahead in the fray.

"Steve [Alseph] got into a little foul trouble, Victor goes down and we're down two guards that started," said Barrette. "I thought Aaron Brown, Mason Stokes, and Tre Blair did a great job today in the minutes they gave us. It's probably not as many as they want but they're valuable minutes. And you have to be ready to play at any time."

And to start the season, an opponent tried to slow things down. It didn't work.

That just meant Central dug in even more defensively and every miss by Southington hurt that much more.

But the Knights outscored Central 15-10 at the beginning of the second half after trailing just 26-22 at the half.

Then the defense dug in the third period.

"Teams are going to want to slow the pace down" against us said Barrette. "Teams are content with being down 12 [points]. It's a hard thing to do, it's a hard thing to teach your kids, but I thought we were locked in defensively no matter if the possession was 20 seconds or a minute long. I thought we were locked in all day defensively."

Central buzzed Southington over a 9-0 run to open the final period.

A steal and two charity shots from Rivoira and four consecutive points by Glasper gave the No. 1 team in the state a 45-24 cushion with 5:22 remaining.

Late in the game Alseph found Clingan for a loud alley-oop—a soon to be staple of the program on almost a nightly basis.

"One down and we're back to work tomorrow morning," said Barrette. "We have a big one Monday night [against East Catholic]. This is one of those games they call a trap game [against Southington]. I was happy to have it on the first night of the year because these guys were excited to play."

Mason Brown hit the only three-pointer of the game for the Rams; Southington's Ryan Hammarlund dropped in three 3-pointers on his way to a team-high 15 points.

Southington would eventually endure a very tough 4-16 campaign, something that seldom happens at a competitive school. The Knights lost their first four games but then went on a four-game winning streak from Dec. 30 to Jan. 13 with victories over New Milford (47-32), playoff bound Enfield (45-38), Hartford Public (63-46), and Glastonbury (53-33)—moving to 4-4 on the season.

Southington would then lose its final 12 games, including a 24-22 loss at Simsbury on Jan. 26. They did not qualify for the Division II playoffs.

***

It was a great weekend of basketball from Trinity College—as the Doc Hurley Classic always is.

That Saturday was a telling day for several of the programs around the state because once Central defeated Southington, four tremendous games followed. In the end, the tournament featured three future state champs and one runner-up.

Those results included:

Bloomfield 82, Weaver 46—Bloomfield snuck by Granby 58-54 in the state title game. The Warhawks finished the regular season at 16-4 and were the sixth ranked team in the Division IV Tournament.

Bloomfield's run included a defeat of Bristol Eastern by fifty points on Jan. 24 (86-36). The Warhawks were only up 32-24 at the half but then blitzed the Lancers into oblivion, even after the outcome was no longer in doubt.

Prince Tech 69, Capital Prep 66—Tech had a rather good year, going 15-5 overall and was ranked sixth in the Division II fray. But Tech was dropped by No. 11 Middletown in second round play, 71-52.

Wilbur Cross 72, Northwest Catholic 68—Cross was a tough squad, eventually forcing Bristol Central to overtime on Feb. 2.

But the story here was Northwest losing to the Governors by four points and then reeling off 21 straight wins until bumping up against Central in the finals of the CCC Tournament—dropping a 63-56 decision to the Rams before the start of the CIAC Division II Tournament.

Cross fell to East Catholic (73-63) in quarterfinal round play of the CIAC Division I Tournament.

East Catholic 70, Middletown 32—The Eagles ended up one of the most deceiving No. 8 seeds of all time in state tournament play—being tested early and often across the regular season of the 2021-22 campaign.

East Catholic went 15-5 in the regular season and lost to programs such as Bristol Central (74-59, more on that later), Mater Dei, California (73-58), Windsor (70-66 in OT), and Northwest Catholic (54-51).

The Eagles were just about as battle-tested as Central was that year. In the Division I finals East Catholic defeated Notre Dame-West Haven 50-49 to seize the championship.

Middletown was a quality program, despite losing three times to the Rams over the regular and postseason play.

***The Rematch was coming...**

After that epic 69-68 overtime victory by Bristol Central over East Catholic—resulting in the Rams capturing the CC Tournament Championship, every fan knew an in-season rematch was in the works. And why not play that game at the same facility Central expected to be playing at in its final game of the season?

That exciting contest, pitting the Rams versus the Eagles, was sponsored by *The Day* newspaper—dubbing the event "The Day of New London Holiday Classic Tournament."

And an impressive two game line-up was assembled for the inaugural event.

Ledyard battled Waterford in the undercard of the event while Bristol Central/East Catholic was slated for 8 p.m. on day one. The game, pitting the top two teams from Connecticut from 2021, was streamed live. In the previous meeting, Clingan had roasted East Catholic for 33 points and 26 rebounds.

But once Central got rolling in the game, the Eagles were left in the dust— eventually trailing by twenty points.

***

Clingan's First Game—at Manchester (Friday, Dec. 14, 2018)

Donovan Clingan, in his first scholastic game, posted an impressive line: 14 points, 16 rebounds, and six blocked shots. Still, the Rams lost badly, 88-43.

Central was blitzed from pillar to post over 32-minutes of fast break hoop. Even so, Central's 6-foot-9, 14-year-old loomed over the Manchester players. It was impressive.

However, the home team had a roster 12 seniors-strong and simply overwhelmed the younger squad from Bristol. It was a 42-16 game at the half, and BC never came back. D'Ante Ross scored 11 points to complement Clingan while Austin Brown added six.

"The game got out of hand, but this was a very tough opening night for my guys," said Tim Barrette to the *Bristol Observer* that night. "This is a perfect storm. I'm starting freshmen and sophomores, [and] Manchester has 12 seniors."

Clingan ended the regular season averaging 21.5 points-per-game and then sank a season-high 37 against New Milford in first round state tournament play. The Rams lost that one in overtime, 65-61, as the home team bombed away from behind the arc, missing several long-range field goals— attempting to stay away from one of the state's best shot blockers.

Because of the pandemic, the Rams did not play another official CIAC playoff game until 2022, making New Milford the only program Clingan and Central lost to in CIAC state tournament play over his four seasons.

***

There was a rumor spread that Tim Barrette hid a $20 bill in the locker room at the Mohegan Sun Arena after defeating East Catholic and the goal was to get back there—for a CIAC Division II championship game—to collect it.

Barrette said when the squad got back to Mohegan in March his team was put in a different locker room for the championship event.

That probably meant an employee at the venue got a $20 raise sometime between late December and March.

Twenty bucks at the Mohegan Sun Arena could buy you half a hot dog and three nachos (with no cheese of course).

***

East Catholic—the eventual CIAC Division I champions—had a difficult 2021-22 season, even by the team's standards, falling to Northwest Catholic in the CCC Boys Tournament and then entering the Division I tournament fray as the eighth ranked squad.

After a first-round bye East Catholic defeated No. 9 Farmington (57-46), No. 16 Wilbur Cross (73-63), and then No. 4 Fairfield Prep (47-40) in the semifinals.

And in one heck of a battle, the Eagles ended up beating No. 2 Notre Dame-West Haven by a single point to tally the Division I title.

Like Central, East who played plenty of challenging competition to prepare for postseason play.

And what did that lead bring to squads like the Rams and the Eagles? Postseason glory and additional banners and hardware for their respective schools.

What did Central's and East Catholic's stacked schedule prove that year? Never duck the stiff competition that in the end it will only make you stronger.

***

Week 2—Game 2

Game 2—Bristol Central versus East Catholic (Monday, Dec. 20)— The Day of New London Holiday Basketball Classic (from the Mohegan Sun Arena, Uncasville)

The Score: 74-59

There was a ton of hype surrounding the Central/East Catholic game as two of the three top programs in the state were sharing the hardwood. But there was only one Donovan Clingan to go around, and the E.C. Eagles did not have him. Clingan burned them for 29 points, 17 rebounds, and seven blocked shots as the Rams walked off with a 15-point win against a top-ranked program.

He started the game with a sweet hook shot, then nailed one while in motion, and towards the tail end of the first frame, canned a long jumper to keep his team ahead against the third-ranked squad in the state.

Damion Glasper also started draining threes, two during the first 2:50 of the game and, combined with the offense from Clingan, the Rams led 12-5 with 4:10 remaining in the first.

Leading by three early in the second (19-16), Central went on a 10-0 burst as Glasper canned seven points—including another three—while Carson Rivoira hit a lay-up and with 5:11 before the half. The number one squad in the state led 29-16.

East Catholic trimmed the deficit to eight late, but two Clingan free throws and a blistering baseline three by Steve Alseph gave the locals a 36-23 cushion at intermission. Although the Eagles never trimmed the deficit to less than ten, the game got chippy in the second half.

A double technical foul with 4:20 to play in the third period meant Clingan had to leave the game. (He had apparently responded to some trash-talking with thank-you that offended someone.)

That meant Powell was subbed in and, thanks to two big buckets by the reserve center, he spurred Central on a 16-11 run—including a buzzer-beating three by Glasper at the end of the third—and when Clingan re-entered the game, the Rams led 62-44 with 5:18 remaining.

Clingan came in hot with a loud dunk which led to a 10-2 run that ended with a three-point play from Rivoira and another slam by the 7 ft. 2 in. giant and with 2:39 left, the Eagles trailed 72-48 and this one was all but over.

Stokes ended the score for Central with a hoop, missing out on an and-one, as the Rams dominated, 74-59.

It was one Catholic school down, one more to follow…from Mohegan Sun in mid-March (or, maybe before then at the championship round of the CCC Tournament).

***

The game also put Glasper on the state map in terms of his offense, mainly because the showdown was broadcast on the internet for free, giving coaches statewide a chance to see Central against good competition.

And Glasper had one of his biggest games of his scholastic career— dropping in 19 points and canning five three-point bombs. It was a tremendous effort.

Defenses were geared to help limit Glasper's offense, but luring the focus away from Clingan helped open things up for the big man in the middle.

Glasper proved to be a hardwood assassin all season hitting clutch shots, and even a two-point effort from the senior standout would help shift a bit of the focus off of Clingan.

***

Before the pandemic-shortened campaign, Central was just 2-6 against the Eagles. In fact, last program to hang a loss on Central before the team won

43 straight games was East Catholic in 2020 CCC Tournament play. On Feb. 27, 2020, the Eagles foiled the Rams 85-48.

Before that incredible run Central lost to East Catholic twice that season, falling by a combined score of 155-79. A CCC Tournament championship to end 2021 and that Mohegan Sun whipping helped the Rams improve that ledger.

***

There was an undercard at the event: Waterford picked off Ledyard 59-47. Waterford, the last Division II champs crowned before the pandemic, ended up playing Bristol Central in the quarterfinal round of the CIAC tournament later in the year.

Ledyard—a Division III program—ended up losing to Waterford three times that season, including a 40-38 loss on Feb. 24 in conference tournament play.

***

Sports in Bristol on hold until after Christmas—pandemic

Like every other town, Bristol could not ignore the pandemic, and after seeing the 2020-21 winter campaign modified, everybody was extra cautious. Even at that, an uptick in COVID forced the Bristol Public schools to postpone scholastic games and practices until after Christmas.

An email obtained from the Bristol Public Schools read as follows: "Due to an increase in positive COVID cases and confirmed transmission among athletes, all BPS athletic programs, games and practices will be paused immediately, the status of all programs to be reevaluated on December 27."

But Central ended up playing all its games, as did the boys basketball team at Eastern. The Rams were slated to be in action against Middletown before the holiday break, a pleasure that was simply deferred to another date.

Division I, II, III or who cares?

Was it such a big deal that the boys basketball program at Bristol Central didn't play in the CIAC's most competitive division? (Was this a complaint? If so, say so.)

For some reason, observers forgot that the likes of NWC, Conard, Simsbury, Amity, Crosby, Stratford, Westhill, and Prince Tech were all strong competitors in Division II that season.

The better argument would be against NWC being allowed in Division II because the program could recruit and stack the deck. (I'm not saying you're wrong, but this may be an argument for another time.)

But the road to the Division II Championship for Central was full of Division I challengers.

"Between scrimmages and regular season, we play seven out of the twenty teams in Division I," said Tim Barrette. "If you're already playing seven teams, I don't know what the advantage is about [moving] up. We've already played those teams."

Central battled New Britain before the regular season and then took out eventual Division champ East Catholic by fifteen points.

Throw in East Hartford, Wilbur Cross, and Windsor—squads that went a combined 61-37 (62.2 winning percentage). And don't forget the Springfield Central showdown could have been classified as a Division I program in Connecticut, and Northwest Catholic, ending the year at 25-3— the best team in the state not to win a championship that season.

"To be honest, the second-best team in the state to me is Northwest Catholic and they're in our division," said Barrette. "So, I mean, we're going to get tested up and down our schedule."

Simply battling all those Division I teams, despite not being a team in that set-up, truly didn't matter in the end.

The focus was on winning the Division II championship, and those battles against programs from one level up simply helped Central get better in the end.

"Our job is to be there at the end of the year" in the championship round said Barrette. "We had an opportunity to play at Mohegan Sun in our second game of the season [against East Catholic], and our message is definitely we want to finish our season there as well."

***

Week 3—Games 3 & 4

Game 3—Bristol Central versus Bristol Eastern (Tuesday, Dec. 28)— The Bristol Central Holiday Classic (from the Charles C. Marsh Gymnasium, Bristol)

The Score: 73-24

Game 4—Bristol Central versus South Windsor (Thursday, Dec. 30)— The Bristol Central Holiday Classic Finals (from the Charles C. Marsh Gymnasium, Bristol)

The Score: 77-33

In what turned into a weird and unusual situation, Bristol Eastern was slotted into an early season game against Central.

In a normal year, maybe the first city series battle occurs around January 9.

In a couple of those Colonial Conference seasons, the first BC/BE showdown was held at the end of January (in 1981-82, the first game commenced on February 5) and that became standard in the 1990's during CCC South wars.

So a mid-January or early February encounter was always expected.

But in December?!?

As it turned out, the month really didn't matter, since Central was the more established team of the two: several members of Eastern's team were underclassmen. Even more significant, Eastern was down a player or two due to COVID.

None of that mattered much as Central rolled out to a 31-3 lead with 6:16 left to play in the first half.

Everybody from Central shared the ball extremely well.

"Defensively, I thought we were really active," said Tim Barrette. "But I was more impressed on how we shared the basketball tonight. Talk about the ball movement, no one was looking for their own tonight. Everything was *share the basketball, look for the open guy*. I thought it was total team game tonight for thirty-two minutes."

Donovan Clingan didn't play much after the third period but collected 23 points and eight rebounds while Damion Glasper added ten.

"They're the number one team in the state," Eastern coach Bunty Ray said of Central. "We're struggling a little bit. We're going to have struggles against teams that are physical [and tonight], that's beyond physical. That's just a team that has a lot of answers, a lot of Division I players."

Julius Powell tallied a career-high eight points while Victor Rosa, Steve Alseph, and Jayeson VanBeveren all scored six with Mason Stokes nabbing five.

Eastern's Ben D'Amato hit two threes on his way to six points as the sophomore led his squad in scoring while fellow sophomore Isaiah Lawrence-Bynum added five points and four rebounds.

The Lancers were pesky to start. Lawrence-Bynum hit a long jumper over Clingan, and his charity toss made it a 6-3 game with 5:04 left to play in the first.

Then Central turned defense into offense. Eastern went scoreless over a seven-minute span and never recovered.

Clingan dropped in back-to-back dunks, Rosa made a steal and lay-up, and on a Glasper hoop the Rams put the game out of reach early—quickly establishing a double-figure tally—and after one, the Rams led 22-3.

"In the beginning of the game," Ray said, " you think 'all right, let's see if we can hold it, move it, you've got to shoot a high percentage, some shots go in here and there,' [but] it just doesn't take long for a mistake and a dunk [or] a turnover for Central to increase its lead I was more upset about our lack of awareness to get shots. I thought we turned the ball over more than we should have against a team that wasn't forcing that kind of tempo."

"They were kind of playing physical and strong. They weren't trapping us. We were just kind of throwing the ball away from young mistakes [and] not being in the passing lane."

As Eastern's misses began to pile up, Central notched the first 11 points of the second stanza, and the game was over at the half with Central in command 44-10. The Rams ran the Lancers off the three-point line, while in the paint there was a Clingan hungry to reject shots.

"It's tough," Barrette said, "because if you take [those three-point attempts] away, then they [Eastern] have to go inside, and there's a seven-foot monster sitting behind. Obviously, one of the strategies for us is to get up ahead, and that zone has been the best defense we've played all year."

Clingan started the third tilt with a 3 as Central ran off 10 straight points against its crosstown rival—getting pulled for good with just over five minutes to play in the quarter.

And then Powell and VanBeveren tallied a combined 10 points to close out the frame as Central held a 66-15 cushion with eight minutes left.

To end the scoring for the Rams, Jaysun Dominguez, Michael Allan, Tre Blair, and Harry Ross scored to help Central win by a 73-24 final.

"I played 15 guys for more than seven minutes today," said Barrette. "Obviously, you try to keep the game in check, but also I want to give these guys an opportunity. They work hard every day, get beat up by the best starting team [that] beats up on them too. They deserve the chance."

***

COVID always seemed to loom over the winter scholastic campaign that season as a program or two around the state still lost games.

Players were also missing games due to the pandemic, but not the Rams.

This team stayed safe, being extremely smart off the court, and those sound decisions proved that players 1-through-15 were all committed to the program and its rules and regulations.

"I'm really proud of my guys," said Barrette after defeating Eastern. "It was a whole team effort, and we have to keep going and hope COVID doesn't stop us."

***

One non-starter, VanBeveren averaged 1.7 points-per-game that season, playing in 26 of the 28 games. He almost subbed in against Northwest Catholic in the CCC Tournament Title game but ended up back on the bench as Barrette played all five of his starters the *entire* game.

But against Eastern that year, VanBeveren kicked in 6.0 ppg.

His biggest moment of the campaign, however, might have been his 3-point against Windsor on February 10.

The look on a certain opposing coach's face after that made three was priceless (*'who's that guy?!?'*).

***

In the undercard of the tournament South Windsor spun Wolcott 70-54; thus the Bobcats' three-point attack would be on display in the finals, challenging Connecticut's number one team in the championship game of the BC Holiday Classic.

Benjamin Brochu took advantage of Wolcott defensively as he burned the Naugatuck Valley League squad for 32 points.

It was a big win for the Bobcats, but sometimes advancement isn't all it's cracked up to be.

The boys basketball program at Bristol Central performed commendably that season in handing out life lessons over 28 games—and 43 consecutive contests overall.

***

Clingan seemingly broke record after record during an otherworldly senior season.

And before the BC/BE game he was honored as the program's new all-time leading rebounder.

His last rebound against East Catholic gave Clingan 1,033 for his career—one more than his late mother, Stacey Porrini Clingan (1,032).

There were a couple reasons why Clingan stayed at Central, and the chance to break his mother's record—being able to put his name in the record book next to hers—was a huge deal.

And you can't put a price on loyalty.

***

All eyes were on the Bristol Central/South Windsor final at the Bristol Central Holiday Classic.

And that was especially true with Rivoira—keeping his eyes on Brochu, the Bobcats' long-range marksman.

After Brochu canned 30-plus points against Wolcott, Carson Rivoira and Central weren't going to let that happen again.

In fact, South Windsor barely scored 30 points as a team in another thrashing in Bristol.

The sharpshooter was held to just 19, with most of that coming after Central held a 30-point cushion as the Rams crushed the Bobcats 77-33 to win its own holiday tournament.

Rivoira mercilessly hounded and harassed Brochu, who tallied seven first-half points and faced an 18-point halftime deficit.

"The difference is he [Rivoira] embraces it," said Tim Barrette of his player's defensive role. "Like right away, during the first game with South Windsor and Wolcott, when [Brochu] was going off for 27 points in the first half, Carson was just smiling at me. And I'm like 'you know?' And he says, 'I know.' And he just embraces it."

"From the time he walked in the door today, he did such a phenomenal job."

"It always seems like the kid hits the first basket and then after that, [Carson] just locks in," said Barrette. "He's the difference in a winning basketball team. Everything he does is winning plays. Everything."

"From the time he walks into the gym until the time he walks out, I can't say enough about Carson Rivoira."

On the offensive side, Rivoira nearly tallied a double-double (10 points, eight rebounds).

One story line in the game was Clingan's not garnering all the headlines. He's perfectly fine with that; besides, his 26 points, 12 rebounds, and five blocks were hard to ignore.

The game was never in doubt.

Leading 18-5 after one period, Glasper canned a hoop off a sweet Alseph feed, Rivoira added a lay-up, and when Rosa made a quick steal and found Alseph for a blistering 3-pointer, Central led 26-5 with 5:52 remaining in the half.

With that 18-point halftime edge in hand, Clingan started the third period with renewed zest.

He crammed in three straight dunks, Glasper and Rosa each hit a lay-up and after Alseph canned in two charity tosses with 3:29 left in the third, Central's cushion reached 48-18 with 3:29 to go in the stanza.

To end the third, Blair dropped in two hoops, Central led 58-24, and even as all the starters were enjoying the festivities from the bench, the reserves continued to attack.

Stokes slipped in five points—hitting a three along the way—as the bench just kept putting the ball in the hoop.

Late in the game Brown hit two hoops, Ross found Manuel Gomez for a basket and Allan's floater with 1:19 left remaining ended the 2021 portion of Central's campaign undefeated.

***

One of the many facets about playing Central was the ability of the squad's second and third units.

Those players competed against Donovan and company all season long in grueling practices, and it just made sense those reserves got better and more seasoned while taking a beating against the number one starting five in Connecticut.

"You've got to play against that team," said Barrette about his second team practicing against the first. "We're the consensus number one team in the state. That's who [the second team] practices against every day. If you practice against them, you can play against anybody. So when they come into the game, [they're ready]. Mike Allan, he said to me tonight after he made that nice basket at the end, 'coach, that's because I face pressure every single day' that he's starting to bring it up in practice. It's only going to make our younger guys better."

"The guys that have been playing JV have been doing a fantastic job at that level and they haven't missed a beat stepping up to the varsity level."

***

Fans not accustomed to seeing what Steve Alseph could do got a major helping of his abilities when he made an under-the-leg pass for a huge Clingan alley-oop jam against Wolcott.

The transfer looked like he'd been playing with this group for years as he helped bring even more stability and chemistry to the program.

Alseph was capable of being a double-figure scorer in his own right, hitting a season-high 13 points against Enfield.

But the senior bought into the program, what Barrette was preaching, and the unselfish nature of the team which was one of the staples to its ultimate success.

"These guys are unselfish," said Barrette. "The turnovers we had were us trying to make the extra pass for us to score half the time. We're going to be a really dangerous team if we continue to play with the unselfishness we're playing with. Guys seem to have more fun making the pass than they do scoring themselves."

***

Central ends the 2021 calendar year undefeated.

After posting a 15-0 record the season before, the Rams went 4-0 to begin the 2021-22 campaign—tallying up a 19-0 record during 2021, defeating teams like Windsor, Northwest Catholic, and East Catholic (twice) along the way.

"Our goal was to end 2021 undefeated," said Tim Barrette. "And we did that. We were 15-0 in the spring [last season] and 4-0 to start the year here. That's a pretty good run."

After that 4-0 start to the 2021-22 campaign by the basketball squad, the football and soccer teams, as well as the basketball squad from last year's COVID shortened season, combined for a 40-6-2 record.

***

After seven days off Plainville was on the docket to start the new year in a historically tough place for Central to play.

"We get to work [Friday] and get ready for Plainville on Monday and go from there," said Barrette. [In terms of being safe from] COVID, hopefully my guys make good decisions. We seemed to have all bought in right now and that buy-in is half the battle."

"I'm really happy to coach this team."

Six words typified what a Tim Barrette program is like for his players:

"There are no off days here."

***

Another History Lesson

There had been some near misses in terms of state tournament qualification for Central in the mid 1970's.

Central head coach Fred Malan had back-to-back 10-win campaigns in 1973 and 1974 and that would be the start of a stretch of exceptionally good basketball by the Central program.

From 1972-1990 the Rams won at least 10 games in all but one season as the talent level at Central began to increase.

The 1972-73 squad fell to Wilby (60-55) in postseason play while the following season, Dennis Hernandez (22.0 ppg) and David Hernandez—a couple of talented and athletic juniors—got the squad back to the postseason but fell 79-72 in first round play against Rockville.

In 1975 the Central program went 17-4, and were Colonial Conference champs. With the Rams' 69-66 victory over No. 11 Naugatuck in first round play on March 5 of that year, things were turning around for the program.

The Rams, ranked No. 6, saw Dave Berlinski score 24 points, Dennis Hernandez add 15, and Mark Masi contribute 10, while Dave Hernandez and Mark Ziogas each chipped in seven.

The Greyhounds led 41-35 at the half but could not maintain the advantage.

Trailing by one late, Central's John Thomas made two critical free throws with 1:47 left to ice the game.

Central missed just six of 29 free throws to advance in Class AA play.

That contest was the Rams' first playoff victory since 1964.

Coach Malan's teams then won twenty games in three of the next four seasons—helping Central claim the Colonial Conference crown over those three seasons.

***

The 2021-22 schedule was like a rollercoaster for Central, sometimes seeing three games in five days in the middle of February to a back-to-back situation on Jan. 17 (vs. Maloney) and January 18 (vs. Middletown).

But there were gaps, a couple due to weather, that saw Central get plenty of practice time in the home gym.

After the Rams won its own Christmas Tournament, the squad played once over an 11-day stretch (at Plainville, January 3).

The Rams then had a full week off between Middletown (January 18) and Enfield (January 25).

However, those were just some of the elements every state championship team had to contend with over a grueling season.

It's always a marathon, not a sprint.

***

Week 4—Game 5

Game 5—Bristol Central at Plainville (Monday, January 3)—CCC South Game (from the Ivan Wood Gymnasium, Plainville)

The Score: 81-42

The most interesting fact, when Central plays at Plainville, is that the Rams' team always has a tough time shooting in that well-lit gym.

Frankly, the Ivan Wood Gymnasium is one of the best facilities in all of the Central Connecticut Conference.

It's bright, the court is big, and the games always seem competitive. Moreover, Central seems to struggle against the Blue Devils.

During the Rams' 15-0 dash in 2021, only three teams came within striking distance against the undefeated program.

Avon made a huge comeback on February 10 but fell to Central in Bristol, 78-76.

And later on against Plainville, the Rams nabbed a huge 64-61 win from the Ivan Wood Gymnasium (February 27).

Of course, the final game against East Catholic needed overtime as Central hung on to take the CCC Tournament championship as Rosa found Clingan for the game-winning hoop in the 69-68 final.

But Barrette's teams have absolutely struggled in Plainville, a pattern that would not repeat itself on January 3.

***

Central started the game off a bit slowly as early unselfishness led to miscues and turnovers.

And Plainville's Brennan Staubley got off to a hot start. Staubley, who was slated to play baseball at the University of Hartford but switched to Franklin Pierce once UHART moved from Division I to Division III for athletics, canned eight of his team-best 15 points early on.

Staubley's corner jumper with 4:25 to play in the first period made it an 8-8 game as the Blue Devils continued to around.

But the Rams scored 27 of the next 32 points over a nine-minute suffocating burst and rolled to an 81-42 win to move to 5-0 overall. Plainville fell to 1-5.

Damion Glasper started the run with a baseline lay-up, Donovan Clingan put back a miss, and when Carson Rivoira made a steal for a hoop, everything started clicking for the visitors.

Central led 23-12 after one, and a Rivoira lay-up with 1:35 to go made it a 39-17 contest at the half, sparing the squad a tongue-lashing from its coach.

"This place has been our death trap for three years," said Tim Barrette of Plainville. "I literary said to my guys before the game, 'can I not come in here and have to punch a locker [or] kick a locker to get us going because it's a one-point game?' Don't get me wrong, we were up 22 points at the half but at the same time, defensively we allowed [Plainville] to get a couple of easy looks early on, and they made them."

"Give Plainville credit, but we were a little unselfish early where we probably just could have scored and if we scored, we could have probably been up even more at the half."

Defense leads to offense, and the 81 points to that point of the season was Central's scoring high for the year.

Balance was the key for Central once again, and this was one of the rare games that Clingan did not lead the squad in scoring.

Glasper attacked the hoop, scoring a game-high 17 points, while Clingan eased his way to 16 points and 12 rebounds.

Rivoira added 13 points and simply hit offensive rebounds for second shooting opportunities, while Mason Stokes made the most of his minutes. He hit two three-pointers as he dropped in a career-high eight points, as did Aaron Brown with seven.

Steve Alseph also flipped in seven while Tre Blair and Julius Powell each had four

At one point of the contest, a floater by Blair with 6:31 left made it a 44-point game (73-29), a lead that allowed some bench players to get some minutes..

Zach Vanasse made a free throw while Brown had a put-back to end the scoring as the Rams won by 39 points.

It was the 30th[t] all-time victory against Plainville. Central has won 78.9-percent of its all-time games against the Blue Devils (30-8).

***

Carson Rivoira (Larry Bird)

Over the early days of the three-point shot in the NBA, Boston Celtics' legend Larry Bird was one of the first good shooters from deep. And while Rivoira didn't start his career off as a long-range marksman, he worked hard to improve his 3-point shooting. He improved it so much that he started taking—and making—those threes in games, to the astonishment of other teams.

The evolution of big men shooting the three-pointer is becoming commonplace in the scholastic game and the Rivoira/Clingan combo proved to be long range threats opponents couldn't ignore. Those two were responsible for 22 of Central's 86 threes that the starting five made.

When your forward/center cash in over a quarter of your three-pointers, defenses have to stretch even further to guard those threats, opening up everything else on the court.

The Larry Bird moniker for Rivoira is appropriate because both athletes simply love to compete (and shoot threes). On the court Bird was a bulldog on both sides of the ball and, like Rivoira, had a tremendous basketball IQ, loved to rebound, box out, and even talk a little trash.

Was Rivoira ever the player Bird was on the scholastic level? No. But Rivoira hounded and harassed opponents, played every minute like it was his last, and knew where to be on the court—one of those in-the-moment guys who makes every teammate around him better.

Rivoira was just as tenacious as Bird and his competitiveness—on and off the court—was the attitude every young player should want to emulate. In addition, Rivoira earned All-New England honors in soccer as a midfielder— the first player in Bristol Central history to achieve that honor.

He tallied 19 goals and eight assists over a complete season, and on corner kicks he was simply bigger than most defenders, heading in more than his share of scores. This outstanding young man achieved on the field, on the court but also in the classroom. At the beginning of May, he received the Connecticut Association of Boards of Education Leadership Award— a prestigious honor and well deserved.

He's also an eloquent speaker and, at Donovan's UConn signing, was the most polished individual who took the microphone that day. Years before, Coach Barrette was the glue while playing at Bristol Eastern; Rivoira did the same at Central.

***

Even though COVID never derailed Central in 2021-22—with the exception of the stoppage of play before Christmas—the squad had a 10-day layoff before the schedule began to heat up again.

Because of a snowstorm, the game against East Hartford, scheduled for Friday, January 7, was pushed to the following week. But that just meant more practice time for the top-ranked squad and a chance to really prepare for those three clashes (Newington, at East Hartford, at Springfield Central) over the second week of January. And at 2-4, that squad from East Hartford was much better than advertised.

"This is what we want," Barrette said of playing tough competition. "These guys want to play the best teams [and] that's why we have the schedule we have," said Barrette. "But every game counts."

The break from in-game competition gave a chance for plenty of reflection of what the 2021-22 campaign turned out to be for the Rams.

***

Clingan hadn't put up his monster scoring totals as of yet but was certainly heading towards Bristol's all-time scholastic scoring records.

After the contest in Plainville, Clingan netted 24.5 points-per-game, Glasper came in (13.5 ppg) followed by Rivoira (7.2 ppg), Alseph (6.3 ppg) and the surprising Stokes (4.2 ppg).

Not lost in the shuffle was the contribution by Rosa who started the season with a little tape around his lower leg. No one really noticed because it didn't affect his play much, even after 11 grueling football games.

His defense was always on display, and the havoc that he and Alseph caused in Central's 1-3-1 defensive schemes was nightmarish to opponents.

***

The GameTimeCT Top10 Boys Basketball Poll from January 10 had the Rams in first place, scoring 17 of 18 of the first place votes. No. 2 Northwest Catholic (6-1 overall) earned the other vote. They had won six straight to that point in the campaign since losing to Wilbur Cross (72-68) back on December 18.

Barrette had mentioned that the team from Northwest could be better than East Catholic, and the long-time Bristol Central coach expected to see the Lions somewhere down the road.

And twice along the way to a state title, the talented Northwest Catholic team stood in the way.

***

At that point, Central was second in the Division II standings: Conard of West Hartford (7-0 overall, 19 power points) was in front. Central had 17.

The Chieftains (In 2022 they would adopt a new mascot—the Red Wolves) had super sophomore Riley Fox and a lot of talented individuals surrounding him.

The problem for Conard was that Central, NWC, and Wilton were just a bit stronger.

A Conard/Central clash would have been entertaining, but the schedule did not provide for it. (Little known fact: former Hartford Public and NBA standout Marcus Camby started his scholastic career at Conard).

***

Donovan's path to Bristol was somewhat untraditional, and once the Waterbury transfer arrived, he still had to force his way into the lane every game and face attempts to block the path to the basket.

It seldom mattered.

Week 5—Games 6, 7 & 8

Game 6—Bristol Central versus Newington (Monday, January 10)— CCC Interdivisional Game (from the Charles C. Marsh Gymnasium, Bristol)

The Score: 69-35

Game 7—Bristol Central at East Hartford (Wednesday, January 12)— CCC Interdivisional Game (from East Hartford High School)

The Score: 70-47

Game 8—Bristol Central at Springfield Central (Friday, January 14)—Spalding Hoophall Classic (from Blake Arena at Springfield College, Massachusetts)

The Score: 53-44

After seven days off, Central had an interesting week that started off with a beatable Newington squad, then took on East Hartford, a squad that could be a bit unpredictable, and ended with a prime-time battle against then-undefeated Springfield Central.

As the week went on, the competition increased in toughness.

The Nor'easters from Newington could have brought thunder, lightning, and the Indiana National Guard to Bristol that night, but hurricane Donovan Clingan left another path of destruction in Central's 34-point thumping.

Clingan was responsible for 29 points in that mauling, Steve Alseph buried a 3 in his 11-point effort, and Damion Glasper added 10.

It was good to see Jelani Walton get some floor time, adding a then season-high five points to the effort, Jayeson VanBeveren drained a 3 to pace Central's onslaught.

Not all the starters got into the scoring column. Carson Rivoira did not score a point that night, and it was the first of five games that season in which a starter from Central went scoreless.

Of course, the game of basketball isn't always about scoring.

Sure, we'll rush to the stat sheet after every game and normally the first thing you're looking to see is who scored what. But Rivoira, Victor Rosa, and Alseph were so much more than just scorers. They provided hustle, guile, and intelligence.

That trio—along with Glasper—were stat-stuffers in terms of rebounds, assists, steals and all the intangibles that constitute a winning team.

Gavin Gray led Newington (3-4) with nine points as the program absorbed its 40th loss to the Rams.

***

Two days after thumping Newington, Central traveled to East Hartford to play a squad that also came into play just under .500 but who were not playing like a middle-of-the-road program. The Hornets were 3-4 and had added a player Central did not get a chance to scout.

It was one of those games in which, even though Central led comfortably throughout the second half, pulling Clingan out of the game early was difficult.

The Hornets could quickly throw 10 points up on the board, forcing Barrette to keep the starting unit in a bit longer.

However, the results weren't much different. Clingan played one heck of a game, scooping up a career-high 40 points to go along with 22 rebounds and five blocked shots en route to a 70-47 victory.

East Hartford elected not to respect the outside shooting barrage from Rivoira, and so the senior dropped in three 3-pointers on his way to a career-high 18 points. He just kept shooting threes.

Alseph, Glasper, and Rosa combined for ten total points as Central moved to 7-0 overall. Zander Robinson flipped in a team-high 17 for the Hornets, but the home squad trailed Central 38-22 at intermission.

The Hornets never tasted the lead though Robinson dropped in two 3-pointers over first period action to make it a 12-10 game with 2:16 left in the frame. A three by the Hornets' Chris Brown chopped the deficit to 28-22 with 3:10 remaining in the first half before Central's defense took over.

Highlighted by an Alseph steal and massive dunk by Clingan, the Rams' 10-0 push to end the stanza gave the visitors a 16-point edge at the half and that same duo notched the first six points of the third—ended on a steal and spinning lay-up by Alseph—as the cushion reached 20 (44-24) with 5:20 left.

And then over an eight-minute span, Clingan dominated—scoring 16 of Central's next 22 points. His offensive rebound and put-back with 4:02 to play made it 66-38 as the 7-foot-2 center tallied his 40th point—his then career-high.

Powell got in late to kick in a miss as the Rams were 70-47 winners in East Hartford. But just two short days later, it was time to get real…

***

Travis Knight?

Sometimes you read an unbelievably bad comparison in a newspaper or online . Right around the start of 2022, the Hartford Courant printed a story on Clingan as one of UConn's featured recruits.

Some of the article was a bit on the wild side, claiming that Clingan tended to be frozen in time on the defense end and let guys go by him. Sometimes that was necessary to avoid a third foul. The article claimed he chased blocks—a rare occurrence.

But it pointed out that he could get into foul trouble— the Springfield Central game was one such occurrence—and he needed to improve his foot speed, endurance, and athleticism.

Those are all things every scholastic player must improve at the collegiate level, burt the laughable part of the story was comparing Clingan to former UConn player Travis Knight, a six point, six rebound-per-game guy for his career. He didn't have 3-point range (until Rick Pitino, a coach that also tried to recruit Donovan at Iona, had him shooting those in Boston), and nearly wasn't as polished as Clingan was entering Storrs.

Knight's official visits were to UCLA (he lived out in California, then Utah), Arizona State University and UConn.

Both players won championships as seniors, but Clingan has such a bigger upside than Knight did at the time.

Unlike Knight, Clingan was already prepping for his move to NCAA Division I hoop by losing a few pounds and getting stronger.

Clingan could be much more than six points and six rebounds if everything works out for the impressive big man from Bristol.

at Springfield

Here was the star-studded line-up for the Hoophall Classic that night.

FRIDAY, JANUARY 14

3:00 PM (Women)—Springfield International Charter School, MA vs. Wahconah Regional High School, MA

4:30 PM (Women)—Springfield Central High School, MA vs. Cathedral Catholic High School, CA.

6:00 PM (Men)—East Catholic High School, CT vs. Mater Dei High School, CA.

7:30 PM (Men)—Springfield Central High School, MA vs. Bristol Central High School, CT.

9:00 PM (Men)—Westtown School, PA vs. Vertical Academy, NC (shown on ESPN+).

Talk about a star-studded card...

Barrette wanted to get his team as much non-conference exposure as possible, obviously getting his center the best possible competition possible.

But due to COVID in 2021, a trip to play in the Hoophall Classic was not going to be allowed by the CIAC. Due to the pandemic out-of-state-trips were not allowed.

That all changed in 2022 when Central traveled to Springfield College to square off against Springfield Center in a major league bout.

And for the few times that year the Rams had to play for a big stretch without Clingan in the mix due to foul trouble.

Against East Catholic Powell and company held the fort, but this time around an incredibly talented Springfield squad made Central pay with full court traps that led to turnovers.

In the end Central triumphed again—squaring up a 53-44 victory as the Rams ended the campaign 1-0 outside the state of Connecticut.

The Rams led wire-to-wire, though Springfield closed to within six (45-39) with 2:09 left.

But then Rosa found Clingan twice for hoops—one coming off a goaltending call—as Central had the lead back to 10 again (49-39) with 1:13.

There was a report that Clingan tallied a triple-double, but a couple of competent stat guys (one of those statisticians went by the name of Keith Lipscomb) recorded the big man with 24 points, 16 rebounds, and seven blocked shots.

Several publications had Clingan with 10 blocked shots, but while he didn't reject that many, he altered several attempts as the home team shot just 19-percent from the field by the halftime break.

The Rams went up 8-0 right off the bat as Alseph hit a lay-up then found Rivoira for a quick hoop.

Rosa added a bucket, and when Rivoira missed an attempt Clingan was there to follow it in as Springfield Central was misfiring from the onset.

It was 14-7 after one and off a hoop by Springfield's Joseph Griffin the deficit was trimmed to 14-9 with 6:58 left before the half.

From there the Rams used a 18-7 burst as Rivoira and Rosa drained back-to-back threes late in the second as Clingan was being triple-teamed.

Rosa ended the half with a jumper as the Rams scooped up a 32-16 edge by intermission.

At one point Springfield misfired on 30-of-37 of its first field goals and was just one-for-11 from three-point territory.

Rivoira hit another 3 early in the third, and Clingan put back another miss as Central took charge at 37-18 with 5:27 remaining.

But Clingan picked up his third foul with 4:33 left in the stanza and was subbed out.

Aaron Brown came in, but the full-court pressure caused havoc for the Rams. Springfield went on a 10-0 push to trim the deficit to 37-28 with 30 seconds left in the third.

Clingan reentered, making 3-of-4 free throws and, off a lay-up from Glasper, Central restored order—leading 42-30 with 6:55 remaining. However, he picked up a fourth foul with 6:26 to play, and wound up back on the pine.

Springfield used a 6-1 burst to cut the deficit to seven—sandwiched around a steal and 1-of-2 free throws by Powell—as the home team trailed 43-36 with 3:53 left.

But by the time Clingan came back, Springfield had run out of gas and missed five consecutive foul shots, Clingan scored seven consecutive points for the Rams, and when Alseph went to ice the event at the free throw line, he and one of the Springfield players started chatting.

Alseph quickly pointed to the scoreboard as the opposing player barked something in his direction (something about not giving a *flying frisbee* about the score and refused to shake Alseph's hand) with 15 seconds to go.

In the end Bristol Central passed the Hoophall Classic challenge with its nine-point win at Springfield College.

Springfield Central had won 29 straight games going into the game versus Bristol Central. Overall, the Rams defense held Springfield to 16-of-63 shooting from the field—a 25.4-percent shooting clip. And to the surprise of absolutely nobody, Clingan was named MVP of the game.

*****

There aren't many defensive "answers" for a player whose fingertips are above the rim, other than hoping he'll miss. Clingan didn't miss very much.

***

Clingan ended up making the All-Showcase Second Team that weekend, another noteworthy accomplishment over a remarkable career at Bristol Central.

The Springfield Central showdown was the only game that season in which Glasper did not score a single point.

He was also harassed and hounded the entire evening, but when he wasn't scoring, Glasper simply did all the winning things a successful player would do. He was the guy who would pass the ball that got someone else the assist and he knew how to play off Clingan to perfection.

Glasper scored over 300 points in his senior campaign and more than carried the scoring load when needed.

In another program, Glasper could have been a 20-25 point-per-game scorer, but for the Rams, he fit in perfectly as the squad's second leading points generator.

While a Michael Jordan/Scottie Pippen comparison isn't exactly the one to use here, Glasper's value to a successful cannot be underestimated. He was a tremendous competitor and in the end, a state champion.

***

After that trip to Springfield, Central had a slew of home games to deal with to end the month of January.

Maloney and Middletown made a unique back-to-back, and that was followed by yet another week off!

From there, Enfield in Bristol, a road game at Hartford Public, and a home confrontation against Platt were on the docket for the Rams.

***

On January 17, the GameTimeCT Boys Basketball Top 10 Poll had Central in first place once again.

The Rams garnered 17 of the 18 first place votes for 538 points in the poll.

Here's the rest of the poll as voted by media members around the state.

Second: Northwest Catholic (one first place vote, 492 votes) was 7-1 overall.

Third: Windsor (458 votes) hung in at third with a 6-1 record. Both teams would place Central later in February (The Rams ended the year a perfect 4-0 against those two top ranked squads).

4. Notre Dame-West Haven

5. Ridgefield

6. Kolbe Cathedral

7. Naugatuck

8. East Catholic

9. Norwich Free Academy

10. Wilbur Cross

***

During week six of the scholastic campaign, Central was about to hit the midway point of the season after battles against Maloney and Middletown in Bristol.

The Rams ended up winning those two showdowns by an average of 37 points.

Week 6—Games 9 & 10

Game 9—Bristol Central versus Maloney (Monday, January 17)—CCC South Game (from the Charles C. Marsh Gymnasium, Bristol)

The Score: 74-30

Game 10—Bristol Central versus Middletown (Tuesday, January 18)—CCC South Game (from the Charles C. Marsh Gymnasium, Bristol)

The Score: 80-50

The Maloney team was a squad in the middle of rebuilding, and the young team was completely overwhelmed against the veterans across the court when they showed up to play in mid-January.

This would turn out to be the closer of the two games the squads competed in that season. And the 44-point win proved to be history-making for the Bristol school as well.

With its 80-50 win over the Spartans, Central won its 24th straight contest—tying the school record set in 1989-1990.

The Rams led 21-8 after eight minutes and blew open the game in the second stanza—outscoring Maloney 23-6—on the way to a 44-14 edge at halftime.

Donte Kelly (10 points) hit for double-figures that night, but the Spartans were completely and utterly overwhelmed.

Donovan Clingan toasted Maloney for a game-high 26 points and splashed in two 3-pointers. While no other player scored more than ten other than Kelley and Clingan, Central showed remarkable scoring balance.

Damion Glasper and Steve Alseph each tallied nine points, Carson Rivoira chipped in with seven, Jelani Walton tied his career high of six points, Aaron Brown nabbed five, Julius Powell scored four while Zach Vanasse hit a 3 to lead the offensive attack.

That put the Rams at 9-0 on the campaign with a huge tilt against Middletown on deck the following night—a test that would become extremely physical.

Versus Middletown

The boys basketball team from Middletown had some size and speed and was expected to give the Rams some fits on the court. And being overly aggressive against Clingan was one such method it used early in the showdown.

Middletown coach Eric Holley even brought in big Teejay Jackson to body-up on Clingan—something the referees put a stop to both times the 6-foot-4 giant came into the game for defensive purposes.

The Blue Dragons sealed the big man front and back—a tactic several teams used against Clingan over the years—but it was just a matter of time before a suffocating run did in Middletown.

That physical play seemed to energize Clingan on the defensive end; he started blocking shots left and right. And for some reason another opponent forgot about Rivoira's outside shooting.

Leading 9-7 early in the second quarter, Central blasted Middletown with a 18-2 burst—highlighted by a Clingan dunk and two three-point bombs by

Rivoira—as a Powell putback and two charity tosses from Glasper made it a 27-9 game with 7:27 remaining in first half play.

"Carson, Damion, Victor and Steve made shots early [and] if you're not going to guard one of them, people don't give us enough credit. We can shoot the ball when we're open," said Central coach Tim Barrette.

Middletown trimmed the deficit to 33-20 late in the second quarter but a 9-2 Central run, with two buckets from Victor Rosa kicked in for good measure, saw the home team lead 42-23.

Central never let it get its cushion dip below that halftime push, and the contest became a blowout. With Central leading by twenty Clingan found Glasper for a baseline 3, and later the center notched 10 of 12 points for the Rams, finishing the third with an offensive rebound and put-back, as Central nabbed an imposing 67-34 lead with one period to play.

Aaron Brown cashed in on a three early in the fourth and a Rosa free throw pushed the margin to 34 (71-37) with 6:58 left. In the final minutes, Powell dropped in a hoop, Vanasse added five points—including a 3—to the scorebook. A late floater by Walton concluded the 30-point victory. It was the tenth win for the Central program and 25th in a row, establishing a new program record.

Clingan just missed a first-half triple double as his final line was 19 points, 22 rebounds and that school record of 16 blocked shots. Again, the physical nature of the game saw Clingan do his job well under extreme pressure.

"It's not easy when you've got two guys taking out your knees on every play and obviously, I understand why people are physical with him," said Barrette of Middletown's approach against Clingan. "What I liked most I thought was he didn't take a play off on the defensive end. He led us defensively while allowing guys on the offensive end, taking advantage of the 4-on-3 we were playing because of the double-team."

Alseph added 12 points, Rosa re-tied his season-high of seven points and Rivoira added 11 points—hitting three threes—while Clingan was grabbing boards and making outlet passes to streaking teammates for buckets and hockey assists—passes that made the pass that made the basket).

"I thought we overshared a couple times tonight but I thought our guys are sharing the basketball," said Barrette. "They enjoy playing together and that's very obvious when you watch them on the floor."

Matt Steuerwald led Middletown with 12 points and Chace Petgrave added 11. No other player scored more than five points as foul trouble, missed shots, and rejected field goal attempts by Clingan completely shut down the Blue Dragons' offense. Eli Wilborn, Middletown's top player, was limited to just five points.

***

Glasper's 17 points was a huge contribution to the winning endeavor over Middletown, and when he was able to get into the offensive flow, the game opened up for everyone.

He notched 12 of his 17 points over first half play.

"He found his rhythm last night" against Maloney said Barrette of Glasper. "He made his first shot [Monday] night and things seemed to open up. You've got to understand, he's the second-best basketball player in terms of scoring. And when that happens, everyone saw his performance against East Catholic—that's the film that's out there—so a lot of teams have been focusing on taking him away. But at the same time, he's just got to keep his head in it. He did a good job."

***

Central (10-0) remained No. 1 in the state poll as of January 24, again getting all but one first place vote.

Northwest Catholic continued to hang around—still with just the one loss at 8-1, winners of seven straight. The Lions earned that other first place tally.

Windsor (8-1, 494 points) remained in third place, Notre Dame-West Haven (12-0, 480) took fourth while Ridgefield (8-1, 380) was hanging in at fifth.

The only other notable team in that top-10 was East Catholic, but the Eagles had lost three out of first nine games over a very tough schedule.

***

The pace began speeding up after the holidays with fewer Covid interruptions, though the weather still played a role. Here the Rams are on their way to a decisive 46-point win over Middletown.

***

Central was off again for another week, playing a schedule that ran from Tuesday (January 18) to Tuesday (January 25). In between, Clingan and company continued to win at practice and prepare for Enfield and Hartford Public—two squads below the .500 threshold. Snow days were common in Bristol but it seemed like it snowed just a little too much throughout various points of the championship campaign.

The Rams entered the final week of January as the No. 1 team in the CIAC Division II standings.

And getting to 10-0 was a big deal for the program at Central.

"We're halfway there. We're 10-0," said Barrette "And truthfully, we're a third of the way there because if everything pans out, playing in [the CCC and state] tournaments, we'd like to be 30-0 by the end of this year."

Fortunately, Barrette wasn't teaching math at BCHS because no matter what combination of games were remaining that season, a 30-0 finish simply wasn't in the cards. Thanks to all that amazing regular season play, a first round bye was in the works in the CIAC Division II Tournament. There would be a well-deserved game off.

But there were ten more regular season games to go.

***

Health was the key to any championship season and the Rams were healthy nearly from start to finish.

Barrette's troops bought into the system and program, working hard in practice and keeping away from situations that could make them threatened COVID). The Rams were lucky on that front as other programs around the state lost players due to the pandemic.

"We're trying to stay healthy," said Barrette. "And then we have to get ready for [Enfield this] week.

***

Adding his 1,421 points coming into the season, Clingan had scored 1,677 overall by the midpoint of the regular season. He trailed only Martin Huckaby (1,825) for Central's all-time Central scoring record to that point of the season.

Glasper was second on the team in scoring (10.9 ppg), followed by Rivoira (9.1 ppg), Alseph (7.2 ppg), Rosa (4.1 ppg) and Powell (3.1 ppg). Along those lines, VanBeveren and Blair played in every game to date and this can't be undersold, for consistency counts. With it a successful program gets the job done.

***

Week 7—Games 11 & 12

Game 11—Bristol Central versus Enfield (Tuesday, January 25)— CCC Interdivisional Game (from the Charles C. Marsh Gymnasium, Bristol)

The Score: 91-63

Game 12—Bristol Central at Hartford Public (Thursday, January 27)—CCC Interdivisional Game (from the Hartford Public Fieldhouse)

The Score: 85-71

After a week off, Central was ready to battle Enfield, a program that ended up giving teams in Bristol some real heartburn over the previous three or four seasons.

But the Eagles were in a downward pattern in 2021-22.

And even though Central belted Enfield by a 91-63 final, some defensive letdowns didn't exactly please the Rams' coach and he let them know it at halftime.

The home team, which led by 23 at the half, blasted the game open and quickly. It was a forty-point affair (71-31) with 2:38 showing on the clock in the third quarter.

That halftime message was received, loud and clear.

"I wasn't too happy at halftime to be honest," said Barrette. "I didn't think we practiced very well yesterday, and I thought it carried over to the first half. We threw some lackadaisical passes, but that's how we practiced yesterday. I told the guys at halftime that's on me as a coach because I'll be the first to take one, take it for those guys when we lose but then I have to be the person I need to be in practice and they've got to be better than that."

"We came out in the second half with a new energy, pushed it out to forty real quick, almost doubled them up to start the third quarter and that was kind of my message at halftime."

It was triple-double time once again for the mighty Donovan Clingan as he ripped the Eagles for 25 points, 19 rebounds, and 10 blocks. He collected his triple-double evn before the end of the first half and went over 1,700 points for his career that evening (1,702).

But the fun was only starting for Central.

There was Damion Glasper, scoring 10 points in the first quarter on his way to 18.

Steve Alseph punched home a career-high 13 points, Victor Rosa and Carson Rivoira each tallied six, Jayeson VanBeveren (five points) cashed in on his first three, and the combination of Mason Stokes, Tre Blair, and Jelani Walton all chipped in with four.

And Alseph dropped in his Central high of 13 points, again dishing off the rock with gusto and scoring when the opportunity came about.

He ran the offense extremely well, a fact not lost on Barrette.

"People don't realize that Steve Alseph can score the basketball more than people know," said Barrette. "He just enjoys making a good pass more than scoring itself and you always need one of those [players] around. We're blessed to have him."

The 91 points was the most ever scored by a Donovan Clingan team from Bristol Central.

Enfield fell to 3-8 off the loss while the Rams moved to 11-0.

Enfield's Isaiah Plummer and Tighe Thebodeau each scored as the squad bombed from long-range with some success.

The Rams usually were extremely successful in running teams off the three-point line but the Eagles stayed poised around the arc.

A big 3 here and there kept the visitors hanging around despite never leading.

"Enfield shot the ball really well tonight," said Barrette. "They made [nine] threes."

Central started the game on a 20-4 burst—started by a dump by Rosa to Clingan as he jammed in the first hoop of the showdown.

The home team scored 10 points over the final 1:08 of the first frame.

Glasper canned a 3, an offensive rebound and put-back from Rivoira led to two free throws, Alseph hit a hoop and Blair (notching a career-high tying four points) found VanBeveren for a 3 at the buzzer that made it a 25-6 game through one.

Enfield chopped the deficit to 15 (27-12), but Central eventually pushed it out to 29 again before settling at 47-24 at halftime.

The Eagles trailed by 40 at one point in the third period, and the reserves hit the game midway through.

Late in the game a Walton steal led to a Blair hoop, and Mike Allan made a sweet feed to Stokes for a basket.

Harry Ross put the icing on the cake as his put-back ended the scoring at 91, moving the Rams to 11-0 overall.

***

Over the course of the season some of the opposing coaches going up against Central showed obvious frustration when battling Donovan Clingan.

Here are half-a-dozen of the more entertaining quotes as coaches tried to motivate their players:

"Don't be scared…wake up and play!"

"Everyone is such a fan (in regard to players interacting with Clingan on the court)."

"So what if they got this 7-foot guy?!?"

"That's not a natural talent…"

"You gave up two offensive rebounds to him already…LET'S GO!!!"

"[Is there] three seconds in basketball?!?"

There were more, some unprintable.

Sitting behind the bench of an opposing team battling undefeated Central was truly entertaining as programs tried to navigate the shark infested waters in Bristol.

At Hartford Public

The game against Hartford Public was only close once Barrette had pulled his starters.

Public made a huge comeback against Central's reserves late in the showdown, but the home team could not get over the hump, especially after they gave up 85 points, only six off Central's season high that season.

Coming into the game, the Rams had only beaten the program from Hartford once in eight tries.

The victory over the Owls was the program's 27th consecutive win—the longest winning streak in Connecticut.

Barrette said fans were not allowed into the game—leading to a quiet gymnasium at the field house from Hartford Public.

Clingan scooped up 31 points, 16 rebounds, and seven blocks to lead the visitors. He also tallied four assists.

He ended up hitting 13-of-18 field goals but missed all three 3-pointers he took (Clingan ended up shooting 33-percent from deep for the season).

Glasper had a big night, scooping up 14 points, eight rebounds, and four steals while Rivoira had another gem—posting seven points, 12 boards, two assists, and two steals.

Alseph (nine points, three rebounds, nine assists) just missed a double-double, Rosa added six points and a couple of assists while Powell tied his career high of eight points, posting four boards and rejecting two shots along the way.

VanBeveren hit 3-of-4 field goals on his way to seven points and three rebounds, Walton dropped in two points and two rebounds, and Mike Allan canned a free throw as Central led 26-14 after eight minutes of play.

Central hit 36-of-70 field goal attempts in the game, just over 51-percent.

The Rams stretched the deficit to 48-27 at the half and 71-45 through three. The starters played in the first three quarters before the reserves had to deal with full court pressing tactics until the very end.

Public outscored Central 26-14 over the final quarter but Barrette wasn't interested in reinserting his starters into a game that was all but over. Fifteen-plus turnovers allowed Hartford to hang around a bit, but the Owls were limited to just five offensive rebounds in the game as second chance points were at a premium.

The Rams were without the services of the injured Tre Blair—who spent much of the second half of the season on crutches, and Public pressed Central's second team into oblivion in the fourth frame.

Off that 14-point triumph, Central was 12-0.

But two challenges—one of epic proportions—were on the docket the following week.

The game at Wilbur Cross would put Bristol Central's undefeated streak on the line.

But first it was a showdown with a young but dangerous squad from Platt High School in Meriden.

***

Central, at 12-0, was in first place in the CIAC Division II with 54 power points. Westhill sat in second place (11-1 overall), Conard was third (11-1), and Wilton—a team that was, perhaps, Central's toughest opponent that season—was hanging in fourth (10-1).

The Rams remained in the top position in the race for the top spot in Division II for the rest of the regular season.

***

Up to that point of the year, Central was one of seven squads in the state that had not tasted defeat. Notre Dame-West Haven (14-0), RHAM (13-0), Naugatuck (12-0), Cromwell (11-0), Sports Medical and Sciences Academy (11-0) and Bloomfield (10-0) were also sitting pretty. And a couple of those squads ended up as state champions.

Would Bristol Central be one of those teams?

***

After Clingan's 31 points at Hartford Public, the senior tallied 1,733 scholastic points, just 92 points away from Huckaby's school scoring.

And the big man needed 102 points to tie Bristol's all-time leading scholastic scoring mark held by St. Paul's Carey Edwards (1,835 points).

Averaging 26.0 ppg, Clingan seemed ready to set the record on February 7 at Lewis Mills, unless their head coach Ryan Raponey had a plan to slow the big man down that evening…

***

The GameTimeCT Boys Basketball Top 10 Poll was released on the final day of January with the Rams at No. 1 overall. They were rolling at 12-0—netting 568 points—and ranked first in the CIAC Division II rankings.

Wilbur Cross fell out of the top-10 that week, but the logic was simple: if the Governors defeated Bristol Central in New Haven, the squad would shoot right back up the rankings.

That February 2 showdown promised an amazing pair of games with Hillhouse hosting No. 3 Windsor as the undercard. And by the completion of the night, the SCC proved to be a very tough league against the class of the CCC.

***

But before that Wilbur Cross tilt, Clingan was about to break another record over at Bristol Central when the squad took on a very pesky Platt program.

Could the Rams keep its focus in what turned into "Tournament Preview Week" between the Cross and Platt showdowns?

***

If this looks like a game of four-on-one, it may have felt that way to many of Donovan Clingan's opponents that season. The "one" usually came out on top.

***

Week 8—Games 13 & 14

Game 13—Bristol Central versus Platt (Monday, January 31)—CCC South Game (from the Charles C. Marsh Gymnasium, Bristol)

The Score: 79-48

Game 14—Bristol Central at Wilbur Cross (Wednesday, February 2)—The Robert Saulsbury Invitational (from the Floyd Little Athletic Central, New Haven)

The Score: 71-59 (OT)

Tim Barrette had something special in mind when his squad was preparing for the showdowns against Platt and Wilbur Cross to begin the month of February.

"I told my guys this is tournament week," said Barrette. "When I say tournament week, it's a different mentality you need to have. We had it during the CCC tournament [last year]. We had it yesterday at practice."

Platt was a bit on the youthful side while Cross (8-5) had greatly underachieved that year, even with its having delivered Northwest Catholic's only loss..

But the Governors were going to play at home—a clear advantage for the home team. And quickly, the stakes were going to be at their highest come February 2 on the road.

"I tell you all the time, these guys aren't the greatest practice team sometimes," said Barrette. "But when the time comes to it and it's time to [play], they're ready to go. They were ready at practice yesterday and I'll guarantee they'll be ready [on Tuesday] for Wilbur Cross."

Versus Platt

Platt, who would become a force on the court over the next couple of seasons, didn't have any answers for Donovan Clingan, and the big man posted a new career high over the Rams' 31-point thumping of the CCC South competitor.

Clingan established a new single-game scoring record for the Rams as the center dropped in 47 points—surpassing the 45 scored by Ryan Howse back on February 22, 1994.

"It's crazy," said Clingan of his record-setting tally. "Without my team, my coaches, this wouldn't be happening. It means a lot, you know. It's the reason why I stayed [at Bristol Central], to break records like this and make people proud. I don't even know what to say right now. Forty-seven is crazy. It means a lot to me, it means a lot to my family, [and to] Coach Barrette. Just to hold the record…I don't even know."

Clingan also scooped up 26 rebounds and blocked three shots. His numbers improved to 27.6 points and 16.8 rebounds-per-game off the winning effort.

The victory over the Panthers was the Rams' 78th all-time win against them.

Outside of Bristol Eastern, Platt is the team Bristol Central has defeated the most in its long history. And there wasn't much doubt once Central was able to step up defensively against the program from Meriden.

The game was Central's 28th straight victory while the Panthers dropped to 9-4.

Clingan netted his squad's first ten points of the game—giving a glimpse of what the night would become for the senior standout.

But Clingan also shared the ball well, hooking up Carson Rivoira for a three-point play and off one final lay-up, the 7-foot-2 All-Stater tallied 16 points as Central led 25-16 after one.

Anthony Nimani led Platt with 22 points but didn't have much help, and once Central made some defensive adjustments, all that Panthers' offense quickly dried up as Clingan nearly outscored the entire team by himself.

"We made a couple of changes on Nimani after the first quarter," said Barrette. "Nimani's a really good player. I told him that after the game. He made tough contested jump shots with Carson in his face with pull-ups in the first quarter. Give him some credit. In the second quarter, we changed our mentality. [There was] a little bit more denial, a little bit more double-teaming off the bounce, and it kind of took them out of the rhythm."

Early in the second quarter, Victor Rosa and Damion Glasper buried threes and then over the final 4:15 of the stanza, Clingan scored 12 of his squad's 14 points—three of which were consecutive dunks and slams—and off the power of a 22-3 run, Clingan had 30 points at the half and Central was cruising at 47-19.

"He did a great job tonight," said Barrette of Clingan. "I told him in the first half, we missed 18 shots at halftime and he had 11 offensive rebounds. That's only seven possessions where you're not getting an offensive rebound. And I think Carson had two others. We pretty much were able to convert after the first shot a ton in the first half."

The Panthers didn't have any answer for Clingan in the third quarter either as the offense was flowing.

Glasper later canned a three, Clingan added a lay-up and a baseline three-point bomb to scoop up his 44th point and by the completion of the stanza, Platt trailed 70-33.

But Clingan came out to start the fourth quarter: something was in the works

"I knew I had thirty [points] around halftime," said Clingan. "[Coach Barrette] was like 'you need to stay in for one more' I was like either [there] was some record or I was about to have fifty. So I was like 'I've got to do it. Whatever it is, I've got to get this bucket.'"

"So I went in, I got the dunk and then it was forty-seven."

And with the scoring record in sight, Clingan dunked his way into the record books as Alseph found the center for an and-1, and once he hit the free throw with 7:12 remaining, Barrette immediately pulled him from the game.

Timekeeper Dave Greenleaf made an announcement of the new scoring record, and the center got a standing ovation.

But to get that final basket, Barrette was sweating buckets on the sidelines.

"I wasn't going to leave him in there any longer, trust me" said Barrette of Clingan playing into the fourth quarter. "I was yelling at my assistant coaches [and] they were yelling at me, 'One more, one more possession,' and I was shaking my head. That was the last possession he was getting, no matter what. We had talked about that. He wasn't going [to play with] under seven minutes [in the fourth period]. Obviously, if you're that close with a [school] record at that point…somebody told us [about the record] in the third quarter because that's when he actually got to that point. We were just trying to get one more [basket]."

Jelani Walton and Zach Vanasse hit late shots while Mason Stokes and Harry Ross tallied one free throw apiece as Central nabbed a 79-48 win over Platt.

Glasper netted 10 points, hitting two threes, Rosa scored a then season-high nine points and Rivoira added five points and several rebounds to complete the winning effort.

***

The loss was a little Bristol payback for Platt coach Shawon Moncrief and Platt as far as this writer is concerned.

Back in February of 1997, I was working in the Sports Information Department at New Hampshire College (now known as Southern New Hampshire University) and then-senior Shawon Moncrief was one of the leading players for the men's basketball program.

In one game, Moncrief was on a breakaway and dropped in a massive tomahawk dunk.

As soon as he did that, the fire alarm went off.

The game went on for another thirty seconds as confusion rained down on the NHC Fieldhouse.

The Athletic Director Chip Pollack drew the referees attention, stopped the game, and we were all forced to wait outside—at night, in the cold—until the fire department arrived.

We were probably outside for about 15 minutes, shivering in the wind and avoiding the snow drifts before finally being allowed back inside the gymnasium.

Central beating Platt is called basketball karma because of that tomfoolery by Moncrief.

(In all honesty, a few seconds before Moncrief's monster dunk, a rogue basketball hit one of the many fire alarms in the building. And in a delayed reaction by the alarm system, it finally went off about thirty seconds after getting hit and happened to coincide with the slam dunk. But I'm still going to blame Moncrief for it…).

***

One of the many entertaining twists and turns of Central's season was what happened after the final horn sounded.

People were always trying to get pictures of selfies with Clingan, even opposing players.

In the handshake line after the Platt game, the last player who shook Clingan's hand was not in uniform, but he grabbed Clingan for a selfie anyways, quickly snapping a few pictures. Clingan didn't have a clue to what was going on and the look on his face was priceless.

***

Just getting Clingan to establish the (then) school record for points in a game gave Barrette some real heartburn.

With the contest all but over over and Central comfortably ahead to open the fourth period, Clingan was on the floor—having scored 44 points and needing one point to tie the school record.

Barrette didn't want Clingan on the floor and was a bit desperate for him to score his points and get the heck out. But turnovers impeded the effort as the team was trying to force the ball into him for one final hoop.

"[Clingan] had no idea he was even close" to the school record in points said Barrette. "He couldn't understand why we kept saying 'throw him the ball.' We knew where we were at."

Alseph finally got a pass off to Clingan who dunked with authority, plus a foul, and when his final free throw fell through with 7:12 remaining in the game, the record was set and Barrette glued his 7-foot-2 center to the bench for the rest of the evening.

"Obviously, that's something he deserved tonight, "said Central coach Tim Barrette of Clingan's school record.

***

When naming past centers for the Bristol Central boys basketball program, Jeff Salovski was a good one. "Big Deli" was a 6-foot-11 285-pound pivot man who ended up scoring 1,269 for the program.

But before Salovski, turning the year back to 1994, Class L All-Stater Ryan Howse was ruling the courts at Central. He was also a scoring machine and sank a career-high 45 points and nabbed 25 rebounds against Platt in February of 1994.

Howse averaged a 20-20 when he finished his scholastic career—helping his squad to a 15-5 regular season record and a No. 6 ranking in the Class L postseason tournament where Central was upset by No. 27 Kennedy in two overtimes, 70-64.

While the 6-foot-8 Howse had a distinguished career at Central, neither he nor Salovski could stack up to the abilities of Clingan.

Assistant coach Joe DeFillippi watched both of those players at Central as he was Howse's head coach and an assistant on Clingan's watch.

And he was not surprised in the least when Clingan started breaking all the scoring records at BCHS.

"There are not many people that stop Donovan inside the paint," explained DeFillippi. "He's tough. He's just tough, and now he's developed an outside game and all of that. He's just got a complete game."

"If anybody could do it, I know it would be Donovan. That's a lot of points."

You just couldn't compare any of the eras of the big men from Central whether it was Bruce Kuczenski (Central's only player that played in the NBA…so far), Howse, or "Big Deli" for that matter.

Clingan was simply in a category all his own.

"Ryan wasn't getting seven dunks," said DeFillippi of Howse. "He was hitting threes and hitting midrange and [getting] up-and-unders, stuff like that. Donovan is more a few dunks here, put-backs, he hit a nice 3 tonight [against] Platt, [and gets] a couple midrange."

"And Donovan's has three guys hanging on him, and that's not easy either."

***

After that Platt game, Clingan disclosed the other Bristol records he was trying to accomplish.

"I've got two more," said Clingan in terms of his goals. "[I want to be] the all-time leading points record [at Central], and then [I want to score] 2,000 points. That's my goal."

However, Barrette knew there was one team record Clingan wanted more than anything before his career was said and done at Bristol Central and that was the *elusive* CIAC Division II state championship.

"He only cares about one" record said Barrette. "And that's the truth. The one record he cares about is putting a banner on that [gymnasium] wall."

***

There was a growing possibility that Clingan could seize Bristol's all-time scoring record in New Haven after the 47 against Platt.

Clingan was up to 359 points on the season (27.6 points-per-game) and had 1,780 for his career.

He needed just 45 points to snare the record, and a game against the likes of Wilbur Cross meant the possibility of his playing the entire game.

Fourth quarter minutes were rare for Clingan but as the level of competition increased, naturally, blowouts were less likely. Central's big man never minded those rare fourth period stints.

But the challenge against Cross ended up having little to do with scoring records and the like because, in New Haven, Central was in for its toughest regular season challenge of the year.

***

What made the 47 points against Platt even more special was that no other player in Bristol Public school history has scored more points in a single game at Central *or* Eastern.

The record at Eastern is 46, established by Eli Rodriguez back on January 30, 2012, in a CCC South bout on the road in Middletown.

Rodriguez smashed the old school record of 42, established by Bobby Jones back on January 6, 1967 (in a 99-76 win over, you guessed it, Platt) by dropping in 46 in Eastern's 77-73 overtime loss at Middletown.

Clingan was one point better than Rodriguez's amazing feat from just over 10 years ago and both efforts were simply breathtaking to witness in person.

***

At Wilbur Cross

In the third-ever showdown between Central and Wilbur Cross, the Rams defeated the Governors for the first time in program history at the 6th annual Robert Saulsbury Invitational in New Haven on February 2. The tournament was named after the legendary Wilbur Cross coach and the 92 year old was actually in attendance for all three games that evening.

The Governors, the only team besides Central to hang a loss on Northwest Catholic that season, had size, length and shooting ability.

And what a game it turned into.

How wild was the showdown?

In a rare feat, the Rams were nearly dominated in first half play, leading for just 1:47 around the first and second period break.

Clingan, scoring Central's first 11 points, but when he left the game for a breather to open the second frame, the Governors retook the edge.

Central trailed by as many as nine points in the first half, trailing 29-20 off a made 3 by Fredo Delgado.

Cross had made five three-pointers to that point of the game as the home team's quickness was giving Central early game fits.

A Glasper 3 and Rosa lay-up helped the Rams eventually trim the deficit to two, but the visitors trailed at the half, 35-29—needing to regroup at intermission after allowing a 23-point quarter by Cross.

In the second half, the teams traded haymakers. but neither team wilted over 16 grueling minutes of play—ending in a stalemate.

Cross led by eight early in the tilt, but did not score for over eight minutes.

Suffocating defense saw the Rams ramp up a tremendous 18-0 run—started by an and-1 from Alseph, helped by a couple of offensive rebounds and hoops by Rivoira, and concluded with a banked 3 from Rosa and quickly, Central held a double-figure cushion at 47-37 with 1:10 left in the third.

All five starters from Central posted points during that critical scoring burst.

But a 10-0 run by the Governors, started by another Delgado three-pointer, tied things up at 49-49 with 6:00 left in regulation.

Rivoira and Camar'ee Williams then exchanged hoops, making it 51-51 with 4:46 left in the fourth before the play of the game unfolded.

Two scoreless minutes later, a scrum broke out on the floor and off the play, Delgado drew a technical foul—putting Glasper at the line.

After the two made free-throws, Central fed Clingan for another hoop and with 2:26 showing on the clock, and the visitors were held a 55-51 edge.

However, the Governors ripped off five straight points and when Delgado drained another 3, the team from New Haven led 56-55 with 1:41 left in regulation.

A late steal by Rosa led to another Clingan basket and after another miss by Williams, the Rams were playing a bit of keep away with less than a minute to go, leading 57-56.

Glasper was later fouled, hitting another pair of free throws, as the Rams led 59-56 with 22.7 seconds showing on the clock.

And then a failed boxout led to a three-point play for the Governors.

Elijah Guillaume was fouled and hit his first charity toss but missed the second.

Williams grabbed the offensive rebound and banked in a shot as the hoop tied the vent at 59-59 with 10 seconds to play in regulation.

In the final seconds of regulation, Alseph then tried to weave through traffic—getting the ball over the half-court line.

But in the process Cross stole the ball as time was running out.

A late heave at the buzzer fell short as four additional minutes were added to the clock.

But Cross had nothing left—never scoring in the extra session.

Glasper drew a charge in the paint to open the frame and then drained a dagger three.

Delgado missed a three, rebounded by Clingan, and the big man then hit one of two free throws to make it 63-59 with 2:14 left.

Seven seconds later Cross was called for a traveling violation and on the flip side, Rivoira nailed a floater to make it a six point game (65-59) with two minutes left.

Clingan then made a huge block, later sinking in a backbreaking three-point play, while an offensive rebound by Rivoira led to two more free throws by Glasper as Central iced the game—71-59—with 56.4 seconds remaining.

The Governors were outscored 12-0 in the four minute overtime session, never getting a foothold of the opportunity that came and went in an instant.

Over the final 19:11 of the contest, Cross was limited to just 24 points as the Rams' defense took over the game despite the fifth quarter.

Glasper was the man that day, sinking 21 big points along the way—two off his season-high of 23.

He also dished out seven assists, and his blistering 3 with 2:43 left in OT ended up being the game-winning hoop for Central. Clingan was tremendous on the big stage once again, collecting a triple-double of 29 points, 22 rebounds, and 12 blocks.

Delgado scored a team-high 18 points, hitting six three-pointers, to lead the Governors.

***

Other games from the invite included:

Career Magnet 66, Whitney Tech 42—Career of New Haven and Bristol Central have history. The squads tangled in the semifinal round of the 2014 Class L postseason tournament in a showdown that went into overtime. Central lost that encounter, 66-61.

In the finals, No. 2 Career and No. 4 Windsor duked it out as the Warriors pulled out a 63-59 win. It was Windsor's fourth state title overall and first in CIAC Class play.

Hillhouse 77, Windsor 70—Hillhouse picking off the Warriors was a bit of an upset, one of only three regular season losses for the Windsor program.

The Warriors had won six straight games before bumping into Hillhouse, and the only loss to date for the program was an 81-80 setback at home to Northwest Catholic on January 4.

Eight days after that setback, Windsor traveled to Bristol for a showdown against the Rams, a game whose start was delayed by traffic.

***

There was an excellent Wilbur Cross broadcast of the game online that evening, even though the announcers favored Cross. But the audio was silenced when fans began screaming obscenities, and anyone from Bristol watching the overtime saw the ending in complete silence.

The finish was satisfying nonetheless..

The one that got away at Bristol Central...

Central's 2014 team, 17-3 overall, had all the makings of a state championship finalist, but bad luck seemed to spoil the squad.

That bad luck started in the first round of CCC Tournament play as No. 15 Glastonbury upset No. 2 Bristol Central 63-59 at home.

At the same time Bristol Eastern, the No. 1 ranked team in the CCC Tournament in 2010 (18-2) fell in first round place to No. 16 Manchester 63-60 in Bristol.

It's odd how both the Central squad from 2014 and Eastern's team in 2010 both lost first round CCC games but ended up as state semifinalists before the completion of the CIAC Tournament.

No. 9 Weaver won the CCC's in 2014 with a 59-57 victory over No. 11 Maloney.

At 17-4, Central started Class L play as the No. 3 seed in a very talented field.

The Rams, who scored at least 72 points over its first three tournament games, picked off No. 30 Classical Magnet by a 78-50 final on March 10. Two days later, the Rams beat Middletown 72-59.

In quarterfinal action at home, Central defeated a good Farmington club, ranked No. 11, by a 77-59 on March 14.

The semifinal neutral site was a good one, a short drive to New Britain High School, and the locals showed up in big numbers. Career needed overtime to finally dismiss Central, a 66-61 heartbreaker in overtime.

"I couldn't ask for much more," said Barrette after the game. "I've been telling these guys all year it's going to take all eight guys, and tonight, literally, it took all eight guys I played, even a ninth. I can't commend my guys for any more effort than they just left."

"All I ask for them every day when they come to practice, and every game, is to leave it all on the floor…I'll tell you what, that's the definition of it tonight.'

Joey DeFillippi ended the night with 16 points and seven assists and while he didn't have his best shooting night, he canned two big threes and hit critical free throws to keep Central afloat.

"Joey's a good shooter,' said Barrette. "He didn't shoot the ball great tonight, but I have all the confidence in the world [in him]. I've been saying that all year and I'll [still] go to him. I don't care if he misses twenty shots. I'm still going to my senior captain because he hits big shots all the time."

Manny Severino posted team highs of 18 points and 12 rebounds while Jacob Collins added 12 points and nine rebounds.

"Never say quit, that's all I tell these guys," said Barrette. "It's not about how hard you get hit, it's whether or not you can keep moving forward, and we did that all night."

The game featured a combined 30 missed free throws. Both teams were in it until the end. Severino and Rutledge eventually fouled out, but DeFillippi made a three late that kept spinning around the rim before finally falling in.

Central was outscored in overtime, 10-5, dropping a tough five-point decision to cap a 20-win campaign.

After the game, Barrette said that the 2014 squad was the best one at the school in 25 years—alluding to the state champs from 1989-90.

And he was right.

"I couldn't have been any prouder of my team," said Barrette. "That's [Career] a good basketball team. Like I said, we gave it everything we had."

2014 CIAC Boys Basketball—Class L semifinal game

No. 2 CAREER 66, No. 3 BRISTOL CENTRAL 61 (OT)

from the Chick Shea Gymnasiums at New Britain High School

Bristol Central (20-5) 10 15 29 11 5—61

Career (22-4) 19 14 11 12 10—66

BRISTOL CENTRAL (61): L.J. Johnson 3 0 7, Joe DeFillippi 4 6 16, Manny Severino 7 2 18, Jacob Collins 5 2 12, Kyle Pileski 1 0 2, Ty Hamel 1 0 2, Ladin Rutledge 2 0 4, Devin Francis 0 0 0, Jason Severino 0 0 0. **Totals: 22 10 61.**

CAREER (66): Tyreek Perkins 2 10 14, Tyrell Eaddy 1 4 6, Amos Ford 2 0 4, Justin Campbell 1 1 3, Matt Hamilton 5 4 15, Jordan Lomax 2 2 7, Justice Phifer 8 1 17. **Totals: 21 22 66.**

Three-point goals: Johnson (BC), DeFillippi (BC) 2, M. Severino (BC) 2, Hamilton (Career), Lomax (Career).

Records: Career 22-4 overall; Bristol Central 20-5.

Central had a great postseason run in 2014, getting contributions up and down the roster.

Manny Severino was the leading scorer for the Rams during postseason play—averaging 18.0 points and 9.3 rebounds-per-game while hitting half-a-dozen three-pointers along the way.

He also tallied five steals in the victory over Farmington.

"I'll tell you, Manny played phenomenally this tournament from start to finish," said Barrette. "He's a heck of a basketball player."

DeFillippi was hobbled a bit with a nagging knee injury but still averaged 12.8 ppg while draining seven threes over postseason play.

"Give Joey some credit," said Barrette. "Joey's been battling a pretty bad knee injury. He's been going to the doctor every single day for the last week. But he made the big shot when he needed to."

Collins averaged 14.3 points over the playoffs and augmented that effort with 8.3 rebounds-per-game.

Johnson averaged 10.0 ppg over the postseason, hitting eight threes over that stretch run.

Contributions came from all over the court for Central and proved to be the best squad Barrette coached until Clingan and friends delivered the program its second ever championship in 2022.

However, that 2013-14 crew was a good one.

"These seniors leave a legacy [and] that's what I told the guys" after the Career game said Barrette. "I'm really proud of them. Finishing the season at 20-5 in a league we are [in] and I'm going to tell you what, I think we represented the CCC South pretty well in the state tournament."

***

After his outstanding career at Central, DeFillippi moved on to Mount Ida, a former NCAA Division III, just outside of Boston in Newton, Massachusetts.

And he was simply tremendous in the Mustangs' program.

He took home team MVP honors in 2018 while also being named the school's "Male Athlete of the Year."

In terms of hardwood play, DeFillippi started all but one game for the program and is the all-time leader in several statistical categories.

DeFillippi left the program as its third all-time leading scorer (1,224 points) while his 191 three-pointers ranked him first.

He left the team third all-time in steals (146), fourth in assists (281), and sixth in defensive rebounds (326).

He dropped in 275 free throws, hitting 80-percent of those attempts.

Of note, DeFillippi was one of many former Bristol Central players that traveled to Mohegan Sun to see their scholastic program win the Division II championship in Uncasville.

***

The victory over Wilbur Cross was a tremendous feat, but a possible trap game was on the horizon.

After a short break, Central eventually traveled to Lewis Mills in Burlington to battle the Spartans—coached by Bristol's own Ryan Raponey.

Raponey, like Barrette, was a disciple of former Bristol Eastern boy basketball and baseball coach Mike Giovinazzo.

Barrette knew this showdown could turn into an ugly mess if things started to breakdown, but Clingan was on the verge of something big, and on Tuesday, February 8, Donovan Clingan put himself on the top of Bristol's scholastic scoring record book.

***

The victory against Cross was Central's 29th straight win—pushing the squad to a 14-0 record overall.

The Rams were running away with things in the CIAC Division II playoff rankings as Northwest (11-1) was hanging in at No. 2.

But, as the postseason was a bit on the horizon, the top-two teams in Division II were locked in the rest of the way.

***

To that point of the year, Central was one of just a handful of teams that were still undefeated. Notre Dame-West Haven and Naugatuck were two of them.

Northwest Catholic (12-1, 490) continued to snare that other lone first place tally. Notre Dame-West Haven (476 points) placed third, Ridgefield (12-1, 442) was fourth and Windsor (11-2, 394) was fifth pending a showdown with Central.

***

Week 9—Games 15, 16 & 17

Game 15—Bristol Central at Lewis Mills (Tuesday, February 8)— CCC South Game (from the Thunderdome, Burlington)

The Score: 68-40

Game 16—Bristol Central versus Windsor (Thursday, February 10)— CCC Interdivisional Game (from the Charles C. Marsh Gymnasium, Bristol)

The Score: 83-67

Game 17—Bristol Central versus Berlin (Saturday, February 12)— CCC South Game (from the Charles C. Marsh Gymnasium, Bristol)

The Score: 54-33

***

Opposing teams don't look forward to playing at Lewis Mills because if you're not focused on the task at hand, coach Ryan Raponey and his squad will burn you—usually with five guys who can play, defend, and shoot with range.

Mills is always fundamentally sound, both offensively and defensively, and Raponey's game plans are usually on the mark.

The gymnasium at Lewis Mills, dubbed the "Thunderdome" in Burlington, has seen more than its share of upsets since Raponey arrived.

At Lewis Mills

On February 8 as Central won its 30th consecutive game when Mills fell to Central, 68-40 and Clingan became Bristol's all-time scoring leader. In addition to his 34 points, he had nine rebounds, three assists, and five blocks.

This brought Clingan's all-time point total to 1,843 as he passed Malcolm Huckaby (1,825) for the school record (Clingan received an ovation from the crowd when the game was stopped to honor his newly minted record) and again when he broke Carey Edwards' (1,835) city record.

"We looked inside early," said Tim Barrette of Clingan's offense. "We pounded the ball inside. [Mills] didn't have much of an answer for that. Obviously, he's bigger than most people."

Carson Rivoira chipped in four points while Damion Glasper, Steve Alseph, and Victor Rosa each added four points to the till.

Mills (6-8) hung around due to its long range shooting attack as Jon Schibi (15 points) helped the home team can eight threes. Mills trailed by single-digits toward the end of the first quarter.

Clingan scored all nine points of Central's game-opening 9-2 run—draining a top-of-the-key 3—but Schibi started hitting from deep and another three cut the deficit to 11-8 with 3:52 to go in the first frame.

"Give Schibi some credit. He made some fantastic three-pointers," said Barrette. "He got one going early. One of the things we talked about in the scout was not letting him make one early and he made one early. That's a long night chasing him around. He made a couple of deep ones, played really well tonight."

But Clingan, again shouldering the load, helped Central on an 11-3 burst, and his lay-up with 5:39 before the half gave Central a 28-14 lead. Mills notched the next two hoops as Brice Waldron and Colby Cables (nine points) hit back-to-back lay-ups to make it a 10-point game.

But in Central's half ending 12-3 burst lest the Spartans trailing 40-21 at the half.

"We all know Donovan changes the ballgame out there with his presence," said Raponey. "But, beside him, Central has some very good athletes and, unfortunately, what happened to us at the end of that [second] quarter was we had some missed shots and we just kind of lost track of these other guys in transition. They do a good job of getting to the basket and finishing."

Central used an 18-5 burst to put the game away in the third period as Rivoira cashed in on a miss and Rosa hit a floater. When Alseph—off yet another steal—hit one final lay-up, the visitors led 58-26 and took a 29-point cushion until the final period.

Julius Powell dropped in two shots over fourth period play while Aaron Brown made a nice up-and-under move for a basket.

Mike Allan and Jayeson VanBeveren mopped up with hoops in the end as Central nabbed an important 68-40 CCC South victory with the confrontation against Windsor on deck.

And by the end of the game, news of Clingan's record was spreading like wildfire.

"With 34 points tonight, Donovan Clingan became the all-time leading scorer at Bristol Central and the city of Bristol," said former BC boys basketball coach and current principal Pete Wininger via Twitter. "Couldn't be happier for him, his family, his coaches and his teammates. What a great legacy!"

But quickly after the game, Barrette was already thinking about victory number thirty-one as Windsor was coming to Bristol for an important CCC confrontation.

"Thirty in a row sounds great but I really want a big one on Thursday," said Barrette of the Windsor game. "[The streak] doesn't matter if we lose on Thursday. So, I'll be right to work tonight, getting ready for [coach] Kenny Smith on Thursday. My guys will have a great practice [on Wednesday], lock into what we need to do and obviously, it's going to be a completely different game on Thursday night than it was tonight."

***

Against Mills, Steve Alseph helped to stretch the lead early making steals— setting his big man up for a sweet passes for hoops as the Rams took control of the contest.

Over the course of the season, Alseph's defense was underrated, but he was a master with the ball off other teams' miscues, always finding his teammates for open shots.

"He threw some good bounce passes tonight for lay-ups," said Barrette of Alseph. "I didn't think he played particularly well in the first half offensively. I kind of yelled at him a little bit to kick it in gear. He wasn't feeling great but with that being said, when he wants to go, he's the engine that makes this team go."

***

Steve Alseph brings the ball up as a Mills defender readies himself. Alspeh and Damion Glasper shared most of the ball-handling chores.

After Central defeated Lewis Mills in the first round of the CCC Tournament, Raponey had some great insight on what happens when going up against a 7-foot-2 giant with quickness, size, intelligent, and athletic personnel surrounding him:

"What you've got to understand when you come in to play a team that is athletic at every position with a lot of length and lots of strength [like Central], they obviously can get themselves on you on the perimeter and force you into things that you may not be capable of doing because of the big man in the middle. You make a move, you get by somebody, you get into the lane—typically against normal competition—that's an opportunity for a basket. And we typically capitalize on those opportunities."

"Unfortunately, it's a different ballgame with Donovan in there."

***

As for Clingan's records, Tim Barrette called them amazing.

"One thing I did tell him tonight was to just play and let it happen. Don't force tonight, don't try to get points, and do what you do. It will come naturally. I said I don't want 17 points anyways. I wanted double that and I think that's what he finished up with."

"[It was] perfect, right on the number."

Raponey, who had played for Bristol Eastern and coached there for years, knows the impact Clingan has made at both Bristol Central and the Bristol community as a whole.

"A couple years ago, I remember saying he was a once in a generation type of player," said Raponey. "You hope the best for Donovan moving forward at UConn and whatever follows him after that. Being from Bristol originally and seeing a player that good come through, you don't want those types of things to happen against you but when you see a guy reach a record like that, when you've been watching him play for a long time, you're happy for him for sure."

***

After the Mills game a few students dressed up as 'ESPN' announcers with microphones at a makeshift announce table. Those students were waiting for Clingan to come out of the locker room for an "interview."

But Clingan was already on the bus, waiting to get back to Bristol along with his teammates. There wouldn't be any postgame shenanigans that night. But there would be plenty of tomfoolery with Windsor coming to town for a huge CCC Interdivisional showdown…and a change of plans.

***

The Pandemic still looms

The showdown, pitting Central and Windsor at the XL Center would be a main attraction and a chance for Clingan to be competing in a venue UConn would be playing in for several games the following seasons.

But well before the game, COVID knocked out any chance of playing from that venue.

"That was a COVID restriction, vaccination status" thing said Barrette of the cancellation of the XL Center. "With the new rules the governor put in, you have to show your vaccination status or a negative test within seventy-two hours. That's impossible to run for a high school venue."

"They don't have the staff."

That only meant Windsor would have to travel even farther now as Central was the home team for the game.

Again, fortune favored the maroon and white.

"They reluctantly pulled the game," said Barrette of the XL Center. "This was our home game. Windsor will be here on February 10."

And Windsor did show up that day. They were just *a bit* late…

***

Getting buses to transport kids in Connecticut was a nightmare due to the pandemic—and was so for years after—but the traffic didn't help Windsor that evening and anyone knows that traveling down poorly designed I-84 into and out of Hartford has always been a nightmare.

***

Versus Windsor

Windsor was another state tournament test for Central and to the start the contest, the visiting aggression raced out to an 11-7 lead.

But the Rams posted a 12-3 run, never trailing again, as Central zipped up a more than impressive 83-67 win over.

Central moved to 16-0 overall, winning 31 straight and did so over another state power.

Clingan, fresh off setting two Bristol records in one game, once again put himself into the record books. He bombed the Warriors for 51 points—four more than his previous school record of 47 against Platt—as the big man made quite a statement.

However, that wasn't the only one. Clingan also collected 31 rebounds and nine blocks in flipping Windsor. The center went over 1,900 points for his career and improved his scoring average to just under 30 points-per-game (29.6).

The 51 points were the second most points ever scored in a game scholastically in Bristol, one just behind Mark Noon's 52 scored against Prince Tech back on January 15, 1974.

For the Rams, Rosa canned a career-high 12 points, Glasper posted 10, Alseph sank five and VanBeveren hit the biggest three of the evening. Tyler Betsey notched 19 points to pace the Warriors, falling to 12-3 overall. After busting Bulkeley for 106 in the previous game, Windsor was 34 points off the mark against Central.

That's the difference when you have a 7-foot-2 fire-breathing center standing in the way.

After leading by four with 4:12 left in the first period, the home team went on the attack. Central notched 12 of the next 15 points as Rosa zipped up a steal for a lay-up and when he coolly dropped in a 3, Central went ahead 16-14 and Windsor never led again.

A slick wrap-around by Glasper led to a three-point play as Central led 19-14. Windsor trimmed the deficit to two to open the second period (19-17), but the Rams used another run to nab a bit of a cushion.

Central scored the first nine points of the stanza, and when VanBeveren splashed in a 3—as Windsor coach Ken Smith looked on in disbelief—the squad led 28-17 with 4:50 remaining before the half.

And then a slick 8-0 run—a Clingan dunk, consecutive steals and lay-ups by Rosa and Glasper, and one final hoop from the Central center—gave Central a 17-point edge late.

Clingan had a 16-point third quarter while Rosa chipped in a three as Central extended the lead to 64-44 to start the final period. No margin is ever safe against Windsor, and, to open the final period, Clingan was still on the floor for the Rams. The Warriors got within 14 before Alseph canned a 3 as the deficit was stretched back to 19 late (75-56).

With 1:44 to go, a Clingan dunk gave him points 48 and 49 and with under a minute to play, Rivoira fed his center the ball for his first 50-point game as the Rams came away with an impressive 83-67 thrashing of Windsor.

***

In a story written by Kyle Maher of the *Journal Inquirer*, Windsor coach Ken Smith admitted that his squads have never given up 51 points to anyone in a game.

He called Clingan "good" in the story. It was probably an understatement.

***

Before the pandemic Central was 0-10 against the Warriors.

With three wins against Windsor during the 43-0 streak, which speaks volumes about how strong the program from Bristol Central had become.

Central's run in 2014, where the Rams were one hoop away to advancing to the Class L title game against Windsor, could have been that first victory over the Warriors.

But No. 3 Central fell to No. 2 Career (66-61) and never had that chance to get that first win over Windsor. That was until 2021…

***

The only shame was that Clingan was never able to snare the city record along the way of a brilliant career.

Perhaps few knew of Noon's record ,because Clingan could have easily tallied one late basket to get the record.

But 51 points in a single game? Who can knock that amazing achievement?

***

The victory against Windsor was Central's 29th straight win—pushing the squad to a 14-0 record overall.

The Rams were running away with things in the CIAC Division II playoff rankings as Northwest (11-1) was hanging in at No. 2.

But, with the postseason on the horizon, the top-two teams in Division II were locked in the rest of the way.

Versus Berlin—Bristol Central's senior night

Finally, Berlin came to town on February 12 for a make-up game from earlier in the campaign.

But head coach Stan Glowiak was absent, and an assistant coach was running the show.

At halftime, it seemed that the assistant was in an important conversation with Glowiak who some said was at an island resort. Wherever he was, Glowiak was one of the best boys basketball coaches ever in the CCC

South, putting together many championship squads within the division from his post at New Britain High School.

Glowiak had come out of retirement to help out at Berlin as an assistant, taking the place of Mike Veneziano, who had passed away from cancer at 53, just before the season began.

Glowiak had assisted Veneziano in 2020, and was elevated to the head job. Glowiak was helped by assistant coach Darren Ayotte.

***

Berlin had a plan.

The coaching staff decided the best course of action against Central was to *slow* the game down to a crawl.

And it's the one and only time B.C. fans wished for a 35-second shot clock.

The plan didn't really work outside of holding Central to a season-tying low 54 points.

There was plenty of holding, plenty of stalling, and a whole bunch of snoring, but this also reduced Berlin's chances at the hoop.

The strategy flopped when the Redcoats missed shots, and Clingan didn't seem phased despite the visitors getting a bit overaggressive on the 7-foot-2 center.

Clingan plowed Berlin for 27 points, 11 rebounds, and three blocks as the Rams nabbed its final regular season win at home, 54-33.

Central was a perfect 17-0 and had won for the 32nd consecutive time.

Berlin led 7-6 late in the first, but a 13-0 blast by the Rams put an end to any kind of upset bid.

"We were working our tails off in the first half," said Barrette. "Berlin banked two threes, things like that. But our message at halftime was they can't do that if we get up 17 or 18 points. We play defense for a minute and a half and then take a shot we don't need to take because we have a 7-foot-2 kid that they can't stop."

"Obviously, sometimes it's like you play that 'I want a shot' down at the other end but come state tournament time, we have to make sure we lock in and do what we have to do to combat any style that teams play against us."

Over a stretch that lasted from the end of the second quarter into the fourth, Central's defense suffocated the visitors.

The Redcoats scored four points over a stretch of 10:31 and it was a 58-22 game with under 7:00 to play.

Rivoira scored a dozen points and nine rebounds while his passing helped get his teammates more than a couple of high-percentage shots.

There was a play late in the game that typified the night when Rivoira went after a loose ball off an offensive rebound and got it to Clingan for a mighty slam.

"They shared the ball great tonight," said Barrette of his team. "[Rivoira and Clingan] share the ball great. It's nice that two guys go get the ball every time it goes up and rebounds."

Rosa and Glasper each chipped in five points, Zach Vanasse hit a 3 while Carmelo Thompson—who could be a good one for the Rams—scored a late hoop.

Alseph was a bulldog defensively and even as Berlin tried to muck things up with its physical style on Clingan, the home team remained poised and focused.

Berlin's Marino Fanelli scored all 12 of his points over fourth period play—with the game out of reach—as his three-point barrage was too little too late.

Zach Skinner added nine points while Jake Smalley—attempting to physically frustrate Clingan, living in the All-Stater's jersey on several possessions—had eight.

***

The victory was the 12th all-time win against the Redcoats, pushing the Rams' winning edge against the team to 60 percent (12-8).

And the intent was to get ready for a particularly good Middletown squad a few days later in what should have been another state tournament test.

"We've got to get ready for Middletown. They want us, I know that," said Barrette. "It's always a tough place to play. But I told my guys every game means something at this point. Our goal is to put away our maroon jerseys. If we win out in the CCC [Tournament] and the states, we'll be putting away the maroon jerseys. We'll be the home team throughout as long as we can make it in."

However, the final three games of the season proved not to be the exact postseason warm-up the locals would have hope for.

Over its last three regular season games, Central outscored Middletown, Maloney and Bristol Eastern by a combined 224-114—all on the road.

And the Blue Dragons was going to be down its top player, spelling doom for Middletown.

***

Central honored its senior cheerleaders and boys basketball players before the Berlin game.

Players honored from the 2021-22 undefeated Rams were the starting unit of Victor Rosa, Carson Rivoira, Donovan Clingan, Damion Glasper, and Steve Alseph.

Also honored were the bench trio of Zach Vanasse, Aaron Brown and Jelani Walton—seniors who stuck with the program, working hard in practice and giving the best minutes when they were called upon.

"They deserve everything," said Barrette of his senior core. "The record that [timekeeper Dave Greenleaf] announced for me at the end [for program wins] was because of them. It doesn't happen without them."

Looking at the career wins by that senior group, the legacy left by those individuals should stand for a long time. At least until the next 7-foot-2 center pops around.

"They've won 57 games over the last four years. Those numbers are astonishing," said Barrette. "They've won 32 games in a row to this point. They deserved everything they got tonight."

The evening was also highlighted by the fact that Central took home the CCC South championship.

Again, Barrette passed the accolades off to his senior group.

"I couldn't be prouder of them," said Barrette. "Today was going to be a great day. We clinched a share of the conference title today and celebrated eight great kids, never mind players."

***

That night, another milestone was established over a season of record-breaking events for the boys basketball program.

Barrette's win over Berlin was his 172nd all-time victory, tying him for first place with Ed Phelan—the only other coach in program history to lead the Rams to a state championship.

All the records were falling in what was turning into the squad's greatest single season of all time.

***

On the scoring front, Clingan continued his assault on the state's all-time scoring records.

The big man was posting 29.4 points-per-game—leading to exactly 500 points to date.

The center ended game number 19 with 1,921 career points—a city scholastic record for both boys and girls.

Glasper (11.4 ppg) was leading Central in three-pointers made with 17 while Rivoira (8.5 ppg) wasn't just some third fiddle on a good team.

Alseph (6.4 ppg) canned 10 three-pointers made (10) and Rosa (5.2 ppg), the Gatorade Player of the Year in the state for football, was one of the once-in-a-generation players the Rams employed on a nightly basis.

As it was said best before the Middletown game: Central's starting five has been the best unit in the state, hands down. No other program in the Nutmeg State is even in the same company. Who said this?

And the squad from Middletown was in for an onslaught it never saw coming... With that comment before the game, they probably saw it coming.

***

Central was ranked third overall by MaxPreps on February 16, corresponding to Week 10 of the scholastic campaign.

At that point of the season, the Rams were one of three teams in that poll without a loss.

Notre Dame-West Haven and Naugatuck were undefeated in the middle of the month, but each program would draw losses before and during postseason play.

From a GameTimeCT standpoint, Central was No. 1 again—scooping up 18 first place votes and 568 points. The Rams were 17-0 with three road games left to play.

***

Week 10—Games 18 & 19

Game 18—Bristol Central at Middletown (Tuesday, February 15)— CCC South Game (from Middletown High School)

The Score: 80-34

Game 19—Bristol Central at Maloney (Friday, February 18)—CCC South Game (from Howie Hewitt Court at Francis T. Maloney high school, Meriden)

The Score: 68-30

The Middletown showdown was another rescheduled contest and a highly anticipated bout between two of the top squads in the CCC South.

Middletown head coach Eric Holley scouted the Berlin/Central game and brought along star forward Elijah Wilborn.

The Blue Dragons, playing at full strength in Middletown, might have been an interesting battle against the Rams but that showdown never took place because Wilborn had hurt his ankle and didn't play.

With that, Middletown was no match for surging Central, which won by 46 points in one of the program's biggest blowouts of the season. It was 21-6 after one period of play and 46-16 at the half.

Donovan Clingan dropped in 32 points, 16 rebounds, and blocked three shots. He was fouled continually and went to the free throw line a dozen times. Middletown was quickly out of defensive answers without the 6-foot-8 Wilborn in the mix.

Everyone in a maroon and white uniform contributed to the win that night. Carson Rivoira canned two threes on his way to 15 points, Victor Rosa notched eight, Damion Glasper added four while Steve Alseph scored a hoop to lead the starters—getting another early night off.

The bench produced nearly twenty points, led by Zach Vanasse who canned two three-pointers for a career-high six points. Jelani Walton added five; Aaron Brown, four, and Julius Powell and Jaysun Dominguez two each, helping the Rams to 18-0 overall.

***

Off the Middletown triumph, Central had won 35 straight games—the sixth longest winning streak in the nation.

That's a tremendous feat when sizing up some of the non-public schools the Rams were mixed in with, and by the completion of the season, Central had moved up the ladder a few spots as other elite programs around the United States eventually drew losses.

In terms of the longest winning streaks in the country on February 17, Central cracked the top six. Also, the Rams had the longest consecutive game winning streak in New England.

Things were getting crazy in terms of historic records and marks over at Central.

Longest active wins streaks in the United States—Boys (as of February 17, 2022)

58—Our Lady of Sacred Heart (Coraopolis, Pennsylvania)

41—Weddington (Matthews, North Carolina)

40—Bishop Gorman (Las Vegas)

38—Centerville (Ohio)

37—Avoca Central (Avoca, New York)

35—Bristol Central (Bristol, Connecticut)

***

At Maloney

Even if Maloney could have called in all the ghosts of coach Howie Hewitt from days gone by to hit the hardwood against Central, it wouldn't have mattered.

The Bunch Brothers weren't walking through those doors, fans. Ryan Belote and Rashamell Vereen weren't walking through that door. And former standout Jay Murphy, playing four seasons of NBA ball wasn't coming through those doors.

What Maloney was that season was young, and youth against a squad like Bristol Central only spelled doom in the end.

Maloney fell 68-30 and Clingan played barely half the game on his way to 22 points, 19 rebounds, three assists and five blocked shots—hitting 10-of-14 field goals, including a 3 before intermission.

His night was basically concluded as the Rams led 43-4 at the half.

Central led 21-0 through one period of play.

Glasper scored nine points (4-of-8 from the field) to go along with three assists while Rivoira chipped in with six points, four rebounds, and a steal for good measure.

Walton posted a career-high seven points while snaring two rebounds, Rosa went for five points and five assists, Alseph flipped in five points and four assists, and Powell nabbed four points and six rebounds.

Everyone had a hand in this victory including Aaron Brown (two points, two rebounds), VanBeveren (two points, two rebounds), and Vanasse (two rebounds).

In addition, Carmelo Thompson gobbled up four rebounds, Harry Ross and Jaysun Dominguez each snared a couple of rebounds, Jonmanuel Gomez added two points and three rebounds and Mikey McMahon hit 1-of-2 three-pointers for his season best of three points as the Rams were on the cusp of an undefeated regular season for only the second time in program history.

Donte Collins led Maloney with nine points.

The win against the Spartans was the 34th straight for Central (19-0)

***

Central's fate in the CCC Boys Basketball Tournament was set after the Maloney win, giving the Rams the number one seed.

But before getting ready for the postseason, Clingan went for his 2,000[th] point against crosstown rival Bristol Eastern.

***

Once again, when the GameTimeCT rankings were released before the final week of the regular season, the Rams were at the top with 538 points.

It was a weird week in scholastic hoops throughout the state as East Catholic lost to both Northwest Catholic (54-51) and Farmington (85-76) and Norwich Free Academy also lost.

But that Top-10 remained mostly the same as the final week of the season came and went.

And there was one game left on the regular season docket as the Rams traveled to King Street in Bristol on Monday, February 21.

***

Week 11—Game 20

Game 20—Bristol Central at Bristol Eastern (Monday, February 21)— CCC South Game (from the Thomas M. Monahan Gymnasium, Bristol)

The Score: 76-50

It was twenty up and twenty down for Central in regular season play as the squad dropped pesky Eastern by 26 points (76-50). from the Thomas M. Monahan Gymnasium.

And Donovan Clingan notched his 2,000[th] scholastic point off a slick pass from Damion Glasper for a thunderous dunk—sending the Central faithful into a frenzy.

He ended the night with 2,006 points. For the game, he totaled 31 points, 17 rebounds and four blocked shots.

"It feels great," said Clingan. "My coaches, my teammates, fans, and I mean everyone, I just can't thank them enough. It just means a lot to have all this support."

Victor Rosa netted eight points, Steve Alseph scored six, Glasper added five and Carson Rivoira flipped in a hoop.

With that win, Central's senior core had never lost over the last two regular seasons.

From the bench, Julius Powell scored eight points, Carmelo Thompson scored a season-high six points—dropping in two threes—while Jayeson VanBeveren tallied all six of his points over a stretch of 1:59 in the second period.

The Rams out-rebounded the Lancers by 26 while holding the home squad to 31-percent shooting from the field overall.

But Eastern fought thanks to a career-high 16 points as Lukas Sward hit three threes to made it a single-digit game early in the second period.

Isaiah Lawrence-Bynum added eight while Brayden Dauphinais had seven points, five rebounds, and three assists.

"Even the shots [Eastern] made were contested," said Tim Barrette. "I actually thought they made a bunch tonight [that were] contested. [For] Lawrence-Bynum, those were tough shots early on. Give him some credit."

It was the final Eastern game for seniors Jerry Tatum (seven points, two steals) and Elijah Borgelin—suiting up for his first game since January 13 due to a knee injury that ended his season prematurely.

Borgelin started for Eastern and was allowed to score a quick basket before leaving the game to a standing ovation as Central allowed him one final hoop.

"You've got to credit coach Barrette for allowing us to do that," said Eastern coach Bunty Ray of the Borgelin basket. "I thought that was important for him to get those two points and getting in the box score. I think that was important for everybody, so I appreciate the gesture on their end. Great sportsmanship and great for Elijah to get two points tonight."

And who was in the circle for the opening tap? It was 7-foot-2 Clingan going up against 5-foot-5 Ben D'Amato. But the moment for the jump-ball was prearranged due to the Borgelin situation.

The Rams led by six early but a slick up-and-under lay-up and then a floater from Lawrence-Bynum chopped the deficit to 10-6 with 4:50 remaining in the first quarter.

A pass off the backboard from Damion Glasper, leading to a rim-rattling dunk by Clingan, started a 9-0 surge by the visiting aggressors. And on a steal and hoop by Steve Alseph—plus another jam from Clingan—the Rams increased their edge to 21-6 with 1:16 left in the first.

Eastern then went on an 8-2 jaunt as Nate Fries (four assists) and Sward hit a couple threes, and with 7:40 left in the second stanza, it was a 23-14 game. The home team was hanging around.

But Central's defense went into overdrive as a blazing 16-0 burst by the Rams, capped by a Clingan free throw at the 2:05 mark of the second, and the lead grew to 39-14.

The Rams chased the Lancers away from the three-point line, taking Eastern's best offensive weapon in check as much as possible.

"We wanted to run Eastern off the three-point line," said Barrette. "We knew that would be their focus tonight. We've done a pretty good job the last couple of games in doing that."

Sward hit a late hoop but off a three-point play and one final lay-up by Clingan, Central surged in front, 44-16, at the half.

Ten seconds into the third period, Clingan scored his 2,000th point, earning a loud ovation from the standing-room only crowd. Before retreating to the bench, Clingan dropped in three additional baskets and Glasper canned 3 as Central's edge was 55-20 and with 3:55 to go in the period, the visitors were firmly in control.

Victor Rosa and Zach Vanasse added late threes, and when Dauphinais ended the third with two free throws Central held a 63-25 cushion going into the final frame.

Eastern went on to score a season-high 25 points in the fourth period as the Lancers showed a little gumption to end the season. Sward dropped in two threes, Dauphinais hit a three as well, and when Tatum kicked in a lay-up with 3:51 left, Eastern still trailed 72-38 but continued to show fight.

Eastern then scored ten straight points, hitting 7-of-8 free throws and got a 3 from D'Amato, as the deficit was reduced to 25 late before time ran out.

In the end, Central won 76-50, snared the CCC South championship outright, and seized the number one seeds in both the CCC and CIAC Division II tournament frays. The Rams' 20-0 regular season was matched only by Central's championship campaign of 1989-90.

"The last couple of weeks, we've had a [state] tournament mindset," said Barrette. "The last three games, we've been on the road [for] Middletown, Maloney and [Eastern] and we've come away with thirty-point victories in all three games. We've come out strong, haven't taken long to get going and that's been my message. We've got to jump on people right from the beginning."

And after the Eastern win, Central finally got to return its attention to the postseason and the chance to defend its CCC Tournament title before moving on to the state championship picture.

"I can't wait," said Clingan about the postseason. "We have a lot of competition in the states and CCC's and that's what we're here for. We're here to play the best and to be the best, you have to beat the best."

***

After finishing the season without a loss, Middletown played extremely well—going 14-6 overall—but was six games behind the Rams in the final standings.

The Rams actually finished 7-0 in CCC South games while the Blue Dragons ended the campaign at 6-1.

In terms of CCC games, Central was a perfect 16-0 while Middletown went 12-4.

Berlin went an impressive 15-5 (5-2 CCC South, 11-5 CCC), Platt ended things at 12-8, (3-4, 10-6) and Lewis Mills (11-9 overall) was one game back and also qualified for CCC Tournament play.

And guess who the Spartans drew in the first rounds???

***

Frantz was at it again on February 23 in the MaxPreps state rankings.

Central was still in third place in the state's overall rankings behind Northwest Catholic and Notre Dame-West Haven.

Were they using Mr. Greenleaf's old Radio Shack Tandy computers to figure this stuff out?

Anyone who had Mr. Greenleaf for a teacher remembers those lovely machines in the back of his classroom (are they still there?).

He is probably checking every fact and figure in this book as well, making sure the author didn't forget anything.

Greenleaf has seen just about everything at BC and is steeped in the sports tradition at that school.

The guy is simply amazing, and I was fortunate enough to have him as my Algebra II teacher over at Bristol Eastern (Greenleaf had a 'cup of coffee' over on King Street in 1992-93).

I knew his name before becoming one of his students, seeing his byline in the *Bristol Press* over the years, but getting the chance to know him—later as a colleague for that media entity—has been a pleasure since day one.

Central is lucky to have him but please, don't sneak into his room to use one of his Tandy computers when he isn't there…

***

Bristol Central boys basketball program completed a slick undefeated regular season.

And from top to bottom, the squad was impressive on every level.

"I'm really proud of my kids as a program, freshman through varsity," said Barrette. "We just finished 50-3 as a program. That's a pretty great accomplishment."

Bristol high school's last undefeated squad came in 1943-44. In other words, since the end of World War II, the public high schools in town have enjoyed three undefeated seasons—and Central can claim two of them.

And both of those Rams' programs have similar traits.

That 1989-90 team, headlined by Malcolm Huckaby, Lonnie Brooks, Greg Fradette, and Rod Hickey, helped the Rams average just over 69 points-per-game while allowing just 55.5.

The 2021-22 Central squad and the team that opened the decade of the 1990s managed to play one overtime game on the way to a perfect season.

The Rams' lone non-regulation game against Southington in 1989-90 went into double-overtime as Central won, 59-55.

Central went 8-0 that year in games decided by 10 points or less.

The Class L champs from 1990 earned the top seed in the postseason tournament by lot (there wasn't a CCC Tournament played back then) and ended up battling No. 2 St. Joseph in a game that pitted two of American's top-25 scholastic programs.

Central won the title behind a 66-65 win from Central Connecticut State University in New Britain.

Fradette canned the game-winning jump shot with just seconds to play in the contest.

The Rams of 2021-22 had a more dominating regular season—headlined by center Donovan Clingan who, just like Huckaby, headed to a Big East school after senior year.

The final scores between the two programs differ greatly since the 1990 squad had trouble with Bristol Eastern, a veteran team that year.

In 1990, the Rams won both encounters against the Lancers by seven total points while the Central squad from this past season defeated the King-streeters by a combined 75 points.

So, in terms of scores, how did the two undefeated squads from Central stack up during regular season play? Here's each program's regular season scores as the games played out:

Game	**1989-90 Rams**	**2021-22 Rams**
Game 1	75-46, Conard	55-28, Southington
Game 2	58-48, Rockville	74-59, East Catholic
Game 3	79-65, St. Paul	73-24, Bristol Eastern
Game 4	88-63, Maloney	77-33, South Windsor
Game 5	73-63, Platt	81-42, Plainville
Game 6	80-54, Bulkeley	69-35, Newington
Game 7	52-51, Southington	70-47, East Hartford

Game 8	71-55, Newington	53-44, Springfield Cent.
Game 9	61-48, New Britain	74-30, Maloney
Game 10	84-64, St. Paul	80-50, Middletown
Game 11	47-43, Eastern	91-63, Enfield
Game 12	71-43, Conard	85-71, Hartford Public
Game 13	54-48, Maloney	79-48, Platt
Game 14	72-60, Platt	71-59, Wilbur Cross (OT)
Game 15	75-57, Bulkeley	68-40, Lewis Mills
Game 16	59-55, Southington (OT)	83-67, Windsor
Game 17	87-70, Newington	54-33, Berlin
Game 18	75-61, New Britain	80-34, Middletown
Game 19	59-56, Eastern	68-30, Maloney
Game 20	64-60, Rockville	76-50, Eastern

Points scored: 69.2 per-game (1990)   73.1 per-game (2022)
Points allowed: 55.5 per-game (1990)   44.4 per-game (2022)

Those offensive numbers aren't far off as the 2022 edition outscored the crew from 1990 just under four points-per-game.

Obviously, both Central squads were prolific in their scoring exploits, but it's the defense that splits those two programs apart.

Clingan and crew allowed just 44.4 points-per-game in regular season action—11.1 points better than the Class L champs from 32 years ago.

Overall, the Rams outscored opponents this season by an incredible 574 points.

In the end, both those tallies from Central's undefeated teams are impressive but having a 7-foot-2 monster in and around the paint proved to be the difference maker.

Central had competed against some of the top programs in the state, along with one from Massachusetts, and looked forward to more of the same during postseason play.

"I think playing at Mohegan Sun and playing Springfield Central up in Massachusetts [has] prepared us," said Barrette. "Playing Wilbur Cross, you know, we challenged ourselves as much as we could out of the conference as best we could do. We're excited to have an opportunity to play the best teams in the state and see where we stack up."

***

Alseph (Dennis Johnson)

At the end of September, Bristol Eastern's on-again, off-again assistant football coach Tim Barrette was excited about a new transfer to his basketball squad.

Enter senior Steve Alseph.

Alseph had been a casualty of Sacred Heart of Waterbury closing which, just like the squad from Central, was accustomed to winning, winning and, well, more winning.

The Rams swept their way to the 2021 CCC Tournament Championship and Alseph helped the Hearts to the NVL Tournament title as well.

It was just a small sampling for the then-junior on his way to Bristol.

Alseph blended into the Central lineup flawlessly as the preseason proved.

"I think that's where a lot of people are going to be surprised," said Barrette of Alseph. "Steve plays the game the right way. He plays extremely hard. He's a very, very good defender—on the ball defender. One thing I will say, he did a great job in the preseason getting everyone involved. He doesn't look for his own [offense] that often. He came to this team and he's tried to get all the other guys involved in the preseason."

"He's done a great job fitting into that [starting] group."

Not that this existing group needed any more toughness, but Alseph provided a some ruthless aggression.

He was the ultimate agitator who loved to mix it up when the pressure was at its highest. Who could forget Alseph pointing to the scoreboard as Central was about to knock off Springfield Central?

Alseph was showing an opposing guard the scoreboard (and the TV audience—hopefully, who couldn't read lips—was treated to the opposing player telling Alseph that he didn't give a 'flying frisbee' what the scoreboard said). Alseph probably cost the opponents more than a couple points getting under their skin with his quick hands and, a little on the side chit-chat.

But the senior proved to be a very good Dennis Johnson impersonator, a guy who could score, rebound, hit threes, and play superior defense. It would have been interesting to see who the fifth starter would have been had Alseph's school in Waterbury remained open.

What a pick-up. What a find. Alseph was a huge reason why Central was undefeated in 2021-22.

***

As Barrette and his team had predicted, the squad went through the regular season undefeated with just a few stern challenges (East Catholic, Springfield Central, Wilbur Cross, and Windsor) that pushed the Rams a bit more than the usual non-CCC slate of games.

The opponents all fizzled in the end as East Catholic trailed by 20 points against Central midway through the fourth period, Springfield Central couldn't throw the ball into the ocean, Wilbur Cross was outscored 12-0 in overtime, and there was no stopping Clingan against Windsor as he jammed home a school record 51 points.

But all those games, as tough as some of those were, simply proved to be preliminary in scope. Credit belongs to Barrette and his coaching staff for keeping its focus, winning every practice, and taking games one at a time. That meant a 20-0 regular season ledger and, in turn, top seedings in both the CCC Tournament and the CIAC Division II fray.

This is why Central played out the regular season with zest. And there wasn't any time for a letdown as the Rams entered the 2022 postseason against an awfully familiar opponent in the CCC Tournament's opening round: No. 16 Lewis Mills.

***

IN MEMORIAM—STACEY PORRINI CLINGAN

After a long and courageous battle with breast cancer, Stacey Porrini Clingan, Donovan's mother, passed away on March 27, 2018. She was only 42 years old.

Donovan was in eighth grade when it happened, and the soon-to-be-freshman at Bristol Central knew about all the positive his mother spread across Bristol—in the classroom and on the court.

Stacey Porrini was born on December 1, 1975 and was an amazing four-year performer in three sports scholastically for the Rams from 1989-1993.

She competed in swimming, basketball, and track & field at Central—eventually earning CCC South All-Conference honors in all three sports.

A tremendous swimmer, Stacey also left her mark on the basketball court and ended her scholastic career as one of the top players in Mum City history.

She scored 846 career points (fifth all-time at Central), nabbed a city rebounding record of 1,032, and collected 273 blocks.

Over her senior campaign, she averaged 17 points and 21 rebounds-per-game—blocking several shots along the way.

That put her on the radar of the University of Maine, a NCAA Division I program in Orono, but that offer was one of nearly 70 scholarship offers she received.

After her senior season, Stacey did choose UMaine and the 6-foot-4 forward established herself as one of the best players in program history.

Stacey ranks 17th on Maine's all-time scoring list (1,128), fifth in rebounding (929) in 117 career games.

Porrini-Clingan holds UMaine records for blocks in a single game (seven) and blocks in a single season (79). She recorded 185 blocks over her 117-game career.

A three-time all-conference selection, she was on the first UMaine women's basketball team to make it to the NCAA Tournament in 1995. The team also made postseason appearances in 1996 and 1997.

Clingan was named captain in 1997 and earned a spot on the league's all-first team that season. She had earned all-second team honors in 1995 and 1996.

She graduated from UMaine in 1997 with a degree in elementary education and served as a first-grade teacher for years in Bristol at both Ellen P. Hubbell and Greene Hills Schools, leaving a significant impact on the lives of Bristol students.

Her having played at Bristol Central was a huge motivating factor in Donovan remaining in town. The young man helped to honor his mother by staying put.

In the process, he broke her rebounding record and then became Bristol's all-time leader in points, rebounds, and blocked shots.

By the completion of his career, there wasn't any doubt that Donovan would have made his mother extremely proud. That loyalty to his mother helped Donovan stay at Central though nearly 24 prep schools over the years inquired about his services.

Under the Learning Tree— Mike Giovinazzo.

So many of the scholastic coaches in town have learned a great deal from Mike Giovinazzo.

Anyone who played any kind of basketball in town probably did so under Giovinazzo's watchful eye, whether it was at the varsity level at Bristol Eastern or in the various summer camps he's put on over the years. And so many coaches, not just in hoop, have learned how to be a model coach from playing basketball (or baseball) for Giovinazzo, or in gym class at Northeast Middle School.

Bristol Central girls basketball coach Steve Gaudet, boys soccer coach Nate Jandreau, Bristol Eastern boys basketball coach Bunty Ray, Eastern girls soccer coach Scott Redman, and countless other mentors and leaders carefully watched and listened to what Giovinazzo did and said.

He was a tremendous coach, smart, knew every trick in the book, and Barrette soaked in every minute with Giovinazzo as an assistant coach at Eastern. Many of those teachings and lessons were applied to the undefeated basketball program at Bristol Central this past season.

"I knew if I stuck with the program" we could succeed said Barrette. "I've had teachers and tutors [like] Mike Giovinazzo and worked up at UConn. Coach G has been my idol for a long time. He taught me the value of hard work and never being satisfied and because of that, I am the coach that I am today, because of Mike Giovinazzo."

Giovinazzo led the Lancers to the 1986 Class L state title in baseball, and his squad was the runner-up in 1981.

The Bristol Sports Hall of Fame coach is an icon in town and learned from some other legendary coaches like Jim Bates Sr. And Barrette, and countless others, did the same while Giovinazzo was instructing and teaching the student athletes or yelling at hapless referees and officials over the years.

Every town needs someone like Giovinazzo to teach athletes the right way to play, compete and pass on stories of Bristol's rich scholastic sports history.

Bristol Central's title history

Before the 2021-22 campaign the Bristol Central boys basketball program had gone to the Class L championship games in both 1987 and 1990—going 1-1 over those title confrontations.

Each edition of Central's team had a Huckaby on it, and by the time the season was completed the Rams weren't just state champs but a top-25 ranked high school squad in the nation.

The One title that got away: 1986-87

When junior Martin Huckaby and little brother freshman Malcolm Huckaby joined forces, the boys basketball program at Bristol Central— under the guidance of head coach Ed Phelan—had a legitimate chance of winning a state championship.

But in Class L Warren Harding stood in the way of every title challenger. And no one was able to top the Presidents.

Harding starting winning championships in 1983 and entering 1986-87, and behind the play of such big men like future NBA forward Charles Smith, the squad had won four straight Class L championships.

And the Presidents were looking to add a fifth in March of 1987.

But Smith, a 6-foot-10 giant, was long gone, playing ball at the University of Pittsburg (1984-1988) and was named the Big East Player of the Year in 1988, winning a bronze medal in hoop at the 1988 Olympics before going third overall in the first round to the Philadelphia 76ers and was immediately traded to the Los Angeles Clippers.

However, a fifth straight title was going to prove difficult as Central made it to the finals for the first time in school history, hungry for the chance to take out a nationally ranked program.

The *Hartford Courant* had Harding ranked number one in the state while the *USA Today* high school pool rated the Athletics the 13th best team in America.

Its last loss had come out of state during the 1985-86 season, but Central had more than a little talent.

Along with the Huckabys, the Hickey brothers (senior Lydell and freshman Rod) could ball and 6-foot-4 junior center Corey Smith gave Harding fits on the court early and often.

The playoff bracket was split into two as Central was the top-ranked squad in the East Region while Harding was No. 1 in the West.

And after Central defeated South Catholic, 47-46 on March 18, the Presidents were awaiting the Rams in the finals.

The Rams, allowing opponents just 43 points-per-game, kept up with Harding as a hoop from Central's John Dauphinee trimmed the deficit to 48-47 with just under seven minutes to play in regulation.

But the Presidents scored 21 of the final 23 points, smothering Central defensively, as Harding walked away with its fifth straight championship behind the 69-49 victory at Kaiser Hall in New Britain.

Martin Huckaby shot 10-of-19 from the field for a game-high 22 points, brother Malcolm added nine while Rod Hickey posted eight.

Harding's Frenchy Tomlin was also a force, with a game-high 25 points.

The Presidents ended the year on a 35-game winning streak, going undefeated along the way (26-0) while Central (22-3) found its way back to the Class L title game.

The One title that didn't: 1989-1990

But in 1990 it was a completely different story with Malcolm Huckaby and Rod Hickey leading the charge as seniors.

Hickey had an amazing quote in the Bristol Central yearbook the previous year after the Rams had reached the quarterfinal round for the seventh time the previous season:

"We had a successful year with only two league setbacks. We might not have won the State Championship but we'll be back." Those guys knew it, could taste it, and when winter 1989 arrived, the perfect storm materialized.

The Rams went 20-0 in regular season play—including a tremendous 59-55 double overtime victory over Southington. But in postseason play a familiar opponent was looming.

Harding was back in the finals in both 1988 and 1989 and lost those two contests by a total of seven points—including one in overtime (76-72 to Bassick in 1989). By 1990, Harding was ranked 12th—and 15-7 the day of the showdown against the Rams—while Central was the No. 1 Class L seed.

Before that rematch, the Rams had a couple of rounds to win. Central earned a bye in first round. Round two saw the Rams tangle against No. 16 Seymour (11-9 regular season), and the locals wrapped up a 96-59 win in Bristol on March 9. Huckaby scored a game-high 29 points, Scott McCarthy, 16; Lonnie Brooks, 14; Greg Fradette, 12; and Brooks, 10.

And then in the quarterfinal round, Central put up another 90-plus point gem—this time defeating No. 8 Windham, 92-40, at East Catholic in Manchester, when quarterfinal round games were held at neutral sites.

The Rams led 51-17 at intermission and that cushion ballooned to 73-27 with eight minutes to play. Huckaby single-handily whipped the Whippets for 26 points, 12 rebounds, and 10 assists,. Brooks went for a monster game of 26 points and 24 rebounds. Rod Hickey added 15 points and 10 rebounds as defense ruled. No one scored more than nine for Windham (14-8).

Central had revenge on its mind March 14 in a semifinal showdown against Harding in a postseason rematch from Quinnipiac College in Hamden.

Harding had reached the finals seven times over the past 10 years, and a trip to CCSU and a shot at the Class L finals was on the line. Phelan was 0-and-5 against Harding in state tournament play

In another full-out war on the hardwood, the Rams were able to spin the Presidents—knocking Harding out of postseason play with its 77-74 victory. Central led 62-44 at one point but the Presidents squad stepped up the pressure—notching 17 of the next 22 points—and with just under three minutes to go, the Rams cushion was chopped to four.

But late hoops by Brooks and Huckaby made it a 72-63 game with 1:40 left and BC hung on to win—advancing to the championship round for the second time in school history. Huckaby led with a triple-double of 23 points, 12 rebounds, and 12 assists while tallying four steals and Brooks added 24 points, 11 rebounds, and seven assists. Fradette nabbed nine points while Duane Salgado added six.

Hickey added 15 points and 14 rebounds, along with five blocked shots as Central (23-0) advanced to the title round, squaring off against No. 2 St. Joseph, also undefeated over regular season play.

Central was able to earn the number-one seed over St. Joseph via lot. St. Joseph had the state's number one ranking and was also ranked in USA Today's high school poll. This was a big-time bout in the state, broadcast on WTNH-TV Channel 8, and the contest lived up to its amazing billing.

St. Joe had superior size up front with two players at least 6-foot-7, but Central was ultra-athletic and Phelan was supremely confident in his squad. The game came down to the wire before late game heroics sealed the win for the locals.

Fradette (17 points) answered the bell with a late-game three-pointer that gave the Rams a three-point lead at 66-63 with about three seconds to play. A late game three from Doremus Bennerman (24 points) just rimmed out as the Cadets (25-1) ended up losing by a single point. Huckaby was the MVP, hitting for 21 points and 10 rebounds while Brooks added 19 points—canning 5-of-7 shots from three-point land.

At the end of the season, the Bristol Central boys basketball program was ranked No. 1 in both Connecticut and New England while USA Today's Super 25 Poll had the Rams ranked the 20th best in the state.

The program won a then school record 24 straight games. No other program in the state finished undefeated. St. Joseph was ranked 18th in that same poll before losing to Central.

Roster **1989-90 Bristol Central Boys Basketball Team (24-0)** Craig Yarde, Kevin Komanetsky, Jason Castolene, Matt Drury, Marvin Fitzpatrick, Greg Godbout, Rod Hickey, Greg Fradette, Malcolm Huckaby, Lonnie Brooks, Duane Salgado, Brian Woolley, Scott McCarthy, and Coach Ed Phelan.

Senior
Night
February 12, 2022

Dream Team

THE SECOND "HALF" OF THE SEASON BEGINS

Tournament Time

Coming into the 2022 CCC Tournament, Donovan Clingan was averaging 29.3 points-per-game.

And over his 78-game scholastic career, he scored those 2,006 points for an average of 25.7 points-per-game.

That average is simply staggering, thinking about his beginnings as a 6-foot-9 freshman, putting his team on his back from the start.

The legacy the big man forged—the run before the 2022 postseason as a senior—was staggering to comprehend.

But the ante was upped a bit though it was going to be a chore for any program to knock off the Rams in CCC Tournament action.

Up first was a date against Lewis Mills—this time from the friendly confines of the Marsh gym.. It would be the only home game for Central in the CCC Tournament.

Barrette knew exactly what his team was getting into squaring off against Mills for the second time in February.

"You obviously play who is on your" schedule said Barrette of the CCC Tournament. "But we [just] can't roll the ball out. We know everyone wants to beat No. 1, and I'm not ready for the streak to end. We've got to get to work in practice and be ready to play."

Brice Waldron, the senior standout from Mills, came into the showdown on fire as of late, kicking in a game-high 28 points against Eastern the previous week.

Waldron was a dangerous, proficient three-point shooter.

Jon Schibi and Colby Cables could all shoot from range, and Central's goal was to keep the Spartans from shooting threes.

Central was wary of the "trap game" the first round showdown could turn into, and the locals understood what's at stake in a real tune-up for the upcoming CIAC Division II Tournament.

"Now, [if you] lose, you go home," said Clingan. "We have to go to practice with a positive mindset and just win every practice. From coaching all the way down to players, we've just got to win every practice, and we'll come out a better team every day."

***

Consistency is king in any kind of sports endeavor and that was something Central had in droves that season.

However, the rotation would be even more compacted as the pressure and talent increased.

Along with Clingan's unworldly numbers, Damion Glasper (10.6 points-per-game, 20 three-pointers), Carson Rivoira (8.4 ppg, 10 threes), Steve Alseph (6.1 ppg, 11 threes), and Victor Rosa (5.5 ppg, nine threes) all played—and started—Central's 20-pack of games.

Julius Powell and Jayeson VanBeveren were ready for back-up minutes when called upon, but Central stuck to its five-man starting unit tightly and late in tournament play, "iron man" basketball took effect.

In one CCC bout the five starters played *all* 32 minutes as the margin of error decreased rapidly after postseason advancement.

***

This 2022 CCC Tournament field was loaded up and down the bracket and if Lewis Mills were the last ranked seed, you know the 16-team line-up could do some damage.

When East Catholic (12-4) is ranked tenth and must start play on the road, that's a shocking realization (more so after the squad won the CIAC Division I bracket and failed to advance out of the quarterfinals of the CCC Tourney).

After Central, Northwest Catholic (16-0 in CCC games) was ranked second, Conard (14-2)—and the dynamic Riley Fox—earned the third seed.

Windsor (14-2) came in at fourth and surprisingly RHAM chimed in at No. 5, giving the CCC Tournament a real postseason look and feel.

After Bloomfield (No. 6), Simsbury (No. 7), Middletown (No. 8), and Farmington (10th)—like East Catholic—were all 12-4 in CCC play.

But no matter the opponent, Central had to prepare a little bit extra for scrappy Lewis Mills.

"This team has always been a tournament team so I think I'll see a different level of focus Wednesday at practice," Barrette said of his squad.

***

The field was stacked in the CCC's and this tournament was a get out of jail free card if the Rams needed it.

Win, loss, or draw, Central was already locked into the No. 1 spot in CIAC Division II tournament. But that wasn't the way the locals looked at that tournament.

The defending champions wanted to run the entire table and getting off to a good start in the CCC's would help that become a reality.

CCC Tournament Schedule:

*Thursday, February 24—First Round games (from the site of the higher seed).

*Saturday, February 26—Quarterfinal Games (from Enfield High School)

*Tuesday, March 1—Semifinal Games (from Enfield High School)

*Thursday, March 3—CCC Tournament Finals (from Enfield high School)

Rankings / School / CCC Record (not including non-conference CCC games)

1. Bristol Central, 16-0
2. Northwest Catholic, 16-0
3. Conard, 14-2
4. Windsor, 14-2
5. RHAM, 13-3
6. Bloomfield, 12-4
7. Simsbury, 12-4
8. Middletown, 12-4
9. Farmington, 12-4
10. East Catholic, 12-4
11. Berlin, 11-5
12. Platt, 10-6
13. Manchester, 10-6
14. East Hartford, 10-6
15. Newington, 9-7
16. Lewis Mills, 9-7

First round games—at the site of the higher seed:

No. 1 Bristol Central vs. No. 16 Lewis Mills

No. 2 Northwest Catholic vs. No. 15 Newington

No. 3 Conard vs. No. 14 East Hartford

No. 4 Windsor vs. No. 13 Manchester

No. 5 RHAM vs. No. 12 Platt

No. 6 Bloomfield vs. No. 11 Berlin

No. 7 Simsbury vs. No. 10 East Catholic

No. 8 Middletown vs. No. 9 Farmington

The looming question of the CCC Tournament simply centered on who would advance to the finals to face Central in the championship showdown.

Again, Conard/BC would have been fun, but everyone was excited for a possibility of a Central/Northwest Catholic finals.

And in the end, everyone got what they wanted.

The CCC Tournament was a sampling of what would take place from the Mohegan Sun Arena come the third weekend of March.

And the Division II championship preview was actually better than the eventual state title tilt.

***

Victor Rosa (Danny Ainge)

Comparing Victor Rosa to former BYU standout Danny Ainge is a compliment of the highest order.

The only difference between the two was Ainge would whine a lot—especially on the hardwood.

Rosa never really said much, letting his play do the talking, though it looked like he wanted to thrash one of the guards from the Wilton basketball team in Central's semifinal win in overtime, one of the rare times he lost a cool on the hardwood during an overly physical affair).

Both Rosa and Ainge were amazing scholastic performers (Ainge actually played for the Toronto Blue Jays while attending BYU. I still don't know how he was allowed to do that, since he was the school's top player in men's basketball as well).

Ainge was a high school All-American in football, basketball and baseball as a junior at Eugene High School in Oregon.

And while Rosa didn't receive all the same accolades Ainge did over three sports, Rosa always performed at an elite level.

In football he was an unstoppable force—running the football in all directions at once while making his share of passes to keep defenses honest on the gridiron.

In basketball it was his play on the defensive end, hitting a three-pointer or two along the way.

While in track and field for the Rams, it was his sprinting—along with a toss or two in the javelin—that truly allowed people to see his all-around athletic abilities.

But he was the man in football, and against Hartford Public on October 16, in a 52-48 win over the Owls in what turned into a high-octane back and forth affair, it was a late game-saving tackle by Rosa that propelled Central to the win.

Here's the story from the game in TBE from October 17, 2021:

HARTFORD—Needing one last big play, the Hartford Public football team was twenty-five yards away from the Bristol Central end zone last Saturday, looking to steal away the game from the Rams.

The Owls were down to its final play with just 11.1 seconds remaining on the clock, trailing 52-48.

And when Public's Christian Garcia took the snap, the quarterback went on the attack in what turned into the final play of the afternoon.

He slipped by four or five Central defenders and juked his way to the 10-yard line.

The path was there for a possible Garcia sprint into the end zone—but it was open only for an instant.

As Garcia was streaking over the five, he crashed and burned at the Central two as time expired, ending the contest with the Rams getting to the pay window over the four-point victory.

But who made the final stop for Central?

What player ended up earning the game-winning tackle for the Rams?

Senior Victor Rosa, Mr. Everything for Central, was being interviewed about 10 feet away from head coach Jeff Papazian after the game and the veteran coach asked his star a critical question.

"Vic, who had the last stop?" asked Papazian.

Rosa, who didn't miss a beat on the question, immediately said it was him.

Papazian said of course Rosa was going to say that he made that game-saving tackle with a chuckle.

"I promise you, I got it," retorted Rosa with a smile.

Well, what did the instant replay show?

Someone had filmed the final play, and everyone got to see the last seconds of the gridiron bout unfold one more time.

It showed that it was indeed Rosa—along with teammate Justin Despins—who tackled Garcia two yards short of the Central end zone.

Rosa smiled as Papazian just shook his head.

"Get out of here!" said Papazian to Rosa with a big grin.

It was a great moment between a player and coach of a team that's clearly finding its stride as the Rams are currently on a four-game winning streak (4-1).

***

Central's football squad ended the season at 9-1 in 2021, went to the playoffs for the first time since 1987—winning nine straight games at one point.

Though Central lost to the eventual state champions in quarterfinal play—dropping a 49-14 decision on the road to Maloney—it was an incredible ride by the Rams from start to finish.

And Rosa was at the helm of that playoff team from Bristol. The UConn football program is getting a good one in him.

***

Postseason Week 1—Game 21 & 22

Game 21—Bristol Central vs. Lewis Mills (Thursday, February 24)—CCC First Round Tournament Game (from the Charles C. Marsh Gymnasium, Bristol)

The Score: 66-29

Game 22—Bristol Central vs. Middletown (Saturday, February 26)—CCC Quarterfinal Round Tournament Game (from Enfield High School)

The Score: 73-58

Lewis Mills head coach Ryan Raponey was none too pleased after the completion of the CCC first round game against Central.

A 37-point loss can do that to a coach.

"We left too many guys open," said Raponey. "I understand if Donovan is going to get baskets. I understand if he's going to get rebounds but unfortunately, we didn't do a good enough job on the defensive end of being able to keep the game within striking distance."

Central, as anticipated, ran all those three-point shooters off the arch as Mills had trouble putting the ball in the hoop from the onset

Defense led to some quick offense for the Rams and the Spartans never got into the flow.

Top ranked Central (21-0) had won its 36th consecutive game while No. 16 Lewis Mills fell to 11-10 overall.

"We made them work for everything" offensively said Tim Barrette of Mills. "Every possession was a minute long and not because they were trying to run clock, it's because we weren't giving them a look. I'm really proud of them. I told them [after the game] 'way to lock in there defensively.' We made them earn everything they got."

Donovan Clingan played another partial game, notching 25 points, 17 rebounds, and three blocked shots and when attention was diverted to the big man, Damion Glasper looked like Stephen Curry on the floor—hitting seven three-pointers for 21 points.

Carson Rivoira scored six points, Steve Alseph added four and Victor Rosa creating havoc on the defensive end. His defensive job on Brice Waldron allowed him just two points while Steve Alseph also kept the sharpshooter off-balance

Jon Schibi and Connor Evans each canned two threes, collecting eight points apiece.

But baskets were few and far between for the Spartans.

Clingan scored eight of the game's first 10 points as his final hoop of the first quarter made it a 13-2 contest with 3:52 left, but the Spartans hung around and off an offensive rebound from Jack Stanislaw and floater by Charlie Joiner, Mills trailed just 15-7 with 1:33 left in the first tilt.

"They got seven offensive rebounds in the first half because they were pulling Donovan away from the hoop," said Barrette. "But with that being said, had we just played one trip of defense each time, we would have allowed about five points in the first half."

"I'm really, really proud [of the defense] …we're better defensively than people give us credit for.

With Mills putting extra emphasis on Clingan, throwing out junk defenses and the like, Central simply let somebody else shoot the ball.

Central scored 18 points among Rivoira, Alseph, and Glasper to put the thing away early.

Glasper drained four straight threes over a stretch of 4:30 and after two quick hoops by Alseph, the Rams led by twenty (31-11) with 3:12 remaining in the first half.

"You've got to make a choice," said Barrette of who opponents defend against Central. "In the first half, they were actually [using a] box-and-one on Donovan and leaving guys out there to shoot. I don't blame them. We haven't shot the ball particularly well but we're much better at home as most teams are. Glasper got off to a great start offensively. He got that first [three] to go and from there, you know he's a streaky shooter, but when you get off early, that usually results in a pretty good night."

The home team led 36-17 at intermission as the Rams scored 21 points over the last 9:15 of the first half.

"I thought we did a better job in the second quarter of trying to get what we wanted offensively," said Raponey. "Unfortunately, I just didn't feel we did a good enough job at our primary defense tonight to give ourselves a chance to hang in the game longer."

Central then belted Mills for 17 straight points to turn the game into a blowout.

Clingan had 10 points over the run, Rivoira added four points and when Glasper kicked in his sixth three of the contest with 2:46 remaining in the stanza, it was a 53-17 game.

"I preach that first four minutes out of halftime," said Barrette. "That's generally our bread and butter. At halftime, [we] make a few adjustments but focus in on what we need to do. And our goal is to step on the [opponent] coming right out of halftime, put the game away, and then let our subs finish the thing off."

And then Glasper unleashed a half-court three-point bomb at the third period buzzer, hitting nothing but net, as his seventh and final 3 gave Central a 58-22 cushion—allowing Barrette to empty the pine.

In the fourth, VanBeveren hit two straight hoops, Aaron Brown canned a floater and a Mason Stokes jumper ended the scoring for Central as the squad won the contest by a 66-29 final—advancing in CCC Tournament play against Middletown.

"We're ready" for Middletown said Barrette. "We're ready as we're going to be. I'd love to be able to practice tomorrow because the snow day [on Friday] throws in a wrench but you know what, this team is full of seniors. We'll do something virtually [on Friday] …we'll be locked in and on Saturday and be ready to go against Middletown."

2022 CCC BOYS BASKETBALL TOURNAMENT—ROUND 1

No. 1 Bristol Central 66, No. 16 Lewis Mills 29

No. 2 Northwest Catholic 88, No. 15 Newington 65

No. 3 Conard 71, No. 14 East Hartford 59

No. 4 Windsor 70, No. 13 Manchester 54

No. 5 RHAM 72, No. 12 Platt 54

No. 6 Bloomfield 70, No. 11 Berlin 66

No. 10 East Catholic 44, No. 7 Simsbury 33

No. 8 Middletown 51, No. 9 Farmington 50

CCC Quarterfinal Round*

Game 9—No. 1 Bristol Central vs. No. 8 Middletown (11 a.m.)

Game 10—No. 4 Windsor vs. No. 5 RHAM (1 p.m.)

Game 11—No. 3 Conard vs. No. 6 Bloomfield (6 p.m.)

Game 12—No. 2 Northwest Catholic vs. No. 10 East Catholic (8 p.m.)

*The rest of the tournament commenced from Enfield High School as restrictive COVID protocols were eased from the playing site.

***

For the second round showdown against Middletown, the scene shifted to Enfield High School as Central—the top seed—was forced to play at 11 a.m..

Some wondered why the No. 1 program wasn't scheduled to be in the final game that night?

However, the time mattered little in the end, even as Elijah Wilborn was back in the mix for the Blue Dragons—having missed Central's last game due to injury.

And the showdown was another hard-hitting bout.

Versus Middletown

The final scholastic game for Central in the month of February saw Middletown attempt to be overly physical against Clingan.

It was a tactic that was used repeatedly against the Rams over the season, but all it brought was additional fouls—and frustration—for opponents.

Central had to let the caffeine kick in early because the Blue Dragons came out fighting.

Clingan hit an early 3, but off a floater by Middletown's Marshall Butler (14 points), Central trailed 16-10 with fifty-one seconds remaining in the first stanza.

Poor shooting, missed defensive assignments, and miscues foiled the No. 1 seed early in the bout—leading to the Blue Dragons' fast start.

"We weren't awake for the first four minutes defensively. That was horrendous," said Barrette. "The eleven-a.m. start and playing a team for a third time [didn't help]. People ask why you don't want to play a team a third time, that start today is a prime example of why."

"With that being said, I told the guys in the locker room we haven't seen a lot of game pressure lately so having some game pressure today was probably good for us in the long run."

Central's defense then went into overdrive as the squad scored 20 of the final 23 total points of the first half as the Blue Dragons went scoreless for a stretch of 5:53 going into the halftime break.

The Rams led 30-19 at the half—capped by a Clingan put-back—as Middletown never recovered.

"Give Middletown a lot of credit. They made shots today," said Barrette. "They shot the ball great, kept them in the game, and we could never really finally push that away. I'm proud of my guys for hanging in there, that's for sure."

Clingan scored Central's first 13 points as he ended the fray with 38 points, 15 rebounds, and 10 blocked shots.

Glasper pushed in 14, Alseph added nine, Rosa had seven, and Rivoira flipped in five to pace the scoring attack.

Middletown's Matt Steuerwald netted a team-high 15 points.

Central led by 13 late in the third period as Alseph found Rivoira for a lay-up with 1:18 left, but Nasir McDaniel hit for five straight points, and when a Clingan dunk ended the stanza, the Rams were still in front at 49-39 but were not fully able to run away from Middletown.

But the Blue Dragons never made it a single-digit affair in the fourth quarter. Every Middletown basket was countered by Central. When Clingan tapped in a miss with 3:21 remaining, Central led 62-46 and won by 15. Windsor was next.

"We've got to be better than that on Tuesday night when we play Windsor," said Barrette. "If we play like that, we'll lose by ten."

That was certainly an ugly 11 a.m. game leaving at least one Central coach talking about taking a nap later that afternoon (I think it was coach Barrette).

***

The Blue Dragons were held to just three free throws attempts, making two, while Central canned a more than credible 20-of-26 from the foul line.

Glasper made 6-of-7 while Rosa was a perfect 4-of-4. And all that effort in practice and preparation certainly paid off in the end.

***

Of note at the tournament, Northwest Catholic defeated East Catholic in quarterfinal round play by 12 points (69-57) as the Eagles were foiled once again.

A Central collision course with Northwest seemed unavoidable as the top seeds in postseason play continued to win.

2022 CCC BOYS BASKETBALL TOURNAMENT—Quarterfinals

Quarterfinal Round—Saturday

Game 9—No. 1 Bristol Central 73, No. 8 Middletown 58

Game 10—No. 4 Windsor 91, No. 5 RHAM 64

Game 11—No. 3 Conard 74, No. 6 Bloomfield 70

Game 12—No. 2 Northwest Catholic 69, No. 10 East Catholic 57

*All Quarterfinal round games were played at Enfield High School

***

At the end of February, GameTimeCT released its final poll for the month and Central finally tallied all the first place votes.

The Rams were unbeaten at 22-0 overall, had all 18 first place votes, and 568 points overall.

The only team within striking distance was Northwest Catholic. And the Lions were able to tangle with Conard one more time in the CCCs.

***

The final four games of the CCC Tournament featured three of the state's top five squads which included Central, Northwest, and Windsor.

Conard was in that mix and was playing a superior brand of hoop behind sophomore Riley Fox.

But the then Chieftains just couldn't get over the hump against West Hartford rival NWC.

***

Postseason Week 2—Game 23 & 24

Game 23—Bristol Central vs. Windsor (Tuesday, March 1)—CCC Semifinal Round Tournament Game (from Enfield High School)

The Score: 56-37

Game 24—No. 1 Bristol Central vs. No. 2 Northwest Catholic (Thursday, March 3)—CCC Tournament Finals (from Enfield High School)

The Score: 63-56

The final four of the CCC Tournament was set as the top seeds were No. 1 Central, No. 2 Northwest Catholic, No. 3 Conard, and No. 4 Windsor.

Both the Rams and the Lions had already hung losses on their semifinal opponents, and it was just a matter of seeing which opponent would advance.

Conard gave NWC a good first half run but faltered the rest of the way, losing by 16 points.

And Central's game against Windsor?

Well, that showdown was 'fun' for about three quarters.

Versus Windsor

Three lead changes and four ties highlighted a back-and-forth first quarter as the Rams tangled against the Warriors.

But in the end it was another game but with a predictable ending as Central defeated Windsor 56-37.

Over the two games that the Rams and Warriors played, Central outscored Windsor, 139-104.

Central trailed early, but an 11-4 burst, finished by a baseline 3 from Damion Glasper, gave the No. 1 seed a 14-11 edge with 1:49 left in the first frame.

Windsor never held the lead again.

It remained close until the fourth when it was just a 38-33 game, but Central's defense suffocated the Warriors—holding the squad to only *four* fourth quarter points, sending the Rams back to the CCC Tournament finals behind the 19-point victory.

Windsor (18-4) was held to a season-low 37 points—scoring just two points over a stretch of 6:04 that started at the tail-end of the third period and lasted until the 3:16 mark of the fourth when the game became a blowout.

"We knew they were going to change it up" defensively said Tim Barrette. "We missed a couple of bunnies early. We were two of eight from the line in the first half. If we had done a better job in the first half, we should've been up 15 at halftime but with that being said, I can't be prouder."

"To hold a Windsor team to 37 points, that's something to be proud of."

Central (23-0) was one victory away from tying the school record for wins in a season as the Class L champs in 1989-90 went a noteworthy 24-0. The Rams also won 24 games back in 2002-03 (24-2) under then head coach turned principal Pete Wininger.

The Rams notched their 38th straight victory, another school record that simply grew after every Central triumph.

Donovan Clingan once again proved why he was Connecticut's top player as he drilled the Warriors for a 20-20, specifically 28 points, 24 rebounds and six blocks.

And when Windsor's defense sealed off the 7-foot-2 center with its physical play, Glasper added timely threes early as he dropped in 14 points.

"They spent a lot of attention on [Clingan] in the first half," said Barrette of Windsor. "Damion Glasper picked us up on the offensive end."

Steve Alseph scored nine points, Carson Rivoira added four, and Victor Rosa scooped in a bucket. Julius Powell and Jayeson VanBeveren made important contributions off the bench over second-half play as Windsor was clearly frustrated and limited offensively. Tyler Betsey scored a team-high 20 for the Warriors.

Leading 14-13 early in the second stanza, Central went on an 8-0 run as Clingan dropped in a dunk, added a lay-up, Glasper hit 1-of-2 free throws when Windsor coach Ken Smith picked up a technical foul and Alseph hit a blistering 3 that made it 22-13 with 5:00 minutes showing on the clock.

Clingan and Alseph scored the rest of the points for Central to end the first half as the top seed led it by eight, 30-22.

"We gave [Windsor] six points in transition in the first half…I can't ask for a better defensive effort in the first half," said Barrette.

It took nearly three-and-a-half minutes for Central to hit its first bucket of the third quarter, but Windsor wasn't exactly lighting the nets on fire either.

A floater from Glasper, a jumper by Alseph, and a quick Rivoira lay-up made it a 36-25 game with 2:39 left in the third.

But when Clingan picked up his third foul with 2:23 left in the frame, VanBeveren came in, Powell helped out as well, and the Rams held the fort though the Warriors went on a bit of a run.

Windsor ramped up the pressure, allowed an offensive rebound put-back from Rivoira, but an 8-2 jaunt from the Warriors cut the deficit to 38-33 with eight minutes remaining.

"Every game that we've won, he's been in a little bit of foul trouble," said Barrette of Clingan. "Julius and VanBeveren did exactly what they needed to do. I can't be prouder of the subs tonight [over] the limited minutes they gave me."

With Clingan back for good to open the fourth period, it was all over for Windsor. Rosa started a Central 10-0 burst with a runner, Clingan canned two free throws and a couple rim-rattling dunks, and when Glasper connected on a driving lay-up, Central was back in control at 48-33 with 3:28 left.

Windsor simply couldn't connect from deep as the squad scored only two late hoops. "We wanted to run them off the [three-point] line," said Barrette. "We'll give up as many elbow jumpers as we need to in the fourth as long as the 3-ball doesn't go in. We felt that we had a comfortable enough lead that we could finish the game off."

Central ended the fray with a 9-2 burst, highlighted by an and-1 from Clingan—eventually advancing the locals to the CCC Championship round for the second straight year.

***

Central-Windsor Part II didn't live up to the hype, but that often happens when the opponent is mismatched. The Warriors were riding a six-game winning streak coming into the showdown against the Rams since losing to Central back on February 10. However, anyone who knew anything about scholastic basketball in the state wanted to see two specific teams clash in the finals of the CCC Tournament.

After NWC fleeced Conard over a suffocating second half of play, it was time for the main event. Enter Bristol Central and Northwest Catholic for the Boys CCC Tournament Championship. And this showdown on March 3, didn't need an ounce of hype.

In early tournament action against Lewis Mills, (above) Clingan seems somewhat uncontested near the hoop, while (left) a Mills player gets ready to absorb a hoped-for charge from Damion Glasper.

2022 CCC BOYS BASKETBALL TOURNAMENT

Semifinal Round—Tuesday, March 1

Game 13—No. 1 Bristol Central 57, No. 4 Windsor 37

Game 14—No. 2 Northwest Catholic 66, No. 3 Conard 50*

*Jalen Hamblin tallied a team-high 22 points while Riley Fox pumped in 20 as the sophomore struggled from the field over the semifinal bout.

***

After the game against Windsor, Clingan, Alseph, Glasper, and Rivoira were all honored as CCC South All-Conference recipients.

The other players from the CCC South that earned All-Conference recognition were Jon Schibi and Brice Waldron from Lewis Mills.

Plainville and Bristol Eastern did not have representatives on the team that season.

Rosa, frankly, deserved recognition with the grouping as well but I guess that entire starting unit couldn't be honored.

Or could they?

Windsor somehow got five players from its team on the All-Conference squad in the Northern Division while East and Northwest Catholic both had four teammates earn postseason honors.

***

Finally, the top two programs in the CCC—in the state for that matter— were about the lock horns in the Central Connecticut Conference Boys Tournament Finals.

Bristol Central (23-0) squared off against No. 2 Northwest Catholic (22-1), two programs with a combined 45-1 record.

And it was a tournament preview as the gymnasium was packed. Tickets were available only online and many people were turned away at the door.

Coming into the contest, Central has won a school record 38 straight games while looking to defend its CCC Tournament crown from last year, pitting Central's Tim Barrette against Northwest's John Mirabello.

They're a lot alike. They are the winningest coaches in their respective program's history, both know the game inside and out and are great mentors for the players that compete for them—elevating those young men and the schools they represent.

Both love their respective programs and community. The set-up between the squads didn't need much hype, as all the names involved were familiar ones.

Clingan (29.4 points-per-game) was on the cusp of 2,100 career points but upped that to 30.3 ppg in the CCC Tournament—scoring 91 points over the first three postseason games.

He also averaged 18.7 rebounds and 6.3 blocked shots-per-game to go along with those 30-plus points in CCC tourney play.

Glasper drained 10 three-pointers over postseason play while averaging 16.3 ppg.

Alseph (7.3 ppg, three threes) directed the offense to near perfection while supplying one 3 per tournament game, and anyone could see that his defense and leadership were certainly underrated.

There was Rosa and his defense, and Rivoira treated opponents like bowling pins—rack em' up and he'd knock them down.

Rivoira posted five points-per-game over the three CCC Tournament games and his rebounding average was nearly double his scoring output.

The Rams' opponent, Northwest Catholic, was a talented group, boasting plenty of height and skill at every position.

Matt Curtis could explode for 25 points on any given night and had dropped in 32 points over a huge win against Windsor back in early January.

He was a good shooter from deep but streaky as well.

Against Conard in CCC play, London Jemison netted 17 points while Gianni Mirabello and Badara Diakite each kicked in 11 over the 16-point victory.

Jehyvic Spencer and Hayden Abdullah helped out in the paint and most of those players had three-point shooting abilities.

Mirabello has made half-a-dozen threes in a game earlier this season while London Jemison, Abdullah and Diakite could make threes as well.

Amazingly, when Central won its opening game of the season at Trinity College against Southington that was the same venue that the Lions lost its only contest of the regular season.

NWC fell to Wilbur Cross, 72-68.

Versus Northwest Catholic

The CCC Tournament finals was an epic bout from start to finish. And for the second straight campaign, the Rams scooped up the CCC Tournament championship over a Catholic school program.

But unlike the last two years, a showing in the CCC's wasn't going to end the season for Bristol Central.

Central led for the final 28 minutes against Northwest Catholic as the Rams posted a satisfying 63-56 victory over the Lions in what Barrette termed a "once-in-a-lifetime experience".

And the beat continued on for the Rams over the seven-point victory.

The win moved Central to a perfect 24-0, tying the program's record for wins in a season with the CIAC Division II Tournament on deck.

It was Central's 39th straight victory while Northwest fell to 22-2 overall, dropping a game for the first time since mid-December.

The victory was the first back-to-back CCC Tournament titles in school history and the third one all-time.

In 2003 Central won its first tournament but needed 18 years to get back to the championship.

Clingan was an unstoppable force against NWC, as he smashed in a game-high 45 points, pulled down 28 rebounds, and had six blocks to claim a little more hardware for his team and school.

"It feels great," said Clingan of the win. "We've still got four more [games] to go. This is one more step to where we want to be. We're all happy, we're all proud of each other. We love each other. It's great."

Northwest tried to be physical, but Clingan was on another level and even when he was double-teamed, Central's tremendous passes schemes found the mark just about every time—leading to high percentage hoops and rim-rattling dunks by the 7-foot-2 giant.

"We have the x-factor standing in the paint," said Barrette of Clingan. "He's the best player in the state of Connecticut, hands down."

And when the game was on the line, Clingan notched 15 of his team's final 17 points to clinch the championship—accomplishing another lofty goal as CIAC Tournament time was at hand.

Trailing 10-9, a behind the back pass by Alseph to Clingan led to one of those thunderous dunks with 3:51 left in the first quarter as Central went on a 10-2 run and led the rest of the way.

Curtis was sensational in defeat, posting 28 points—hitting from outside-in—and nearly helped his squad draw even by the halftime break.

"Curtis is one heck of a player," said Clingan of the NWC sharpshooter. "I'll give all the love to him. He shoots it, he scores it…that's my guy. No matter what, win or lose, I love Matt to death. That's my guy."

But Rivoira took over on Curtis defensively after Rosa did an excellent job over the first half as the shooter was limited to just four early points in the third and not much else.

Central's defense was on-point as no other player from the Lions notched more than eight points. Rosa and Rivoira did an incredible job slowing him down.

"We threw everything we had at him," said Barrette of defending Curtis. "I appreciate Carson and Victor, the way they took that personally and tried to stop one of the best guards in the state. It was a total team effort tonight."

Central had all five of its warriors, its starting crew, play the entire thirty-two minutes without any substitutes.

Alseph's arm was scratched with 5:54 left in the third quarter and was nearly lifted for VanBeveren.

But the game was stopped due to the blood, Alseph (three points) was bandaged up and quickly returned—meaning the entire starting crew went the distance against the second ranked team in Connecticut.

"Iron man basketball tonight," said Barrette. "That's a testament to the shape we're in because I only used two timeouts and we got through thirty-two minutes using only five guys."

Rivoira hit for five early points—including a 3—but when Northwest's Jehyvic Spencer, filling in for Diakite who picked up his second foul 4:38 into things, hit a three-pointer of his own and the Rams trailed 10-9 nearly halfway through the first frame.

From there, Central used a 14-4 run as Clingan nabbed 12 of those points while Glasper (seven points) added a jumper, and with 6:28 to go in the half, the Rams nabbed a 23-14 lead.

The Lions responded with a 12-2 burst as Curtis posted nine points over the jaunt to make it a 26-24 game with 1:11 left before the break. Check the math

Clingan held his ground on a couple of those Curtis drives, staying out of foul trouble over first half action.

"We had to play a little bit smarter tonight," said Barrette. "We gave up a couple lay-ups early to Curtis without [Clingan] contesting because we didn't want to get him into foul trouble early. We knew we needed him in the third and fourth [quarters]. We didn't want him playing tentative in the second half."

To end the second, Alseph hit Rivoira for a lay-up and Rosa threw a pass over to Clingan for a dunk—leading to Central's 30-26 margin at intermission.

At the half, Clingan had collected 20 points, 17 rebounds, and blocked three shots with more to come over the final two quarters.

A Diakite 3 trimmed the deficit to one to open the third period and after Clingan and Curtis exchanged hoops, Northwest still only trailed by one—this time at 34-33 with 5:15 remaining in the third.

Ahead by four (39-35), a 7-3 run—highlighted by a three from Alseph—made it a 46-38 game with 50 seconds remaining in the third. Leading by five through three quarters (46-41), the teams exchanged hoops to open the fourth but off a three by Mirabello, Northwest was still hanging around, trailing 52-48 with 4:08 left.

Central then stalled the game out and went exclusively to Clingan in the paint—the Rams' closer of closers. And the big man, in MVP like fashion, sent the Lions packing.

Rivoira found Clingan for a lay-up and then three consecutive dunks later, the Rams established its biggest lead of the evening—60-48—with 1:52 remaining.

"We didn't work on that until last week because we've been winning games by so much," said Barrette of the stall. "At the same time, I thought we executed it to perfection in the last three minutes."

Curtis hit the Lions last eight points, but the squad got only as close as seven the rest of the way. Clingan drained a late three-point play, another dunk plus a foul, to ice the game as Central won the 2022 CCC Tournament.

"I can't be prouder of my guys," said Barrette.

And after a little on court celebration with the 2022 CCC Tournament Championship banner, the CIAC Division II Tournament was on deck for the Bristol Central boys basketball program.

***

Central ended the CCC Tournament winning its 39th consecutive game, moving to 24-0 on the season.

And the seven-point victory over Northwest was just a sampling of what the Division II title tilt could look like—if Central got by some talented programs in the bracket.

That year, once Central established a lead—with its grouping of five seniors strong—it was nearly impossible to make a comeback, as the Lions experienced in Enfield.

"This is a preview of what's coming in the states," said Clingan after the CCC title win. "We're locked in, we're ready to go and we've got four more games to win a ring."

The Rams were on a collision course with Northwest Catholic despite a number of strong challengers standing in the way.

But that starting five of Clingan, Rivoira, Rosa, Alseph, and Glasper—a grouping of what could have been five NCAA Division I athletes over various sports—displayed an ability and chemistry no other scholastic program in Connecticut was able to match through 24 games.

"It all comes down to heart," said Clingan. "Everyone loves this, everyone wants to win. Everybody cares about other. In order to win, it takes everything. It takes heart, it takes [the right] mindset…it's big.

It wasn't a stretch to say that Bristol Central had the best starting five in the tournament.

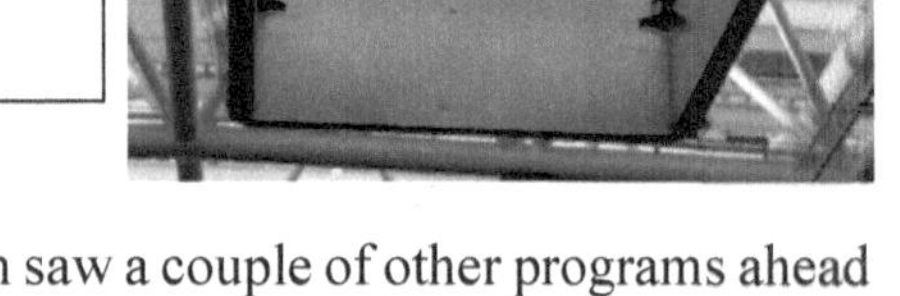

The 9-7 overtime score made all the difference as Bristol Central overcame a determined and talented Wilton Squad in the semifinal in New Haven

Those MaxPreps rankings once again saw a couple of other programs ahead of Central in the standings.

Frantz had the Rams—ranked via whatever computer program it used—rated third in the state on March 2 behind Northwest Catholic and Notre Dame-West Haven.

Both those teams carried one loss apiece while over at GameTimeCT, the Rams were first again and tallied all but one first place vote.

That vote went to Northwest Catholic.

On the following day, it was worthy of note that Central defeated Northwest by a 63-56 final to collect back-to-back CCC Tournament championships.

***

Watching Clingan compete against other "peers," his size was simply eye-opening over the campaign because he simply dwarfed everyone.

Elijah Wilborn from Middletown was a tremendous talent at 6-foot-8 but Clingan could easily rise above him.

And that's how it went for every center that challenged Clingan.

Northwest had a big frontline, including 6-foot-9 freshman Badara Diakite who showed great potential.

But Clingan was bigger than Diakite, and more imposing.

And when Diakite badly missed a dunk attempt over Clingan in that CCC Tournament game at Enfield, it just reinforced the fact it was difficult to go over Central's 7-foot-2 giant.

You couldn't go around Clingan, you couldn't go over him, and you couldn't go through him.

What ended up being the best defense against Clingan over his four seasons at Central was praying that he missed. Regardless of the prayers, that didn't happen very often.

* * *

At times it seemed the masks and interruptions would never end.

* * *

EVENTUALLY IT WILL COME DOWN TO ONE GAME

CIAC Division II Rankings—The postseason finally arrives!

The results from the CCC Tournament did not factor in the Division II rankings so Central could have fallen in the fray and would have still been ranked No. 1. Coach Barrette was eyeing a clean sweep.

2022 CIAC Division II Boys Basketball Rankings

School	Rating	PCT.	Record	Total Points
Bristol Central	1	1.000	20-0	190
Northwest Catholic	2	.950	19-1	213
Conard	3	.900	18-2	153
Wilton	4	.850	17-3	158
Holy Cross	5	.800	16-4	146
Prince Tech	6	.750	15-5	152
Crosby	7	.750	15-5	139
Waterford	8	.750	15-5	132
Staples	9	.750	15-5	127
Stratford	10	.750	15-5	109
Middletown	11	.700	14-6	124
St. Joseph	12	.700	14-6	122
Newtown	13	.700	14-6	118
Westhill	14	.700	14-6	115
Simsbury	15	.700	14-6	106
Amistad	16	.650	13-7	101
Amity	17	.632	12-7	81
Greenwich	18	.600	12-8	108
Xavier	19	.600	12-8	99
Avon	20	.600	12-8	74
Newington	21	.550	11-9	64
Jonathan Law	22	.500	10-10	68
Stamford	23	.500	10-10	66
Sheehan	24	.450	9-10	61
Enfield	25	.400	8-12	54

*Teams 1-7 earned a first-round bye. Minimum qualification for state tournament play in Connecticut is eight wins (40-percent).

***

When the dust cleared in the semifinal round, the top four teams (Bristol Central, Northwest, Conard, and Wilton) were all in the mix.

Division III panned out the same as No. 1 Kolbe Cathedral made it to the finals.

However, the script was flipped as No. 3 Daniel Hand pulled off a 56-39 upset in the finals.

The Rams, however, were on a mission and playing with all the motivation in the world.

First Round—Bristol Central (bye)

Bristol Central earning a bye was a no-brainer with that 20-0 regular season finish.

Only two teams had 20-0 ledgers that season. Naugatuck was the other. The Greyhounds opened the CIAC Division I tournament with a perfect 23-0 record, defeating Kennedy 58-42 in the Naugatuck Valley League Finals.

But off that bye, Naugatuck lost in second round play to No. 16 Wilbur Cross (58-50). Then Cross was bounced by the eventual champs, No. 8 East Catholic, by a 73-63 final.

In Division II number 18 Greenwich defeated No. 15 Simsbury 43-34 while No. 23 Stamford was a 65-62 upset winner over No. 10 Stratford.

Other than those two games, the first round went according to plan.

***

It seemed as if there were Central, Northwest Catholic, and *everyone else* in Division II that season.

But that *everyone else* appeared to be just No. 4 Wilton—perhaps Central's toughest challenge of the year—but no matter what team advanced, it appeared that Central and Northwest were on a collision course for the CIAC Division II finals at Mohegan Sun over the weekend of March 19-20.

"I told [Northwest Catholic coach] John [Mirabello] that" after the CCC Championship game in Enfield said Barrette. "I said 'let's do this again on March 19' as we walked through the [handshake] line. I know they'll throw something else at us."

"It's a great game every time we play Northwest Catholic."

***

The postseason wasn't always a given for the boys basketball team at Bristol Central.

From 1965 until 1974, the Rams did not have one postseason victory.

But in 1975, the Rams—with help from a couple guys with the last name of Hernandez (Dennis and David)—they finally tallied a postseason victory.

That 1975 squad went 17-4 overall as the Rams picked off Naugatuck (71-69) in first round play.

But in the next round, Central allowed nearly 100 points to Bridgeport Central—falling 99-85 in the end (Bridgeport Central was one of principal Pete Wininger's *favorite* teams to play in the postseason when he coached the squad although he had limited success against the Bridgeport program).

Around that time of the Hernandez boys, John Thomas established the Bristol Central school rebounding record of 31 in a game.

Didn't some 7-foot-2 guy break that record recently?

I think his name was Harry Ross.

***

For years, the Boston Celtics franchise was a model of consistency and excellence— a team that always did things the right way. In 2022, for example, they missed another NBA title by two games.

There's tradition with the Celtics and there's tradition at Bristol Central. They're always looking forward to the bigger picture.

After Central defeated Northwest Catholic in an epic 63-56 battle to seize the Central Connecticut Conference championship—it's like when the Celtics won the Eastern Conference title in 2008.

Again, it's a great accomplishment and some NBA teams even put up a banner like that in their home arena to celebrate those types of things (like the Nets did in 2002-03).

But for Bill Russell or Larry Bird, that's not the banner they wanted displayed at Boston Garden.

And for the starting unit of Clingan, Alseph, Rosa, Glasper, and Rivoira at Central, they also had a different banner in mind.

For both of those programs, once that conference title was obtained, the goal was to seize the ultimate prize.

That's how the Celtics always operated and that's what Barrette instilled into his troops after the CCC Title win.

"Our exact words in that huddle is that we're never satisfied and we're always hungry," said Barrette. "With that being said, what we said [after beating NWC] was 'four more [games] to go. Four more to go and we'll have won every goal that we have checked off along the list."

The state championship journey, which was four games away thanks to a first round bye, started in the second round.

Central (24-0, ranked No. 1 in Division II) remained the top-rated team in the state, and awaited the winner of No. 16 Amistad and No.17 Amity.

Here's what the first round looked like in Division II that year:

DIVISION II—FIRST ROUND (Tuesday, March 7)

No. 1 Bristol Central—Bye; No. 16 Amistad (13-7) at No. 17 Amity (12-7); No. 25 Enfield (8-12) at No. 8 Waterford (15-5); No. 24 Sheehan (9-11) at No. 9 Staples (15-5); No. 4 Wilton—Bye; No. 20 Avon (12-8) at No. 13

Newtown (14-6); No. 5 Holy Cross—Bye; No. 21 Newington (11-9) at No. 12 St. Joseph (14-6).

No. 2 Northwest Catholic—Bye; No. 18 Greenwich (12-8) at No. 15 Simsbury (14-6); No. 7 Crosby—Bye; No. 23 Stamford (10-10) at No. 10 Stratford (15-5); No. 3 Conard—Bye; No. 19 Xavier (12-8) at No. 14 Westhill (14-6); No. 6 Prince Tech—Bye; No. 22 Jonathan Law (10-10) at No. 11 Middletown (14-6).

***

On February 21, 2022, the scholastic boys basketball landscape changed in the city of Bristol forever when Donovan Clingan—Bristol Central's All-State dynamo—tallied his 2,000th point over the Rams' 76-50 victory against Bristol Eastern on February 21.

Tallying 2,000 points was one of Clingan's many lofty goals and when he hit his first shot of the third period against Bristol Eastern in Central's last regular season game of the year, the big man tallied that amazing milestone.

"It felt good," said Clingan of the milestone. "To do this at a Bristol Central/Bristol Eastern game meant a lot because that's just a big rivalry that we always loved."

Since that Eastern game, the big man was on fire—romping through the Central Connecticut Conference Tournament as the Rams went 4-0 against some of the best squads in the state.

Clingan posted 136 points over CCC Tournament play, averaging 34.0 points-per-game, and notching 45 points in Central's exciting 63-56 victory over Northwest Catholic.

Clingan came into Division II tournament play with averages of just over 30.0 ppg for the season and 2,142 total points for his career.

Just this season alone, Clingan scored over 720 points before the Division II state tournament game were even played.

To that point of the year, Clingan was 17th all-time leading scorer in state and was just a mere 50 points away from tying all-time great Calvin Murphy (2,192 points) of Norwalk for 12th place.

"He'd be chasing the state record, I believe, if he hadn't had so many games cancelled due to COVID," said Barrette. "With that being said, what an accomplishment."

Connecticut's all-time leader in points, Walt Luckett, played scholastically at Kolbe Cathedral high school, went on to Ohio State and was drafted by the Detroit Pistons in the second round of the NBA draft.

However, no matter how you slice it—2,500 points or not—the 2021 *and* 2022 Gatorade Connecticut State Player of the Year left BCHS as one of the greatest scholastic players in Nutmeg State history on both sides of the ball.

"He's been a hell of a player for four years," said Barrette. "The best this city has ever seen [and] the most impactful player this city has ever seen. And I'm going to tell you something, every time people play against him, they can't believe the impact he has, especially on the defensive end. He gets his hands on everything and he can deter so much and generally after that happens, people stop going at him."

Here's a look at Connecticut's all-time leading scorers in boys scholastic hoops:

CIAC Boys 2,000-point scorers (as of the start of the 2022 state tournament...)

1. Walt Luckett, Kolbe Cathedral, 2,691 points

2. Tom Roy, South Windsor, 2,501

3. Anthony Harris, Danbury, 2,491

4. Alex Jensen, Stonington, 2,357

5. Rashamel Jones, Trinity Catholic, 2,301

6. Tyshon Rogers, Crosby, 2,292

7. Matt Curtis, Cheshire, 2,263

8T. Jordan Williams, Torrington, 2,228

8T. Kahlil Dukes, Capital Prep, 2,228

10. Phil Lott, Wilby, 2,212

11. Kris Dunn, New London, 2,201

12. Calvin Murphy, Norwalk, 2,192

13. Stepfan Holley, Capital Prep, 2,180

14. John Pinone, South Catholic, 2,174

15. DeJuan Ransom, Wilcox Tech, 2,154

16. Dave Vigeant, Litchfield, 2,149

17. Donovan Clingan, Bristol Central, 2,142

***

For the 25th consecutive game, the Rams rolled out the same starting line-up of Clingan (30.0 points-per-game), Glasper (11.1 ppg, team-leading 31 three-pointers), Rivoira (7.9 ppg), Alseph (6.1 ppg), and Rosa (5.0 ppg).

How many scholastic programs could say that it used the same starting line-up 25 times in a season without a significant injury, suspension, or sickness? And during COVID? That was even more impressive.

That starting cast began its trek against Southington at Trinity College on December 18 and the same five players that went a full thirty-two minutes against Northwest Catholic for victory number twenty-four were right back at it.

In terms of the Division II Tournament, it was win and stay home for Central as the No. 1 seed continued its onslaught.

Advancement by the Rams meant a Friday night showing at home against No. 8 Waterford—a back-to-back tournament challenge. The Division II playoffs were about to go into high gear.

***

How could we mention a scholastic basketball season from Bristol Central without talking about "Coachie?"

Jason "Coachie" DeCarolis is an icon over at the school on the hill in Bristol (so is scorekeeper Randy Forrest. But Forrest should have been thrown out of that state tournament game at Bethel years ago due to the tomfoolery he caused at the scorer's table during a heated game. Well, maybe not…).

"Coachie" worked countless games at the scorekeepers table, making the opening announcements, helping chase down footballs on game day in the fall and is a track and field judge to boot.

He is a unique soul and a huge fan of professional baseball and football, though he detests hockey. He even took a selfie with the mayor at Mohegan Sun Arena after Central won the state championship. He does he get around.

Once again a fixture of BCHS hoops program over the boys championship run, he'll be remembered for these three quotes from the 2021-22 campaign:

"First horn!"

"Second horn!"

And the ever-popular COVID related *"Masks are required…"* over and over. There's no one better at what he does than Jason.

***

Here's how the first round went down in first round play and the second round matchups:

CIAC BOYS BASKETBALL TOURNAMENT DIVISION II PAIRINGS AND RESULTS—

Round 1

Amistad 65, Amity 62

Greenwich 43, Simsbury 34

Middletown 58, Jonathan Law 47

Newtown 50, Avon 38

St. Joseph 77, Newington 61

Stamford 65, Stratford 62

Staples 70, Sheehan 23

Waterford 65, Enfield 31

Westhill 70, Xavier 47

SECOND ROUND—Thursday, March 10 (due to a snow day)

No. 16 Amistad (14-7) at No. 1 Bristol Central (20-0); No. 9 Staples (16-5) at No. 8 Waterford (16-5); No. 13 Newtown (15-6) at No. 4 Wilton (17-3); No. 12 St. Joseph (15-6) at No. 5 Holy Cross (16-4).

No. 18 Greenwich (13-8) at No. 2 Northwest Catholic (19-1); No. 23 Stamford (11-10) at No. 7 Crosby (15-5); No. 14 Westhill (15-6) at No. 3 Conard (18-2); No. 11 Middletown (15-6) at No. 6 Prince Tech (15-5)

***

Damion Glasper (Scott Wedman)

Throughout this book, I have made comparisons between players from championship squad at Bristol Central and the 1985-86 NBA champion Boston Celtics.

That Celtics team started, perhaps, the greatest 'Big 3' of all time in Larry Bird, Kevin McHale, and Robert Parish. But Central really started three guards and two forwards.

There wasn't anyone with whom to compare Damion Glasper in that Celtics starting line-up. Glasper actually had more in common with former All-Star Scott Wedman than with Parish.

Wedman had been a star for the Cleveland Cavaliers before getting traded to Boston. He was a seamless fit for the Celtics just like Glasper at Central.

Glasper had the talent to be a 20-25 point scorer on any other team, but on Central, he sacrificed, deferring when necessary but ready to take over in an instant.

Like Parish, however, Glasper wasn't big talker on the court and let his long range shooting and defense do the talking instead.

But he was no second fiddle either.

East Catholic learned that when Glasper dropped 19 points on the Eagles and then buried 21 against Wilbur Cross.

In all the pressure-filled games of the season, some televised, it was Glasper making a tremendous impact. He had a keen eye from downtown, draining seven threes against Lewis Mills in CCC play. He was a leader the rest of the Rams' squad could turn to.

The guard hit for over 300 points over his senior campaign, and Central doesn't go anywhere in 2021-22 without the contributions from Glasper.

He dropped in one out of every three-pointer, amassing a total of 35 of Central's 107 trifectas. Over postseason play, Glasper hit for ten or more points in eight games, averaging 12.1 ppg and just missed scoring 100 points. He was a huge part of Central's three-year run—leading to an eventual Division II championship.

***

Between Central's First and Second Titles

Assistant coach Ed Phelan took over the BC boys basketball program in 1981 and by the completion of the decade, Central had appeared in two state championship games.—winning it all in 1990 as the top team in Class L.

From there, current assistant coach Joe DeFillippi helmed the squad over the ensuing nine seasons, going a noteworthy 15-6 in 1993-94.

And then Principal Pete Wininger took charge for the 1999-00 campaign—winning 10 or more games over his first five seasons.

Some amazing athletes played under Wininger, many from the football team.

Timmy Washington, D.J. and Aaron Hernandez, Jim Bayne, and Billy Givens all suited up for Wininger.

Later on, Steve Hasler, Brandon Dudzinski, Chris Klepps and 'Big Deli' Jeff Salovski helped Central tie a school record in wins—finishing 24-2 in 2002-03.

But Bridgeport Central got in the way of more than a couple of the Rams' playoff runs.

Over the next two seasons (2004-05 and 05-06), Central won 17 total games, qualifying for the postseason tournament.

Wininger's final game took place on February 21, 2007 as Bristol Eastern defeated Bristol Central 70-65—keeping the Lancers (7-13) from going to the playoffs that season.

But so did Central (7-13) and St. Paul—a rare time all three high school programs failed to have a state tournament qualifier.

In 2007, Tim Barrette took charge of the program—qualifying for the playoffs in his first season but dropped a 57-56 heartbreaker at Branford on March 3, 2008.

Central didn't play a state tournament game again until 2012 but fast forward 10 years and the program had its season state championship in hand.

CIAC Division II Playoffs—Week 1

Game 25 (CIAC, Division II second round)—vs. No. 16 Amistad (March 10)

The Score: 65-38

Location: Charles C. Marsh Gymnasium, Bristol

Game 26 (CIAC, Division II quarterfinal)—vs. No. 8 Waterford (March 11)

The Score: 70-48

Location: Charles C. Marsh Gymnasium, Bristol

Snow would cause havoc with Central's second and quarterfinal round games as the Rams, off a first round bye, were going to have to play tournament games back-to-back.

But after a week off, it was back to work.

And No. 16 Amistad, a 65-62 winner over No. 17 Amity, was first. The squad from New Haven trailed 10-0 out the gate. Included in that run was a sizzling one-handed slam by Clingan off a feed by Alseph. The visitors never got any kind of footing, dropping a 65-38 decision.

With the victory, Bristol advanced to play No. 8 Waterford—a 51-48 overtime winner over No. 9 Staples—in a quarterfinal.

It was another historic night for the Rams, and each win continued to fuel a couple school records. Central was on a 40-game winning streak, and the team's 25th victory also established a new school record for wins in a single season.

But there was a little rust early as Central was just a step behind offensively, watching as that early edge was reduced to five (10-5) with 1:47 to go in the first.

"It looked like it, definitely early on," said Barrette of the early game rust. "No matter what, you can only practice so many days. Coming off a snow day yesterday, [it's] not ideal. I also think that sometimes we read our press clippings too much and we weren't ready to go."

However, Central led by 13 at the halftime break and flipped the script to begin the third period.

Central forced several early turnovers in its 1-3-1, leading to high-percentage buckets to make it a 47-25 contest with 3:13 left to play in the stanza.

Amistad trailed by at least 18 points the rest of the way.

"In the second half, we tried to push that primer button with that trap coming out, kind of got us going a little bit more defensively," said Barrette. "We got out on the break and got some easy hoops early. And then we were able to push that lead out to thirty."

Donovan Clingan started his second CIAC state tournament run with 26 points, 24 rebounds and five blocked shots. He was hacked and held repeatedly, then went into beast-mode—attacking the rim with zest and then blocking and altering shots on the other end.

However, Carson Rivoira channeled his inner Larry Bird once again and posted a tremendous game—doing a little of everything against the Wolves.

Rivoira squared up 14 points, five rebounds, and two assists while being an absolute pest on the defensive end. He had four steals while rejecting two shots and restored balance to the game on both sides of the ball.

"He's my glue guy…he's blue-collar," said Barrette of Rivoira. "He's a grinder, he's a bulldog and if I'm going to war with anyone, Carson Rivoira is on my team."

And the unit of Damion Glasper, Steve Alseph, and Victor Rosa combined for 24 points and tallied steal after steal from overmatched Amistad players.

Glasper chipped in with 10 points, Alseph added nine and Rosa floated in five.

Tre Blair, Aaron Brown and Jayeson VanBeveren all made timely contributions for the Rams.

Arion Robinson and Aden Goffe both scored 12 points to lead Amistad, which ended its season at 14-8.

Leading 10-5 with 1:47 to play in the first quarter, the Rams rattled off 12 straight points to put some distance between the squads. After a Rivoira lay-up, Alseph hit a 3 while Glasper added in his own trifecta and a floater and with 7:01 left in the second stanza, Central led 22-5.

Amistad hung around by hitting four threes over the final 5:53 of the half, but Clingan scored eight straight points for Central, and after Rivoira and Alseph dropped in hoops, it was a 34-21 game at the half.

To start the third period, it was turnover city for the Wolves as Central used its zone—and its vaunted 1-3-1 defense—and got off a 13-4 skein, sealed with a Clingan dunk and a 3 by Rosa, the Rams were leading 47-25 with 3:13 left in the frame.

"Once we get into our zone [defense], we get really difficult to score against," said Barrette. "We tend to like to play man first and then go to zone just because I think it gets you a little more in tune to your assignments when you start man. And then we go to that zone and once we extend like that, it's very difficult for teams to score."

A jumper by Robinson made it a 52-34 game with 22 seconds remaining in the third, but a quick 10-0 push from Central—ended by a Rosa drive and hoop—gave the Rams its biggest lead of the evening at 62-36 with 4:47 left. One final dunk by Clingan, coupled by a free throw from Brown, ended the scoring.

"When you hold a team in the state tournament to under forty points, you can't complain defensively," said Barrette. "I wasn't happy at halftime defensively and it's funny because I said to our guys 'we're just better than that.' I said at halftime we played a C- game when we were up 13."

"We can't do that against Waterford tomorrow night."

***

The only surprise of the second round came towards the bottom of the bracket.

No. 11 Middletown shelled No. 6 Prince Tech by a 71-52 final—advancing to quarterfinal round play against No. 3 Conard. That wasn't much of a reward.

Waterford/Staples went to overtime (51-48) while Stamford gave No. 7 Crosby (62-57) a bit of a scare.

CIAC BOYS BASKETBALL TOURNAMENT DIVISION II PAIRINGS AND RESULTS—Round 2

Bristol Central 65, Amistad 38

Conard 70, Westhill 61

Crosby 62, Stamford 57

Holy Cross 69, St. Joseph 58

Middletown 71, Prince Tech 52

Northwest Catholic 72, Greenwich 45

Waterford 51, Staples 48 (OT)

Wilton 57, Newtown 49

QUARTERFINALS (Friday, March 11)

No. 8 Waterford (17-5) at No. 1 Bristol Central (25-0); No. 5 Holy Cross (17-4) at No. 4 Wilton (18-3).

No. 7 Crosby (16-5) at No. 2 Northwest Catholic (20-1); No. 11 Middletown (16-6) at No. 3 Conard (19-2).

***

Central had less than a 24-hour turnaround as the locals, at 25-0, were in the quarterfinal mix and still playing at home.

No. 8 Waterford (19-6) won its second round game against Staples, needing overtime to do it. There wasn't any rest for the weary.

"It's an interesting scenario," said Barrette about the Waterford game. "There's no prep [time] for either team."

The showdown marked the final home game for Central's senior core of eight seniors—including the two-time Gatorade Connecticut Boys Basketball Player of the Year, Donovan Clingan.

The winner of Central/Waterford would move on to semifinal round play on Tuesday, March 15 against the winner of No. 4 Wilton and No. 5 Holy Cross.

Staples (18-7) let an excellent opportunity slip by in its second-round showdown against Waterford's Lancers but a huge 3-pointer by Sean O'Connell tied the game late—forcing an overtime session.

From there, an 8-0 Waterford run knocked out Staples over the final four minutes of play.

The Lancers had some size and length and O'Connell—a talented 6-foot-4 senior—collected 20 points and 11 rebounds against Staples.

Clingan had to match up against sophomore center Juan Morel Jr (10 points, 10 rebounds, five blocks versus Staples), an athletic 6-foot-8 center.

But did Morel have enough length to slow down a motivated Clingan?

It was one final time to see Clingan and those seniors in action at home.

***

Finally, Waterford came to Bristol! And there's a story behind Waterford on a local front.

As the Bristol Eastern boys basketball program was putting together its 2006-07 schedule, Waterford was looking for another opponent for a home game.

The school from Waterford hugs Route 1, and it takes some doing to get down Interstate 95 to get to that high school.

Those Lancers asked Bristol's Lancers to travel down to Waterford for a non-conference game, and the contest was scheduled.

On December 29, 2006, Eastern made the long trip down to the shoreline and absorbed a tough 61-46 loss.

At the end of the game, when it was mentioned if Waterford was going to come up to Bristol the following season, Eastern head coach Mike Giovinazzo was basically told 'thanks for coming down' and that was it.

Waterford did not have any intention of playing at Bristol Eastern in 2007.

And that annoyed Eastern's coaching staff.

Like many squads of the CCC during the 1990s and early 2000s, programs would have up to six open dates for Christmas Tournaments or non-conference games each season.

And typically, teams would return favors to one another.

The Lancers did the same with programs like Bunnell and Stratford which allowed Eastern to see a different brand of basketball.

Stratford wasn't exactly down the street, but each program made it work, saving a little extra gas money for the trips.

But back to Waterford in 2006.

That same season, two weeks previous, Waterford had said the same thing to Plainville—inviting the squad down for a game ('we need one more home game') and didn't return the favor on the flip side the following year.

The Blue Devils lost their game 69-53 to Waterford and that was that.

Those Lancers ended the season at 15-5, went to the 2007 Class M finals but got drilled by No. 4 Weston, 59-35.

Waterford won a state title in 2019, beating New Britain 63-56, and was the last defending champion in Division II before Bristol Central won in 2022 with the pandemic knocking out the CIAC postseason in 2020 and 2021.

And Giovinazzo was in the house that night for the Central-Waterford quarterfinal, enjoying all the action and wondering how much in gas it took to get from Waterford to Bristol.

Gas was a lot cheaper back in 2006, wasn't it?

Versus Watertown

In the final scholastic game for the seniors on the Bristol Central boys basketball team, the Rams were able to top No. 8 Waterford by a 70-48 final at home.

With that triumph, Central moved to 26-0 overall, winners of 41 straight games, and headed back to New Haven the following Tuesday to square off against No. 4 Wilton.

The Lancers from Waterford (19-7) gave a fantastic effort against the Rams, never letting the lead get into double-figures over the first half of play.

And a big 3-pointer from Evan McCue (eight points) just ten seconds into the third quarter made it a 31-28 contest.

But Central turned up the intensity over the next seven minutes or so, turning defense into offense and off a 23-5 burst, the home team nabbed a 54-33 edge—rolling into the fourth frame with a 21-point edge in hand over a vicious quarter of play.

"We've been a third-quarter team all year, let's be honest," said Barrette. "The first four minutes of third quarter, I preach it in that locker room."

Clingan ended his evening with 45 points, netting 29 of those over first half play, to go along with 18 rebounds and five blocked shots in his final game at BCHS.

The rest of the tournament would be played from neutral venues.

His teammates joined the offensive party in the second half as Rivoira (nine points), Alseph (eight), and Rosa (four) netted all their points over second half play.

Glasper added four points, playing through a bit of sickness, and was the only player not named Clingan to score a hoop over first half action for Central.

Clingan ended up scoring 29 of his squad's first 31. Waterford played tough. Sean O'Connell scored a team-high 12 points, Jordan Elci nabbed nine while Logan Peabody, Evan Piotrowski, and Juan Morel all had eight.

That diverse offense helped keep the game from getting out of hand early as the visiting aggression attacked the hoop, then used a little long ball to pile up the points, as the Lancers chopped the deficit to two possessions (31-25) at the halftime break.

"They make [good] adjustments," said Barrette of Waterford. "They run their stuff and any mistake you make on the defensive end, they expose. Give Waterford all the credit. O'Connell, he was really crafty. The way he spins the ball around the hoop, he doesn't have much elevation when he's going to the rim but I'll tell you, he's a crafty player."

Clingan notched the first 12 points for Central, including a 3 from the top of the key, to give the home squad an early edge, and when Glasper made a steal and a hoop with 2:18 left to play in the first quarter, the Rams held a 14-9 push.

Missed Central shots kept Waterford in the contest, and a three from McCue chopped the deficit to 16-14 to end the first period.

Clingan netted 15 points over the following frame and after a lay-up from O'Connell made it a 20-18 contest with 5:29 remaining in the half, Clingan upped the ante.

He went on a personal 8-2 burst as he slammed in a hoop, hit a slick hook shot, just missed out on an and-1, and Central was up eight at 28-20 with 1:50 remaining before intermission.

And when one final free throw fell in for Clingan to end the half, Central's edge was just six as missed opportunities from deep slowed down the home team.

"We were 1-for-12 in that first half from 3-pointers," said Barrette. "We couldn't shoot the ball any worse than we had. The one being Donovan who made the 3. He had 29 of the 31 points in the first half. He kept us afloat, and we knew if we had just chipped in a little bit in the second half, we'd be able to push this lead out."

Elci canned a 3 to open the third but Central turned up the heat ran off a slick 17-3 run.

And once misses and turnovers began to pile up for the Lancers, the Rams took complete advantage.

"Once we got going, we turned them over a little bit in that 1-3-1 [defensive press], kind of sped up play a little bit. We got out in transition, got some easy looks and then once we started making shots, it gets a lot easier for Donovan because then there's only two guys they can throw at him."

Alseph started the run with a 3, Glasper later added a jumper, Rosa dropped in a lay-up and when one final three from Alseph hit nothing but net, Waterford was trailing big at 48-31 with 2:28 left in the third.

"I can't praise Steve Alseph enough," said Barrette. "Let me just tell you, we came out of the huddle at the end of the third and we said 'we're up 19 guys. Now it's time to feed the monster the ball. Don't take another three unless we get the ball inside first.' But Steve made some big shots in that second half and really put us up a bunch."

O'Connell put back a miss to stop the run, but Central then went on a 9-0 push and when Clingan ended the jaunt with a 3-point play, the center had 40 points in the bank and the Rams had built a 57-33 cushion with 7:00 left in the contest.

Midway in the fourth, Rosa dropped in a basket, Alseph hit a hoop, Clingan scored five straight points and when Rivoira ended the scoring with two consecutive hoops, Central's edge reached 70-42 with 2:23 remaining. And in the end, Central moved on to the semifinal round off the 70-48 win— sending the seniors out as winners on their own home hardwood.

"I congratulated them in the locker room in finishing the regular season at home undefeated. It's an accomplishment," said Barrette.

***

Former *Bristol Press* sportswriter Matt Hornick began his online story on the Waterford/Central game with the following opening for the online edition:

"The Bristol Central boys basketball team is accustomed to beating up on the Lancers, but this team came from much further away than the other side of Bristol…"

That didn't go over too well with certain members of the coaching staff from boys basketball team on King Street.

***

All the top seeds advanced to the semifinal round in Division II play. Wilton had to hang on to dear life against Holy Cross (63-62), Northwest Catholic scored 100 points against Crosby (101-63) while Conard was 12 points better than Middletown (55-43).

The CCC was impressive with three of the final four teams in the Division II bracket coming from the Central Connecticut area. Again, there was a collision course ahead between Northwest Catholic and Bristol Central.

But before that championship tilt, the semifinal showdown between No. 1 Central and No. 4 Wilton had World Wrestling Entertainment written over what turned into a game of the ages from New Haven.

And for the second straight visit for Central, a little overtime was needed to determine the team heading to Uncasville.

CIAC BOYS BASKETBALL TOURNAMENT DIVISION II PAIRINGS AND RESULTS—Quarterfinals

No. 1 Bristol Central 70, No. 8 Waterford 48

No. 4 Wilton 63, No. 5 Holy Cross 62

No. 2 Northwest Catholic 101, No. 7 Crosby 63

No. 3 Conard 55, No. 11 Middletown 43

Semifinals—(Tuesday, March 15)

No. 1 Bristol Central (26-0) vs. No. 4 Wilton (19-3)*

*from the Floyd Little Athletic Center

No. 2 Northwest Catholic (24-2) vs. No. 3 Conard (22-3)**

**from Enfield High School. The West Hartford site did not pan out.

Against Amistad, the Rams were overpowering, winning 65-38

Donovan Clingan is interviewed after an early-round victory. It would be the first of many such interviews on the way to the championship.

Championship Week

It was Championship week for the Bristol Central (26-0) boys basketball team. Central drew a tough assignment in the semifinal round as the top ranked Rams battled No. 4 Wilton from the Floyd Little Athletic Center in New Haven. This game would be one of the hardest the Rams played all season.

"Listen, I've been talking about it. Every coach that's talked to me talked about everyone wants to knock off number one," said Tim Barrette. "[They want to] end the streak, all this stuff. But my guys are one game at a time."

And that payoff of taking the one game at a time method led to an undefeated ledger and 41 straight victories.

However, similar statements could be said of the other top three squads in the Division II tournament.

In the semifinals of Division II, No. 2 Northwest Catholic squared off against No. 3 Conard from Enfield high school.

It was a rematch of the semifinal round of the Central Connecticut Conference tournament and a similar result came to pass that night.

NWC was headed for Uncasville.

Barrette and crew weren't looking too far ahead as Waterford was the game of the night on Friday.

And after another blowout win, it led to the confrontation against Wilton.

"We have a three-game winning streak we had to go on" with Waterford in the middle said Barrette. "You can't win three without winning one. We talked about it in our last huddle in my classroom. When we came down, we were ready to play."

And those Lancers were legit and had weapons all over the court, inside and out.

But once Alseph (nine points, two threes) started to make shots from long range over third period action—coupled with Central's staunch defense—that close game became a blowout rather quickly.

The Lancers ran out of gas midway through the third period as Central's energy rose with every made hoop.

"[Waterford] gave us a good shot, we knew that, but we asserted ourselves so much that Waterford put so much effort to stay close in the first half and we had shot the ball so poorly, once we started making a couple threes, that lead really ballooned quickly," said Barrette.

And the crowd went wild when Rivoira rejected a Waterford field goal attempt with 4:52 remaining in the third period.

The hole in the wall made by Rivoira's loud rejection cost the city thousands of dollars to repair (Carson was sent a bill but sent it to Coachie to pay).

***

This senior crew was ready to capture Central's first championship since 1990 and the city of Bristol was waiting for that monumental moment with the UConn-bound Clingan leading the way.

"Coming out of COVID, we needed something positive," said Barrette. "Donovan has put this whole community and school on his back. I can't be prouder of being the coach of these great men."

The bright lights never phased Central's basketball team in the least and via the 26-0 record and 41 straight victories—Connecticut's current longest winning streak and being a top-five mark in the nation—propelled the locals on.

"One word I'll use is composure," said Barrette of his squad. "My five guys have composure. It's hard to rattle them. Pressure doesn't bother us at the end of games and [Clingan] is the ultimate press-breaker because you then have to play him one-on-one inside."

"And that's impossible."

***

Glasper scored four points against Waterford but had a critical second period basket to keep Central in the lead.

The shooting guard was not his normal self after being sick on Friday, but he made some outstanding contributions over the quarterfinal victory nonetheless. With a healthy Glasper in the mix against Wilton, Central had its A-team at full strength which would spell doom and demise for Wilton—eventually.

"I give Damion Glasper a lot of credit," said Barrette after the Waterford game. "He was laying on the bleachers before the game. He was so sick trying to gut through this [game]. With that being said, he gutted through it the best he could. I know we'll have a better Damion on Tuesday night [against Wilton].

***

The lowest seed still left alive in CIAC tournament play in 2022 came in the Division V bracket as No. 20 Windsor Locks upset No. 12 Suffield (54-39) in the quarterfinal round.

Amazingly, the Raiders were a sub-.500 team coming into the postseason (9-10) and became a bit of a Cinderella story.

But the squad fell to No. 8 Windham (53-50) in the semifinals, ending its run against the future Division V champs.

Anything can happen in state tournament play, but were the Rams about to be tripped up by Wilton?

That script sure could have panned out differently if Wilton could have scored a few baskets in overtime because after thirty-two minutes of grueling hardwood action, the game between the first and fourth ranked teams was still not decided. It was another tough game in New Haven…

***

CIAC Division II Playoffs—Week 2

Game 27 (CIAC, Division II semifinal)—vs. No. 4 Wilton (March 15)

The Score: 54-52, OT

Location: Floyd Little Athletic Center, New Haven

One common theme between all the squads that have gone up against Central in state tournament play was that those programs had to go the distance against its opponents to advance to face the Rams.

Working hard, having to play to the buzzer in nail-bitters or worse, battling through overtime sessions to advance to square off against Central was exhausting. For schools like Amistad, and Waterford, nothing was easy over postseason play.

Wilton's Warriors, too, were trailing late against No. 5 Holy Cross by two late in the contest. But Wilton's Thomas McKiernan hit the game-winning 3 with 13 seconds to play to help his team secure a 63-62 victory.

The reward for Wilton? A date with the top-ranked program in Connecticut. But to Wilton's credit, that senior-laden program pushed Central to the brink of elimination in what turned into the best postseason game for the Rams in 2022 at the state and CCC Tournament level.

***

With Wilton's tallest player listed at 6-foot-5, it would be difficult to stop Clingan without turning the game into a certifiable war zone. Clingan would be too big to control despite the multiple bodies Wilton would throw at the big man.

And when that happened, would Glasper, Rosa, Rivoira and Alseph start splashing in three-point bombs and lay-ups?

"It makes it impossible to guard Donovan," said Barrette of Clingan when the offense is coming from multiple players. "It's hard to guard him with three [players] as you saw in the first half [against Waterford]. But once you start making shots, those are back-breakers for most teams because they know they're going to give up some to Donovan inside. But once we start making threes from the outside, that is why we could win a state championship."

If Central did its normal excellent job defensively, with the likes of Glasper, Rosa, and Alseph pressuring the guards, it was going to be a long night for Wilton.

The winner of this game punched its ticket to Uncasville and got a shot at the Division II championship against No. 2 Northwest Catholic.

It was the battle for Uncasville (via New Haven) on that Tuesday night affair.

***

Versus Wilton—from the Floyd Athletic Center (New Haven)

After surviving the onslaught of an overtime game against Wilbur Cross in New Haven six weeks previous, why would the next game there be any different?

And in the match-up against the fourth ranked squad, the Rams and Wilton went to the buzzer…and then some.

With a win Central would be 27-0, winners of 42 straight games, and travel to Uncasville the following Saturday for a championship showdown against No. 2 Northwest Catholic (25-2) with all the momentum in the world on Bristol's side.

But Central had to survive all the elements as the game turned into physical onslaught that was centered on Clingan. Again, he was everywhere that night, including on the floor at times, putting together another outstanding performance.

He dropped in game-high 30 points to go along with 21 rebounds and eight blocked shots. The contest was downright nasty at times. Battling three defenders at a clip, tripped on at least half-dozen occasions, and mauled time after time after time, the senior never lost his composure on his way to another sizzling performance.

"Tonight was a little more than usual," said Clingan of the game's physical nature. "I just [did] my best to keep my head, stay strong, work through contact and just play my game."

Bringing the ball into the paint was a futile method of scoring for Wilton because Clingan blocked almost everything. Wilton ended up shooting just 33-percent from the field, missing 40 of its 60 attempts as Central's defense was clutch.

While the Warriors took just four free throws, making two, the team hit 10-of-32 from deep but was just one charity toss away from stealing the game away from the Rams.

That one, late free throw by Wilton never materialized—forcing overtime.

Tommy McKiernan led the Wilton charge with 15 points, going 5-for-5 overall from the field (all three-pointers), but the rest of the squad was 15-of-55.

Parker Woodring added 13 points, eight rebounds, and four assists while Kevin Hyzy sank 11 points and grabbed four rebounds.

Central kept the high-scoring Hyzy nearly seven points under his scoring average of 17.7 ppg.

Early in the overtime session, Wilton lost its two best players to fouls. Central lost Steve Alseph for the same reason.

"This was a rugby match," said Tim Barrette. "I didn't realize we'd be playing rugby but it is what it is. My guys sucked it up tonight, played through the contact."

Central never trailed in overtime.

Wilton (21-5) truly put together an amazing game but too many lulls on offense—due to an over-the-top defensive effort by Central—doomed the Warriors, though they held Central to just 19 points at the half.

Wilton made a hoop with 3:42 left in the second period, seizing a 16-12 edge, but did not score again in the half as the Rams snared a 19-16 lead at intermission.

Later the Warriors were silent over the first 3:30 of the overtime session as Central grabbed a 50-45 cushion.

"I thought we did a great job defensively all night," said Barrette. "Then when [Wilton] got into a little bit of foul trouble in the end, we were able to close the game out."

The only place where Central struggled was at the free throw stripe—making just 14-of-24 shots—before overtime.

From there, the Rams did not make a field goal over the fifth period. Instead, Central coolly canned 9-of-12 charity tosses—making its final six in a row—to ice the showdown.

"If we had made some free throws in the fourth quarter, we could have put this thing away" in regulation said Barrette.

That would have helped because Central, via 1-of-2 free throws from Clingan, made it a 44-34 game with 1:51 remaining in the fourth frame.

But Central just couldn't put together one final hoop which would have knocked the Warriors completely out. Give the fourth seed credit because everything had to fall in the basket for the squad to force OT.

To start the rally, Hyzy canned a baseline 3 and off a quick steal, he kicked in another one—over a stretch of a Reggie Miller-like 10 seconds—and with 1:32 showing on the clock, it was a 44-40 game and Wilton was back in it.

Clingan was eventually fouled, again making one of the two free throw attempts with 1:18 in regulation, but when Wilton's Parker Woodring hit a little fallaway in the lane with 1:06 left in the fourth, it was a one possession contest at 45-42.

Five seconds later, Central committed a turnover on the inbounds and from there, Alseph fouled McKiernan as he was launching up a 3. The shot fell in for McKiernan, giving him another 3-pointer, and with 40.8 seconds left, the contest was knotted at 45-45.

Wilton was looking for its first lead since 1:19 of the second half via a possible four-point opportunity—coming all the way from a double-figure deficit.

"Give Wilton some credit making some threes in the end," said Barrette. "Those were contested [but] they made some shots."

But the charity toss by McKiernan was off target, Alseph grabbed the rebound, and Central was looking for Clingan for the go-ahead hoop. But his contested attempt was off the mark and after a scrum, McKiernan had the ball and the Warriors called timeout with 22.9 seconds showing on the clock of the 45-45 game.

Wilton worked the ball around but committed an offensive foul with 7.8 seconds left. But Central returned the favor when a pass to Clingan went too far over the center's head and out of bounds. After a long desperation 3 by Woodring failed to fall in at the buzzer, an extra four minutes were added to the scoreboard.

"Apparently, we like to play in overtime down here at Floyd Little," said Barrette with a bit of a grin. "We're 2-0 in overtime [in New Haven]. It shows the maturity of my team."

Wilton never got on track in OT as Central slowed the pace down, getting the ball to its shooters.

McKiernan fouled out as Glasper (12 points) made a free throw and off another Wilton miss, Clingan was fouled with 1:40 to play—calmly sinking two foul shots to make it a 48-45 game.

Soon after, Hyzy was disqualified, but Alseph missed two charity tosses as the Warriors were looking to draw even with 1:18 left I the extra session.

Wilton then misfired on two shots, and when Clingan snared the ball with 35.8 seconds remaining, the big man made it a five-point game.

He connected on two free throws as Central's edge reached 50-45 as time was running out on Wilton.

Alseph fouled out with 31 seconds left as Central did a respectable job in using the combination of Tre Blair and Jayeson VanBeveren to fill in for Alseph, Central's disqualified senior.

Woodring missed the front end of a one-and-one, but Wilton's Eusebe Zarius was fouled, making two charity tosses with 30 seconds remaining, as the deficit was down to 50-47, making it a one possession game once again.

A foul on Clingan led to two additional free throws less than a second later, but the Warriors missed four straight field goals on the ensuing drive. Still they were in the ball game with 7.3 seconds left.

Woodring hit a floater with 3.6 seconds remaining, Glasper was then fouled—kicking in two free throws with 2.7 seconds to make it a five-point game once again (54-49).

Even as Woodring banked home a 3 at the buzzer, Central started the celebration—winning the contest by a 54-52 final—and a trip to the Mohegan Sun Arena was on for a second time for the Rams.

***

It was physical from the start against Wilton as neither team grabbed any kind of early first period advantage.

Rosa (five points) connected on a three-ball and Clingan notched the final five points of the first frame for the Rams but after eight minutes of action, the game was all tied up at 8-8.

Wilton started the second stanza on an 8-4 burst as threes by Hyzy and McKiernan fueled the squad to a 16-12 lead with 3:42 remaining in the period. However, Central tallied the remainder of the points in the half as Clingan cashed in on a foul shot and Alseph hit two of his own.

Clingan then sank a hoop and when Rivoira found Glasper for a baseline jumper, it was a 19-16 game going into the break.

Wilton was never able to take the lead over the third, fourth, or fifth frames—only tying it up late to force the overtime on McKiernan's huge

3—but when the final buzzer sounded, the boys basketball team from Bristol Central was Uncasville-bound.

"When you get lucky, you've got to win one of these if you want a chance to [play] at Mohegan," said Barrette. "We obviously did enough to win tonight."

***

Division II—Semifinal Results from Tuesday

No. 1 Bristol Central 54, No. 4Wilton 52 (OT)

No. 2 Northwest Catholic 62, No. 3 Conard 35

Division II—Finals (from Mohegan Sun)

No. 1 Bristol Central (27-0) vs. No. 2 Northwest Catholic (25-2), Saturday, March 19 at 8:15 p.m. (way past Principal Wininger's bedtime…)

***

Clingan (Kevin McHale)

Donovan Clingan's father, Bill, said he once told his son that his game was a lot like that of former Boston Celtics great Kevin McHale—one of the NBA's Top-50 players of all-time, and a three-time champion.

McHale had some of the slickest low-post moves of all time and was unstoppable in a one-on-one situation.

Sound familiar?

McHale could hit his free throws, rebound, block shots and was a pest on defense.

Towards the end of his career, McHale even started hitting 3-pointers.

Clingan's play reminded us all of McHale hitting a little hook, canning free throws, blocking shots, and using his long limbs and length to play defense

But unlike McHale, Clingan wasn't a secondary option like the Celtics icon was to Larry Bird. Not for the Rams!

Both big men were always having fun, putting up enormous numbers and, eventually, winning championships. It turns out that Clingan didn't even know who Kevin McHale was. Of course McHale retired ten years before Clingan was born. Maybe someone can find Donovan a YouTube video.

***

The Player of the Year in Connecticut drinks Gatorade?

To no one's surprise, Clingan was once again named Connecticut's Gatorade Boys Basketball Player of the Year for 2021-22. It was the second straight season Clingan earned the award. At the time he was averaging 29.9 points, 18.1 rebounds, 6.1 blocks and 3.1 assists per game.

Lewis Mills coach Ryan Raponey was quoted on the official release from Gatorade on Clingan's award and gave an honest assessment of Connecticut's top player.

"Clingan is the most dominant player that I have seen in the last 20-plus years of my involvement as a Connecticut high school player, official and coach. He completely changes the game when you play against Bristol Central. He runs the floor, he can step outside the lane offensively and completely dominates the game defensively."

Clingan was ranked 51st by ESPN for the Class of 2022. Moreover, inside the classroom, Clingan carried a solid 3.5 GPA.

Also according to the release, "Clingan has volunteered locally at basketball clinics with the Bristol Boys & Girls Club and on behalf of the Cambridge Park Youth Sports Clinic. He has also donated his time as a Bristol Central 'Rambassador,' helping incoming first-year students acclimate to high school.

Along those lines, Clingan was also a finalist for Gatorade's National Player of the Year, up for that honor for the second consecutive year.

Other recent Gatorade Connecticut Boys Basketball Players of the Year includes Micawber Etienne (2019-20, Suffield Academy), Tre Mitchell

(2018-19, The Woodstock Academy, and Jaiden Delaire (2017-18, Loomis Chaffee School).

***

Also, the addition of Alseph to the Central boys basketball squad was an amazing acquisition for the Bristol program. The fans came to admire him greatly from the start of the season. Every time Alseph did something well on the court, the crowd would chant "Steeeeeeevvvvvveeeee..."

His name is chanted in a very slow and deliberate way and if you're any kind of trash television watcher, the way the crowd said Steve's name, you know where that particular pronunciation came from.

If you ever caught a minute of the Steve Wilkos Show, the former director of security on Jerry Springer, you heard the live studio audience chanting Steve's name the exact same way.

And when the audience started chanting his name, Wilkos was usually yelling at a guest—for some sort of tomfoolery—and the crowd was agreeing with the host's take on a certain scandalous situation.

Typically, the audience also said his name in unison when Wilkos was ejecting a slimeball off the set in Stamford where the show was filmed.

When Alseph is on the court for the Rams, his name was heard for a tremendous defensive effort, a nifty pass, or a timely three-pointer.

Alseph, a transfer from Sacred Heart, was nothing less than sensational for his one and only season as Central's point guard. He averaged just over 6.0 points-per-game while contributing around four rebounds and four assists every night. In addition, he was a model player and teammate.

The CCC South All-Conference selection did everything, from face-guarding the opponent's top player, to slipping pinpoint passes to Clingan, to just causing general havoc. Alseph is just the type of player Barrette craves for his line-up: a heady guard running the show offensively while taking a no-nonsense approach against opponents on defense.

"He's my engine man," said Barrette of Alseph. "Steve's been a great addition to us. He comes to practice, works hard every day, and says nothing. I couldn't be happier for that kid to have an opportunity to play in the state final."

Against Wilton, Alseph took every assignment to heart and made each possession a nightmare as he was nearly in the jersey of sharpshooter Thomas McKiernan—or whomever he picked up defensively—the entire evening before fouling out with seven points and ten rebounds in the Wilton showdown.

Alseph wasn't shy in the trash-talking department either—always happy to point to the scoreboard when an opponent had a few choice words during on-court battles. In that area he was 27-0.

***

The CIAC Division II title bout, the anticipated championship showdown, was played, of course, at Mohegan Sun Arena in Uncasville on Saturday night, March 19 at 8:15 p.m.

After a long day of scholastic basketball play, was no better way to end it.

Central entered the showdown with a perfect 27-0 ledger while the Lions were 25-2. Northwest's two losses that season had come against Wilbur Cross and Central. The Lions were certainly looking forward to the rematch against Central.

***

Once again, the importance of Central's core group starting and playing in every game heading into the championship showdown against Northwest simply couldn't be ignored.

That senior core played 135 total games between them (out of 135) this season, and the results have been of devastating proportions.

"You can't underestimate the seniors," said Barrette after his squad defeated Wilton.

And that's not an overnight sensation as four out of those five senior players have been in the Bristol Central trenches the entire ride since they were first-year students.

Then this season, Alseph was added to the mix and the result was a 27-0 record.

Along with fellow seniors Jelani Walton, Zach Vanasse and Aaron Brown, that grouping is responsible in scoring 1,715 of the team's total 1,909 points over 2021-22.

That means 90-percent of the program's offense came from that group of eight players — all seniors. That's the value of having senior play, senior leadership and everything that comes along with four-year athletes.

But Wilton had seven seniors of its own, fighting for the same cause—coming up short in the end but leaving it all on the floor over 36-minutes of hardwood warfare.

"[Wilton] had seven seniors on their roster as well so you had two senior laden teams going at each other that don't want to go home. [It was] nothing less than a war," Barrette said. "But I tell my guys all the time I am glad I can go to war with my five seniors any day of the week."

***

The showdown between Central and Northwest wasn't going to hold any secrets for the opposing squad to uncover. After the Rams' seven-point win over the Lions, in the CCC Tournament finals, most of the cats were out of the bag.

Would Northwest try to speed things up, attempting to induce an Indianapolis 500 race? Or would a slowdown, deliberate pace be the way to attempt to hang a loss on Central? How many junk defenses would be in play? And of lesser importance, could "Coachie" announce "first horn" to open the championship game?

It truly wouldn't matter as Barrette and crew had seen it all over 42-straight victories.

"We've won close games that are slow and we've won games that are 85-70 at the other end," said Barrette. "We can play both styles of basketball."

Double-teaming Clingan never worked because Glasper, Rivoira, Rosa, and Alseph hit shots to keep the defense honest. But Northwest brought some incredible size to the court that could have frustrated all those shooters.

On the front line, the Lions had senior Hayden Abdullah (6-foot-8), sophomore London Jemison (6-foot-7) while Badara Diakite (6-foot-9) was the best freshman big man in the state, though when he tried to dunk over Clingan in the CCC Finals, he missed the attempt by a good deal.

Stopping Matt Curtis was the key, and he was capable of a 30-point outing on any given night. He could shoot from deep, hit his midrange shots better than most, and if that frontcourt could just get something offensively over Clingan, the Lions had a chance. But regardless of the players on the court for Northwest, Barrette liked his squad's chances in the rematch.

"We'll be ready to go," said Barrette. "We're just looking forward to the opportunity to play at Mohegan Sun like we had promised our guys. We started there. We want to end there."

"We have a shot this weekend to win a state title."

Said Clingan, "I'll feel good once we go 28-0 on Saturday. I can't wait."

TWO TEAMS—ONE CHAMPION

Here was the breakdown of the title game that was posted in TBE as Bristol Central and Northwest Catholic squared off against each other one more time.

CIAC DIVISION II BOYS FINAL—No. 1 Bristol Central (27-0) vs. No. 2 Northwest Catholic (25-2)

When: 8:15 p.m.

Where: Mohegan Sun Arena, Uncasville

Season Record: Central is 1-0 against NWC. Back on March 3, Central defeated Northwest 63-56 from Enfield high school. The victory propelled the Rams to its second consecutive CCC Tournament Championship.

All-Time Records: The squads are tied 3-3 as the Rams are on a two-game winning streak against the Lions. This is the rubber match between the programs. Central is on a two-game winning streak against NWC.

Title Records: Bristol is 1-1 in championship tilts, beating St. Joseph (66-65) in 1990 while falling in the Class L showcase to Warren Harding in 1987 (69-49). On the flip side, this is the 12th championship showdown for NWC. The Lions are 6-5 all-time in the title game, last winning it all in 2003 (73-71 in overtime versus Wilbur Cross).

Bristol Central's Road to Uncasville: Bye, defeated Amistad 65-38; defeated Waterford 70-48; defeated Wilton 54-52 (OT).

Northwest Catholic's Road to Uncasville: Bye; def. Greenwich 72-45; def. Crosby 101-63; def. Conard 62-35

Coaches: We all know Tim Barrette, the winningest coach in BCHS boys history (182 wins, 140 losses) — recently passing Ed Phelan for the record at Central. On the flip side, John Mirabello is a tremendous coach and mentor for the Lions' outstanding program. He's won over 600 games and is also the winningest coach for the team in West Hartford.

Players to Watch: Bristol Central — Donovan Clingan (Center, 30.4 points-per-game); Damion Glasper (Guard, 10.9 ppg, 34 three-pointers); Carson Rivoira (Forward, 7.9 ppg); Victor Rosa (Guard, 4.9 ppg); Steve Alseph (Guard, 6.3 ppg, 17 threes). Those five players are all seniors for the program and have started all 27 games.

Other Central Players to Watch: Julius Powell (Jr, Center, 2.4 ppg); Jayeson VanBeveren (Jr, Forward/Center, 1.8 ppg); Aaron Brown (Sr, Guard, 1.4 ppg); Jelani Walton (Sr, Forward, 1.7 ppg); Zach Vanasse (Sr, Guard, 1.3 ppg); Mason Stokes (Jr, 1.8 ppg).

Players to Watch: Northwest Catholic — Matt Curtis (Sr, Guard); Hayden Abdullah (Sr, 6-foot-8); London Jemison (So, 6-foot-7); Badara Diakite (Fr, 6-foot-9); Jehyvic Spencer (Sr, guard, 6-foot-2); Gianni Mirabello (So, guard, 5-foot-7).

Question for Northwest: Will the nerves get to Northwest?

Question for Bristol Central: Can Central's core of five-seniors strong end the season at 28-0, winning the school's second ever championship in boys hoop against another elite team?

The other Central victory against NWC: Back on December 19, 2002, D.J. Hernandez jammed in 20 points, Jeff "Big Deli" Salovski hit for 14, while Brandon Dudzinski added six as Central snared a huge 50-49 victory over Northwest at the Doc Hurley Tournament from Weaver High School in Hartford. Chris Bruff scored 16 to lead the Lions. There's simply too much length for Northwest to stop.

True, the Lions have bodies to throw at Clingan, but who is the more battle tested team here?

If Central can make its free throws consistently (that showing at Wilton was not a typical demonstration from the charity stripe) and the Rams' get scoring contributions from the outside, Northwest is in for a long night.

Pick a Winner: Go with Central, 67-64. The pressure is on the Lions to steal this one away. It's Bristol Central's game to lose (the Rams actually defeated Northwest Catholic by more than three points, backing up the reason why this writer did not go into the casino before *or* after the game with a rotten prediction like that...)

***

This Central team should have been playing for a state championship at least once if it wasn't for the pandemic. Maybe even twice as the Rams were a top-four team in 2019-20 when Clingan and that senior class were all sophomores.

And those kids deserved all the success in the world after all the tomfoolery that stalled out the scholastic seasons over a two-plus year stint.

"I hope the town is as proud as I am of these guys," said an emotional Tim Barrette after his squad defeated Wilton. "It's been a long year to be honest. It's been a long two years, three years having the opportunity taken away [from these guys] as sophomores. Junior year, we won everything we could and this year, obviously, 27-0, we've won everything."

"Everything else is gravy."

The way Central played was exactly the way its coach played at Bristol Eastern during his high school days of the late 1990's and early 2000's.

Every game was life or death, the scouting report was the most important part of preparation, and if you weren't wearing a blue and white uniform, you were about to get knocked down and beaten up by Barrette, teammate Eric Carlson, and any other forward from the program.

And he turned himself into one of the best coaches in all the Central Connecticut Conference and the state.

His players have all matched that effort and fire.

"I pour my heart and soul into this," said Barrette. "And so do my guys. The only way this works as a relationship is when we're on the same page, and my team and I are on the same page."

A bullseye was firmly affixed to Central even before the pandemic took hold and when a CIAC state championship opportunity became available, for the first time in nearly three years, the Rams took full advantage.

"We just want an opportunity to play for a state title," said Barrette. "Obviously, we want to win it. At the same time, we want to have an opportunity to take the floor at Mohegan Sun this weekend and I'm hoping that we right this and that the town comes out to support this team because there are no better group of kids in town than the ones playing Bristol Central basketball."

And the players were just as excited as Coach Barrette was.

"It feels great," said Clingan. "We've played there earlier in the year [against East Catholic] but that was just a regular season game. Saturday is for the state championship, and that's why I came and stayed at Central: to bring a state championship to the town, the school, to everyone that deserves it."

"I just couldn't be more excited."

From around the Mohegan Sun Arena...

Fighting for position against the "big man" (left) is a fruitless proposition, but opponents have to try. (Right) Victor Rosa plays some defense against Northwest, Catholic. which was held to 36 points.

Coach Barrette's family was along for the ride each and every step of his 15-year adventure as head coach at Bristol Central.

That includes parents Janet Barrette and Michael Barrette, his wife Katie and son Andrew.

They've seen all the trials and tribulations the coach has gone through and after Central defeated Wilton, Barrette talked about one of the forces driving him forward through the gauntlet of postseason opponents.

During the regular season, Barrette lost his aunt, Sharon Jane Wurzinger who passed on Thursday, January 27 due to complications from COVID.

She was one of Bristol Central's biggest and most dedicated basketball fans—watching the Rams defeat East Catholic at Mohegan Sun Arena in person earlier in the season.

Wurzinger was also there in spirit that Saturday when Central battled Northwest Catholic.

"This is really a special game for me, I'll be honest, going back to Mohegan," said Barrette. "I lost my aunt in January. The last thing she did was go to my game against East Catholic and the next day, she went into the hospital [with] COVID and never came back out. So I made a promise

I would get back there. She got us through a little bit and Donovan just recently lost his grandfather."

"We're playing with a lot of emotion and we have a lot of help on our side."

***

CIAC Division II Playoffs—Week 2

Game 28 (CIAC, Division II championship game)—vs. No. 2 Northwest Catholic (March 19)

The Score: 56-36

Location: Mohegan Sun Arena, Uncasville

In the final game on Championship Saturday, Central and Northwest Catholic went to work in front of over 6,000 fans in the final game of the evening.

Here is the actual game story that ran on the TBE website as the Rams defeated the Lions by 20 points, the largest margin of victory by any team that weekend:

The Bristol Central boys basketball team wins the CIAC Division II state championship, defeating Northwest Catholic, 56-36, on a sizzling Saturday night in Uncasville

MARCH 20, 2022

UNCASVILLE — The Bristol Central boys basketball team is once again on top of the championship mountain.

It was a 32-year odyssey and an incredible journey to get there but behind an elite senior led charge, the top ranked team in Division II — in all the state for that matter—knocked off No. 2 Northwest Catholic in a 56-36 romp from the Mohegan Sun Arena in Uncasville on Saturday night.

The title was the school's second ever state championship in boys hoop and the program — led by seniors Donovan Clingan, Damion Glasper, Victor Rosa, Steve Alseph, and Carson Rivoira — did everything it set out to do since day one.

Over 6,200 fans witnessed history as Central (28-0) ran the table and the squad defeated, arguably, the second-best team in the state and added to its school record of 43 straight victories.

Clingan was easily the game's MVP — posting 25 points, 24 rebounds, two assists, and two blocked shots.

"I just wanted to do this for everyone, for Bristol, the school, my mom," said Clingan of the title victory. "I wanted to do it for myself. I just love the school. [It's] family. I just love it."

Clingan had plenty of help behind him as Damion Glasper (15 points, four rebounds, three assists), Steve Alseph (six points, nine rebounds), Carson Rivoira (six points, 10 rebounds, two assists) and Victor Rosa (two points, two steals) all helped lead the charge to the state championship.

Central's defense was over the top as Northwest (25-3) limped to a 27.7 shooting percentage from the field and drained just 2-of-15 three-pointers.

The Lions were held to just 36 points, a tremendous feat, and didn't have many answers to slow down the motivated Rams.

"I'm going to tell you something, thirty-six points allowed, that's a heck of a defensive effort in state championship game," said Central coach Tim Barrette. "We made [Northwest] work for everything tonight."

Northwest's Matt Curtis was tremendous as he went down fighting with 15 points, five rebounds, and two assists, but no other player on the squad tallied more than eight.

And those 15 points were all tough and contested because Rosa absolutely hounded the outstanding guard while Rivoira took his shot against Curtis with similar success.

"Victor loves a challenge," said Barrette. "He took one of the best players in the state of Connecticut and made him work for everything he got. [Curtis] was tired in the fourth [quarter], that's why all those shots were short because Victor ran him all over the floor."

And Alseph's defense against all the other Northwest ball handlers proved to be a difference-maker as well.

It was a complete whitewash on the boards for Central despite Northwest's size on the frontline. The Rams outrebounded the Lions, 57-29, including an incredible 30-9 tally on the offensive end.

Iron man basketball ruled once again as Rosa, Glasper, Alseph and Clingan all played 31 out of a possible 32 minutes. Credit belongs to Northwest's defense as the unit limited Central to 30-percent shooting from the field and just seven percent from downtown (1-for-14).

But that one three — drained by Glasper at the third period buzzer — propelled Central to a 39-27 lead with eight minutes remaining in the showdown.

Clingan, sealed off and doubled teamed as usual, went nearly nine minutes without scoring a point between the first and second periods, but that didn't matter okay because the rest of Central's squad picked up the slack offensively.

It was back-and-forth early, but a 7-0 run by the Lions, punctuated by a 3 from Gianni Mirabello, made it a 7-2 contest just 2:12 into things.

Central answered with a 6-0 dash and when Clingan put back a missed three-pointer, Central led it 8-7 with 2:02 left to play in the first.

Glasper ended the streak with two free throws — tying the game 10-10 through one.

Those two charity shots were the start of a 10-0 Central burst as Glasper sunk two more free throws, Rivoira scored off a broken play, and two straight hoops by Glasper saw the Rams end an 18-10 push with 5:03 to play in the half. In fact, when Glasper hit his first of two free throws with 7:18 to play in the second period, Central took the lead for good.

Later in the second, Alseph laid in a sweet up-and-under move, and when Clingan notched two consecutive charity tosses, Central went ahead by a 22-15 push with 1:35 remaining.

"We have a great basketball player in Donovan and Damion is pretty good himself but I have three athletes around him that are bulldogs," said Barrette of Rosa, Alseph, and Rivoira. "And that's what won us the game."

To end the half, Northwest's London Jemison dropped in a 3 and when freshmen Badara Diakite (eight points, seven rebounds) saw his hook shot fall through with 30 seconds to play before the break, the Rams were clinging to a 22-20 push at the half.

Clingan and Glasper each had eight points at intermission while Diakite swished in six and Curtis and Jemison added five apiece for the Lions.

The teams traded hoops to open the second half, and when Northwest's Hayden Abdullah put-back a miss with 5:33 left in the third quarter, Central's edge was trimmed to 26-24.

Clingan then went on a personal 7-2 run and, off a sweet Rivoira feed leading to a loud dunk, the Rams inched up to a 33-26 lead with 2:52 remaining in the third. And to end the period, it was all Central.

Rosa slipped in a floater, Clingan cashed in a free throw and at the buzzer, Glasper flipped a shot from the CIAC logo on the court — a 35-foot heave that found nothing but net—and the Rams pushed ahead by 12 (49-37) with the fourth quarter on deck.

"We made some adjustments at halftime," said Barrette. "I thought in the fourth quarter, once we pulled the ball out, we were able to get it inside and [Clingan] was able to finish it with three thunderous dunks."

Curtis opened the fourth with an and-1 to trim the deficit to 39-30 but the bottom fell out on the Lions moments later. A 10-2 Rams' burst nearly put the event away as Clingan started the jaunt with another slam and later on, Rivoira nabbed a steal for a lay-up.

When Glasper hit a free throw with 3:07 left, Central's lead was 49-32 and the building was starting to buzz.

"Carson Rivoira's steal and the lay-up at the end, come on," said Barrette. "You can't teach that. That's just all heart and effort."

Ahead by 15, Clingan ended his scoring with a traditional three-point play and when Rivoira coolly sank two charity tosses, the Rams had a 54-34 cushion with 1:56 to play.

With 56.5 second left, Barrette and Clingan hugged at center court as the senior left the game for good and the Central faithful gave their All-State center a long, standing ovation.

"We were in the locker room together, just him and I before the game. He went in early, he hugged me and said 'coach, one last thing to do together,'" said Barrette. "And I knew with him on my side, there's no way we're not going to succeed tonight."

Moments later, Glasper, Alseph, Rivoira, and Rosa received the same adulation as Tre Blair, Zach Vanasse, Aaron Brown, Jelani Walton, and Julius Powell all finished up.

Brown dropped in a contested lay-up with 14 seconds to play as the Rams' celebration went into full gear.

When the final horn sounded, the Bristol Central boys basketball team was the 2021-22 CIAC Division II.

The game marked the final scholastic contest for Central's senior unit of Damion Glasper, Steve Alseph, Carson Rivoira, Victor Rosa, Jelani Walton, Aaron Brown, Zach Vanasse, and the 2021-22 Gatorade Connecticut Player of the Year, Donovan Clingan.

There was nothing left to prove.

Done and done!

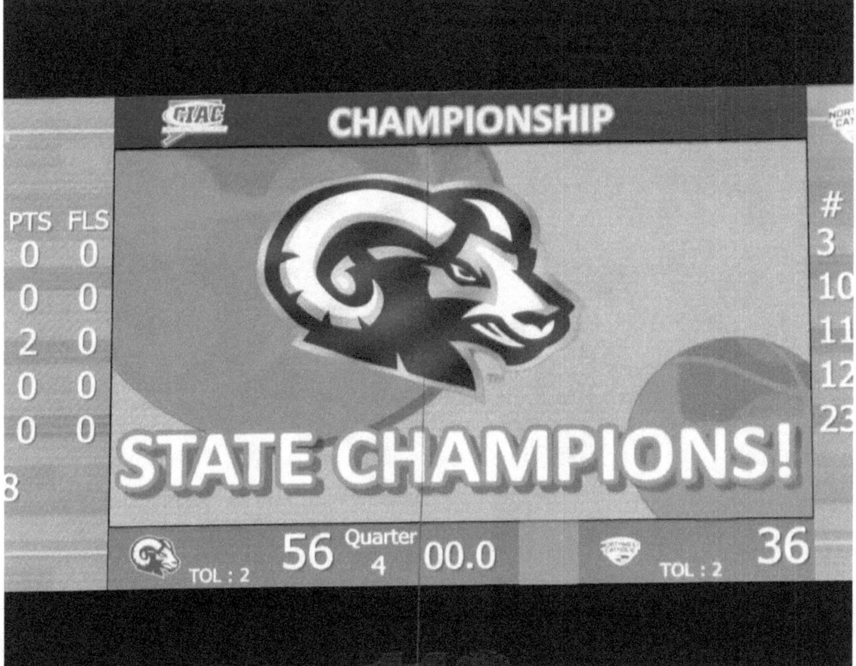
GIAC
CHAMPIONSHIP
PTS FLS
0 0
0 0
2 0
0 0
0 0
#
3
10
11
12
23
STATE CHAMPIONS!
56 Quarter 4 00.0 36
TOL : 2
TOL : 2

Boys Basketball Division II Champions 2022-2023

Bristol Central Rams

RIM DUST…Bristol Central's own Jillian Kovitch sang the National Anthem before the game…Rivoira read part of the CIAC Sportsmanship Code and then turned to the crowd, firing them up, as Central's student section came in droves to see their team win it all. And the crowd was pro-Bristol Central that evening…

***

Once the Central squad finally got out of the arena and onto the bus, the party was on.

When the bus had traveled midway down Route 72, the team received a police escort back to the school. It was a perfect way to finish off the season.

But somewhere along the trip home, DaQuan Brooks contacted his coach via FaceTime in what turned into a full-circle moment for the former player and coach. Brooks has played all over the globe including Canada, got a good look in the NBA's G League, played in the TBT $1 million Winner-Take-All Tournament (We Are D3), and was on the squad for ABA Ancud in Chile.

That's a guy who has never given up on his dream and got a chance to watch Central win the championship and passed along congratulations to his former coach at BCHS.

Those life-long connections are something extremely special between former players and coaches.

***

Clingan's senior year run from start to finish might have been one of the best single-season performances in state history.

The Rams ended the year at 28-0 as the program went 43-0 over the past two years—one of the top streaks in all of America.

And while Clingan will be in a University of Connecticut uniform in 2022-23 when Central continues its school record 43-game winning streak, the All-Stater leaves the BCHS boys basketball program in a better place than when he joined it.

That's all you can ask for as a coach.

The two-time Gatorade Connecticut Player of the Year ended his amazing CIAC, Division II championship run with 2,268 career points—the seventh most scored in state history.

And after Clingan blasted Northwest Catholic in the CIAC Division II Finals for 25 points, he surpassed Matt Curtis's total of 2,263 points from Cheshire.

The second leading scorer in Bristol scholastic history, Carey Edwards (St. Paul, 1,835) trailed Clingan by 433 points by the completion of the 2021-22 season.

For the year, Clingan scored 847 points—good for an average of 30.3 points-per-game.

He hit 360 field goals, splashed in 10 three-pointers, and cashed in on 101 free throws.

If you counted all the games lost due to the pandemic over Clingan's sophomore and junior years, based on his scoring averages over those two seasons, an additional 350 points—or more—weren't out of the realm of possibility.

That 350 could have slated him at 2,618 points overall which would have placed him *second all-time in the state of Connecticut* right behind Walt Luckett (Kolbe Cathedral, 2,691 points).

If playoff runs between CCC and state tournament games could have been extended, Clingan had the potential to be Connecticut's all-time leading scorer.

What an incredible legacy that young man put together during his times over at Bristol Central.

And look at the haul Clingan ended up with when he finished up his career:

*Won the 2021-22 CIAC Division II Championship.

*Took home the last three CCC South Champions.

*Won the CCC Boys Tournament Titles in 2020-21 and 2021-22.

*Holds the school record for points, rebounds, and blocks.

*Leaves as the Mum City's all-time leading scorer for both boys and girls.

*Four times CCC South All Conference, Two-time Connecticut Gatorade Player of the Year, MaxPreps Player of the Year for Connecticut as a senior, CHSCA 2021-22 All-State.

*MVP of both the Boys Basketball Festival, the Robert Saulsbury All-Star Games as a senior.

*As a senior, he averaged 30.1 points, 18.4 rebounds, 3.1 assists, and 6.2 blocked shots per game.

This all happened just before or when Clingan turned 18 years old in February.

Clingan's story is just unfolding and its going be a fun ride to see how the 7-foot-2 center fares at the collegiate level and many of us will be watching live from Storrs, at the XL Center in Hartford, or from home in Bristol.

***

CIAC Boys 2,000-point scorers

1. Walt Luckett, Kolbe Cathedral, 2,691

2. Tom Roy, South Windsor, 2,501

3. Anthony Harris, Danbury, 2,491

4. Alex Jensen, Stonington, 2,357

5. Rashamel Jones, Trinity Catholic, 2,301

6. Tyshon Rogers, Crosby, 2,292

7. Donovan Clingan, Bristol Central, 2,268

8. Matt Curtis, Cheshire, 2,263

***

GameTimeCT's final Top-10 poll had a familiar team at the top of its rankings.

And it was the same program that started there to begin the campaign in December of 2021.

The Rams ended the final standings as the top ranked team. After all the votes were tabulated, Central (28-0) was ranked No. 1—tallying all 570.

Northwest Catholic (25-3) was ranked second coming into the Division II championship game but after that 20-point defeat, there was a new No. 2 team. Division I champ East Catholic (20-6 overall, 512 points) moved into second place to end the year while Northwest (492 points) fell to third.

That meant three squads from the Central Connecticut Conference ended up in the top three spots of the final GameTimeCT poll—just like the final rankings in 2020-21.

Notre Dame-West Haven (25-2, 458) earned fourth place, Hand (23-4, 388) won the Division III championship and took fifth while Windsor (20-5, 368) ended up sixth—making it four of the top six ranked squads that belonged to the CCC.

In seventh place was Fairfield Prep (22-4, 311), Division IV champs Bloomfield (21-5, 259), another prime example of the dominance from the CCC, was eighth.

Kolbe Cathedral (22-4, 237) finished in ninth place and rounding off the top-10 was Wilton (21-5, 198), one of two teams that took Bristol Central to overtime this year along with Wilbur Cross.

Central went 6-0 this season against the final GameTimeCT Top-10 teams.

Conard earned votes as well, ending up in 14th place with 132 points off its 22-4 record.

Wilbur Cross, behind 31 votes, finished in 20th place.

***

Not every scholastic season ends in a championship, but Bristol Central *was* the superior team in Connecticut for most of the past three seasons. Central winning the Division II championship almost seemed like destiny, especially after the CIAC cancelled two straight postseason championships.

To go 43-0 over a two-year window—incredible!

Records fell but Clingan always stayed on the path, kept within the team concept, until the mission was accomplished. And he did everything with a smile.

"I know my mom's proud of me, Bristol's proud, the schools proud. I'm proud, the team's proud, I don't even know what to say," Clingan said after the championship victory. "I'm so excited. This is the reason I stayed at Central."

With that 56-36 championship victory over No. 2 Northwest Catholic, Clingan put himself in the same category with all the other big men in the state of Connecticut who made the same journey.

The first name that comes to mind is former Hartford Public standout Marcus Camby. He was also a Gatorade Player of the Year in Connecticut, going undefeated during a massive senior campaign. The Owls went 27-0 in 1992-93 and Camby was the reason. Averaging 27 points, 11 rebounds, eight assists and eight blocks-per-game as a senior, Camby had two excellent seasons scholastically, accomplishing everything he could on his way to UMASS.

After a 20-0 regular season, Camby and crew absolutely wrecked the postseason and in the Class LL championship game, Camby dropped in 32 points and 14 rebounds as the Owls blasted Danbury, 83-68.

Nearly thirty years later, it was Clingan's turn to shine. He didn't score as many points as Camby did in his title tilt, but the center from Central smoked Northwest with a 20-20 . He came away 25 points and 24 rebounds.

"This is why I stayed here," said Clingan. "This is every high school basketball player's dream and every high school athlete's dream to win a state championship. I mean, it's great especially at a venue like this. Mohegan is a great arena, and I just couldn't be happier."

***

And how many different defenses did Clingan have to go up against over this past season?

He battled the one-on-ones, the 2-3 and 3-2 zone defenses, double-and-triple teams, box-and-1, diamond and one, and triangle and 2s: All defenses that didn't work.

That left the seniors around Clingan open due to some of those junk defenses—hitting threes and attacking the hoop for lay-ups.

Some teams even tried prayer.

Against Central, those defensive methods were never answered.

Teams like Middletown, Enfield, Berlin, and Wilton—especially Wilton—tried to be overly physical and aggressive.

In that Wilton showdown, won by Central in overtime, we even saw a Wilton player flop down to the floor attempting to draw an offensive foul on Clingan in one of the worst acting jobs ever recorded on the scholastic level.

That Wilton game resembled tackle football on the hardwood.

"It's very hard," said Clingan. "I'm getting double, triple-teamed [and] I'm getting beaten up. I just had to stay strong and keep my composure because my team needs me. Without me out there, my team struggles. So they need me out there and I know that. I just have to keep my composure and do what I do."

***

All successful teams understand that a season isn't a sprint, it's a marathon.

Central, the obvious favorite to win the Division II championship that year, never looked ahead of its competition and that one-game-at-a-time method kept the team grounded and in the moment.

"Since the start of the playoffs, coach has said four more, three more, two more," games to go in the state tournament said Clingan. "Today [at Mohegan], he said one more. This is it."

Clingan showed tremendous poise and chemistry throughout the campaign, achieving at the highest level—personally and as a program.

"There's a reason why Donovan stayed," said Barrette. "And those games are why he stayed. That family we talk about, that we broke the huddle with before every game, every time we ended right here, that's what this is really about. This is a family. That's the culture I tried to build 15 years ago when I took this job."

***

How hard was it to do what Barrette and the team did to win the championship?

The boys basketball coach before Barrette, BCHS principal Pete Wininger, had a couple of very good teams—and All-State talent—that just couldn't get over the hump in tournament time, making the feat Barrette and his crew accomplished even more impressive.

"So I think there's a lot of factors that make it nearly impossible," said Wininger. "These kids have been together for the last three years—two of which were kind of taken away from them in terms of the tournament standpoint."

"So to string together the number of wins that he did and to handle all the pressure throughout, with a target on your back and the biggest kid and the best player in the state, to be able to handle that pressure and for our kids to handle that, it's just a credit to Barrette."

"Coach Barrette has been able to manage these kids, kept them focus, their eyes on the prize ahead. They always set goals, focused on them, met them and here we are."

"It's a tremendous credit to [Barrette], his staff, the school community, and players and especially their parents. It's a phenomenal group."

And to pull off that feat against a John Mirabella-coached team—one of the best coaches and mentors in the state—puts Barrette and that victory into another realm. The Northwest Catholic coach has seen it all and to plan against a genius, and program like that, is nearly difficult. But as BCHS boys basketball proved over 43 straight games, anything is possible.

"But you have to be the best to beat the best and we've shown that this year."

***

Which of the two state titlists from Bristol Central had an easier path to the championship?

The 1989-90 squad or the most recent edition?

The two teams were completely different as one star (Malcolm Huckaby) was an All-State guard while in 2021-22, the Rams had a giant hovering in the paint (Donovan Clingan).

The Rams of 1989-90 won their championship against St. Joseph in the final seconds, squaring up an amazing 66-65 victory at CCSU while the last squad spun Northwest Catholic by twenty. Both programs had invisible bullseyes on their backs, and each could have been knocked off in the semifinal round of their respective runs to the championship.

In 1990 Huckaby was joined by Lonnie Brooks and Rod Hickey and the Rams were pushed to the brink in a semifinal showdown as well. On March 14, 1990, the top-ranked Rams had their hands full against No. 12 Warren Harding in a Class L semifinal from Quinnipiac College. The Rams never trailed in the showdown but led just 37-31 at the half and had to fend off Harding over thirty-two brutal minutes.

Central led by 18 in the closing moments of the third period but off a late run, Harding was trailing by just four points with 2:30 to play. Brooks dropped in 24 points while Huckaby contributed a triple-double (23 points, 12 rebounds, and 12 assists. Hickey collected a double-double of 15 points and 14 rebounds, Greg Fradette notched nine points, and Duane Salgado added six for the Rams. Harding bounced back to win the Class L title in 1991 (75-61 over New Milford) and twice more after that as well.

In Central's semifinal battle in 2022 against Wilton, the contest wasn't any kind of picnic in the least. Wilton led by four points midway through the second period but that advantage evaporated as a 20-4 Central burst, finished off by a lay-up from Victor Rosa, saw Central up 32-20 with 3:13

remaining in the third quarter. That 12-point cushion would not be enough, however.

Wilton ended regulation with a 25-13 run and just missed out on a four-point play that would have stolen the lead away from Central late with less than a minute to play in the fourth. throws later, Central punched its ticket to the Mohegan Sun Arena off the two-point win.

***

The biggest benefit of Central's schedule of doom was being able to play a game earlier in the season from Mohegan Sun Arena against East Catholic.

Getting to compete on the floor was a huge deal and crushing the Eagles by a 74-59 score was important. Plus, the Rams were looking forward to the challenge and wanted not just to be there but to win it all.

"We weren't nervous," said Barrette. "My guys were excited to be here, and it was part of the program. I can't say enough about that."

Ironically, while just about every scholastic program in the state had trouble against East and Northwest Catholic, Central did not—beating both programs at Mohegan by a *combined* thirty-five points.

Speaking of Mohegan, Northwest deserved a ton of credit because the squad did just enough to muck things up on the court.

At the half of the Division II championship tilt, it was just a 22-20 game in Central's favor.

But there wouldn't be any blistering speech from Barrette (or kicking of a garbage can or locker) at halftime.

"Here's the good thing about seniors. My halftime speech, there was no yelling," explained Barrette. "There was confidence. We were 0-for-11 from three at one point. We hadn't shot free throws well. [Donovan Clingan] was 3-for-10 from the field in the first half and we're winning by two. It could only get better. We continued to play defense. We held them to 20 [points] in the first half. After that, holding them to 16 points in the second half, how do you beat that?"

And that had a lot to do with the combined defenses of Rosa and Rivoira on NWC star Matt Curtis.

Curtis managed to score 15 points but missed 13 of 18 field goals along the way.

Rosa and Rivoira became experts at frustrating opposing scorers all year.

When Rivoira had that gleam in his eye, it was like back in the day when Frank Purdue was looking at a chicken.

"Victor and Carson did an amazing job on Matt, holding him down to very little points," said Clingan of his teammates and friends. "I just couldn't be prouder of my guys."

Barrette also gave the future UConn football star his due on the defensive end against Curtis.

"What I know about Victor is Victor loves a challenge. He walked in the gym today. He was early. I said, 'Are you ready for the challenge?' He said, 'Coach, I can't wait.' With that being said, he took one of the best players, best guards in the state of Connecticut and made him work for everything he got. And [Curtis] was tired in the fourth. That's why all those shots were short because Victor ran him all over the floor."

Speaking of defense, it wasn't just about containing Curtis.

Central stopped the entire squad in its tracks over second half play as the Lions misfired on 21-of-26 field goals—a 19.2-percent shooting clip from the field.

Now, does defense win championships?

Over at Bristol Central, it does.

"One of the things we wanted to do tonight was out-tough them," said Barrette. "I thought we did that tonight. We made the game physical, we mucked it up and that scoreboard says it enough tonight. We allowed 36 points."

***

Talk is cheap and having a seven-footer on your basketball team doesn't mean a leisurely ride to a state title.

That big man hit the gym at 5 a.m. almost every day to put in the work. But it was Barrette putting in the work as well when "Championship Saturday" was fast approaching.

That work ethic between the All-Stater, the entire Central boys basketball team and the Connecticut Coach of the Year meshed together seamlessly.

"Everyone thought it was easy to coach a seven-footer with all these expectations and I just had expectations [of] we can't lose so the work ethic, I locked myself in a room the other night for seven hours to watch film just to get a better sense even though we played [Northwest] last week," said Barrette. "It's a lot of hard work on my part and their part but it was definitely special."

***

Is Clingan a once in a generation talent? Probably

"Once in a lifetime they said but they also say you better not waste it, and we were lucky enough as a coaching staff to not waste it," said Barrette. "You've got to be able to implement your game plan for thirty-two minutes. I don't know how you do it because that monster [Clingan] eventually is going to get away."

Malcolm Huckaby was also one of those once-in-a-lifetime talents. While Clingan stuck with the once sport in high school, Huckaby was also a talented infielder, and he was good enough to get drafted by Major League Baseball. The third baseman went in the 51st round of the 1990 MLB June Amateur Draft with the Houston Astros.

But Huckaby stuck with basketball and after his time at Boston College (1990-94), he continued on playing. He competed professionally in France, Italy, and in the United States Basketball League with the Portland Mountain Cats, Atlantic City Seagulls, Connecticut Skyhawks and Miami Tropics. Huckaby actually made it to the NBA, suiting up for the Miami Heat in 1996-97 but did not play in a game and was waived before the completion of the season.

***

It's hard to think about the 2021-22 boys basketball campaign over at Bristol Central without mentioning its transfer from Waterbury.

Barrette had Christmas morning made in 2018 when a present under the tree was unwrapped to reveal Donovan Clingan.

And then in 2021, it was Christmas in July.

A summertime present came in the form of Steve Alseph.

Where would the Central program be without him, helping lead the offense and getting his teammates hooked up with the ball at the best possible position?

And that was proven in Central's two biggest wins of the campaign against Wilton and Northwest Catholic.

"You don't run a car without an engine," said Barrette of Alseph. "Donovan could be the car, but Alseph is my engine. [He's] somebody that wants the ball in the last three minutes in the state tournament. He comes off after Damion hits that 3 to end the third [period with Central up by 12] and he says 'guys, it ain't over. Stop smiling. We've got to dig in defensively.' I can't say enough good things about Steve Alseph."

"He's a bulldog and an absolute worker."

The hockey assists, getting in the way of a passing lane that led to someone else getting a steal, and the underrated leadership he displayed 28 times this season for the Rams spoke volumes of his contributions to the squad.

And the 6.3 points, 4.0 rebounds, 4.5 assists and 2.3 steals-per-game don't tell the whole story. Guile and tenacity are tangible skills you can't just pick up playing basketball one day.

"Steve [is] probably the most underappreciated player in the area," said Central assistant coach and stats guru Keith Lipscomb. "His defense is one of the biggest reasons we didn't lose a game."

Everyone knew who four of Central's five starters would be in 2021-22.

But who would be the fifth man? It was the question people were asking around the state.

And when the fifth man was revealed (Barrette told me of Alseph before the season began), the starting unit for the Bristol Central boys basketball program was complete. He was a major reason why the Rams stayed in motion on the court for thirty-two minutes a game and in that championship contest, the senior played without fear.

Alseph collected five points and nine rebounds as he helped Central navigate through a tough first-half of play over its 56-36 victory against the Northwest Catholic. Alseph was a bully on the boards over his final two scholastic games, snagging 19 total rebounds to help keep opponents at bay.

"You saw him mix it up tonight," said Barrette of Alseph in the championship game. "That man was battling inside because Steve Alseph will win at all costs."

His work on the offensive glass over those two final encounters was just as impressive as the rest of his game. Alseph grabbed a combined seven offensive rebounds during Central's showdowns against Wilton and Northwest Catholic.

Offensively, he drained 17 three-pointers—second on the team—and scored a season-high 13 points when Central rolled Enfield to the tune of 91 points. And in his only season for the Rams, the likeable Alseph made a lot of friends, and fans.

***

Wininger Graduates

But before Alseph joined the crew, Barrette had a selection of players to choose from for that fifth starting slot.

Central lost its third leading scorer, Sean Wininger (8.2 points-per-game), along with talents like D'Ante Ross and Eli Rodriguez at the end of 2021.

Any one of those graduating seniors would also have helped the Rams win it all.

So who would join Donovan Clingan, Victor Rosa, Damion Glasper, and Carson Rivoira if Sacred Heart had stayed open in Waterbury?

Barrette could have selected several players from the bench:

Julius Powell—Center (2.4 points-per-game in 2021-22). The Rams would have enjoyed a twin-towers like situation with 7-foot-2 and 6-foot-8 big men to deal with. They've tried that before at Central in 1992 (Howse and Anderson). Powell had some really good moments this season when Clingan was in foul trouble. He filled in well at critical times, like that game against East Catholic.

Jayeson VanBeveren—Forward/Center (1.7 ppg). He didn't play a lot of minutes but he probably led the squad in points scored-per-32 minutes. He could shoot with a little range, hitting three threes, and could grab a rebound or two. The Powell/VanBeveren combo both played in 26 of 28 games for Central.

Aaron Brown—Guard. He played in all but six games and could have helped in the opening line-up with scoring and three-point marksmanship. Early in the season, he had some decent scoring totals and filled in when needed.

Tre Blair—Guard. Blair is a pure athlete and truly would have been a major contributor in Central's 1-3-1 defense. He was an excellent back-up guard but was lost midseason due to injury.

However, Barrette found himself with an unlikely transfer student in the form of Alseph and history was made from there.

***

Could Central have dropped 100 points on an opponent that season?

Of course as that squad could have just thrown the ball into Clingan fifty times to watch *him* score 100 all on his own. Or, Barrette could have thrown caution to the wind and played his starters 28-29 minutes a night.

That type of play never works in a Barrette run program, and for the health of players, it was the smart thing to do. Still, Central did go off on a couple of teams, such as Enfield. A couple of Central's opponents did run up some scores. Windsor notched 100 points *four* times over regular season play.

On December 23, 2021, the Warriors belted Hartford Public—a five-win program—for 116 points while dropping 107 in a road triumph at Wethersfield. Those kinds of efforts simply were built to bury teams, but at Central, Barrette got those athletes in and out as quickly as possible. That's not how Barrette's basketball education was put together.

But the fact remained that the squad from Bristol Central could score points in bunches. The Rams tallied 80 points or more six times this year which included a season best 91-point showing against Enfield on January 25.

In four straight midseason games which included games at home versus Middletown, Enfield, and Platt, with the road game at Hartford Public in the mix, Central scored 335 total points for a four-game scoring average of 83.8 points-per-game.

***

In terms of defense, opponents netted somewhere along the lines of 724 fewer points over those 28 games, putting up just 44.3 points-per-game in offense against Central. Clingan blocked or altered opponents' shots by the bunches—keeping some of those offenders out of the paint entirely by the later stages of the game.

Having shots blocked repeatedly is demoralizing. Middletown suffered 16 of them one game, and that doesn't include altered shots.

Defense was key. Southington, Bristol Eastern and Lewis Mills all scored fewer than 30 points in games versus the Rams. Scoring juggernaut Springfield Central tallied just 44 .Four teams lost to the Rams by 44 points or more while Central outscored its four opponents in CIAC Division II play by an average of 17.8 points-per-game with three of those teams losing by 20 points or more.

Out of Central's 28 games, only three of those contests were decided by single digits. Even Wilbur Cross, which forced overtime, ended up losing to the Rams by double figures.-

***

Can a feat like that ever be duplicated?

A simple answer is no as the senior core of Victor Rosa, Damion Glasper, Steve Alseph, Zach Vanasse, Aaron Brown, Jelani Walton, Carson Rivoira, and Donovan Clingan didn't share in a losing endeavor since they were sophomores.

"These seniors should enjoy the four-year ride they were just on," said Barrette of the remarkable run.

On Saturday, February 29, 2020, the Rams were soundly defeated by East Catholic (85-48) in second round CCC Tournament play.

In over two years since that defeat, Central never lost again.

But the Rams' run with Malcolm Huckaby over his last three scholastic seasons was just as fruitful. From 1987-1990, Huckaby and crew went 64-5 overall (92.7 winning percentage) while Clingan's final three campaigns—a couple shortened by the pandemic—was 60-5 (92.3 winning percentage).

After a 17-5 campaign in 2019-20 and then the 15-0 jaunt in 2020-21, Central was going to be the featured team in the state of Connecticut. The Rams saw everyone's 'A' game over 28 contests with some coming down to the wire.

And every team with an unblemished record fell in the end…except Bristol Central before and during state tournament play.

The top seeded squad in Division I, Naugatuck, was undefeated going into the postseason before getting booted by old friend Wilbur Cross (58-50) in second round action on March 10.

And then there were a couple of No. 1 ranked programs in the postseason that fell short of their championship dreams and aspirations.

Kolbe Cathedral lost the Division III title game to No. 3 Daniel Hand, Division IV's top seed Cromwell fell to No. 4 Granby (59-48) in the semifinals and our friends over in Terryville were stopped in second round play in Division V—losing to No. 16 Portland (57-52).

That's what makes Central's run completely remarkable, a jaunt as the No. 1 team from start to finish.

"Only one team gets to walk away saying they didn't lose our last game and we've been lucky to do that two years in a row," said Barrette. "I can't give these kids enough credit. Forty-three straight wins without getting tripped up, that's a major accomplishment."

***

Since defeating Middletown in 2020, Central won 50 of 51 games to close out the 2021-22 campaign with just the CCC loss at East Catholic as the Rams' only blemish.

Then at the backend of that 51-game path of destruction was 43 straight wins.

It's a legacy every other boys basketball team at BCHS can and will be striving for, well, maybe 32 years—the time between state titles at BCHS.

"We've won forty-three games in a row. It says it's routine but it's also a mandate," said Barrette. "And my seniors take control of practice. They make sure the younger guys are doing what's supposed to be done. And when you establish that routine and that culture, that's what's expected [and] you're expected to win."

"I told my guys this year 'you know how to win,'" said Barrette. "These other [teams] that are close with us, they fold in the last four minutes where we excel because we've won forty-three straight. Winning is a culture and something that's learned, and this group did it better than anyone else I've ever had."

***

At the end of the 2006-07 scholastic basketball season in Bristol, none of the three boys programs in town did not qualify for state tournament play. And after a particularly good run by Central coach Pete Wininger, the Rams were on the lookout for a new mentor to lead the program.

Barrette pounced on the opportunity, becoming the new coach for the boys basketball program at BCHS for his first ever varsity job.

"I was 23" years old when I took this job said Barrette. "But all I knew was I wanted my program to be a family. My family is all here in the stands [at the championship game from Mohegan Sun] because we're all one."

Wininger was just a game off of qualifying for the state tournament and the team still had a scoring machine in the form of junior DaQuan Brooks. An underrated passer, Brooks had the tools to lead to the team back to the playoffs and was a talent Barrette was looking forward to coaching.Barrette's first season started off slowly as the team lost 10 of its first 13 games—including a 106-74 home blowout against Bulkeley back on December 21, 2007.

But those setbacks just fueled Barrette and his squad for a second half of the season run.

The squad reeled off seven straight wins, including his first ever victory against Eastern (58-51 on February 20, 2008) to finish the regular season at 10-10.

Ranked 26th in the Class L fray, Central pushed No. 7 Branford to the limit as the Rams fell 57-56 over first round play but showed a glimpse of what a Barrette run program can do as an underdog.

Over the next three campaigns, Central went a combined 15-45, did not qualify for postseason play, but every loss was a learning experience. The program wasn't that far off.

"We would lose a lot of close games," said Barrette of his early days at Central. "We played teams that were much better than us but always held our own for three quarters. We just couldn't finish."

And after the 2010-11 campaign, the Rams have been playing in the postseason—an 11-year streak that culminated in a state championship. He's posted a record of 158-84 (.653) since his last non-playoff team and his squads have been serious state tournament contenders in a number of those outstanding years.

"As a public school, you go through cycles," said Barrette. "I've been on an up-swing for 12 or 13 years. We've been good."

In 2013-14, Central won 20 of 25 games—falling to Class L runner-up Career Magnet in overtime on March 18 from New Britain high school. The third ranked Rams ended up dropping a heartbreaking 66-61 decision in the semifinal game.

A win against Career would have been Barrette's first big state tournament game against Windsor and head coach Ken Smith. That Central team was a talented group. Jake Collins (14.6 points-per-game), Manny Severino (14.4 ppg), Mount Ida bound Joey DeFillippi (11.6 ppg), Landin Rutledge,Ty Hamel, L.J. Johnson, Kyle Pileski, and Devin Francis all helped Central get within earshot of a state title game.

Four seasons later, Donovan Clingan showed up.

"We've been a good sports town for a long time," said Barrette. "We have good athletes. But Bristol is a hard-working town and they really flocked to this team. Yeah, we have Donovan who's a superstar [but] we have guys around him that work hard, even some of the subs that don't play much. [It's] unbelievable."

***

At one point in his career, Barrette was sitting on a .500 winning percentage all-time at Bristol Central at 140-140.

But forty-three straight victories later, Barrette is currently 183-140 for a slick .560 winning percentage and with those 183 victories, Barrette is the winningest boys basketball coach in school history.

***

When the Connecticut High School Coaches Association released its boys basketball All-State teams for the 2021-22 campaign, Donovan Clingan led a very impressive group of student athletes.

The two-time Connecticut Gatorade Player of the Year helped spur the Rams undefeated season as the program went 28-0 overall.

Finally being allowed to play a complete season due to COVID restrictions being lifted, the 7-foot-2 Clingan started all 28 games for Central, pumping in 847 points for an average of 30.3 points-per-game.

Along the way of a brilliant scholastic career, Clingan showed his ever-improving outside touch as he hit a career-high 10 three-pointers over his final season—dropping in 16 overall.

Over 86 career games at Central, Clingan scored 2,268 points—the seventh most in state history—for an average of 26.4 points-per-game.

Eleven players made the Division II All-State team including Northwest Catholic's Matt Curtis and Conard's sophomore sensation Riley Fox.

* * *

DIVISION 2—2021-22 CHSCA All-State Boys Teams

Donovan Clingan, Bristol Central (University of Connecticut)

Matt Curtis, Northwest Catholic (St. Thomas Moore, Fairfield University) According to GameTimeCT's Jeff Jacobs, "Matt Curtis is the best three-level scorer in the CIAC this season. He's probably the best player not named Donovan Clingan." He averaged 23.5 points, 4.5 rebounds, and 3.5 assists-per-game. He was planning on spending a year at St. Thomas Moore before moving onto Fairfield University.

NOTE…Keeping in mind that Curtis scored 15 points in the championship tilt but Damion Glasper also did the same that nullified Curtis's offense.

Riley Fox, Conard (offer from Central Connecticut State University) The 6-foot-5 sophomore dropped a school record 50 points against Bulkeley that season, averaging 24.3 points. 7.3 rebounds and 2.0 assists-per-game. Shot over 50-percent from the field percent from the floor, scoring a single-season school record of 632 points in a season. Marcus Camby started at Conard but then moved on. Will Fox remain at Conard all four scholastic seasons?

Elijah Wilborn, Middletown (South Kent Preparatory School) The 6-foot-8 center had an offer from Siena but will be doing the prep route instead.

Jeyson Slade, Westhill (Albertus Magnus) The 5-foot-8 senior guard averaged 21 points, 6.0 rebounds, and 7.0 assists-per-game.

Kevin Hyzy, Wilton The 6-foot-4 senior guard gave Central fits in Central's Division II semifinal game. He ended up averaging 17.0 points, 5.8 rebounds, 2.5 assists, and 2.6 steals-per-game.

Jayquan Kirkland, Stratford 6-foot-4 senior guard was a 1,000-point scorer for the program.

Jonathan Rivera, Crosby 6-foot-2 senior guard played AAU ball for the New Haven Heat.

Tyson Mobley, Newtown 6-foot-1 junior guard averaged 10.8 points, 3.4 rebounds, 4.1 assists, and 2.0 steals-per-game.

Elijah Parker, Holy Cross 6-foot-3 freshman guard dropped 30 points in a showdown against St. Paul Catholic to open February.

Sean O'Connell, Waterford The ECC forward could do a little of everything. Opened the 2021-22 season with averages of 19.0 points, 10.0 rebounds, and 6.0 assists-per-game.

Central's postseason chances in a Clingan built line-up at Central

Over his career, Clingan had a chance to play in 14 postseason games with the Rams winning 12 of those contests.

It's an incredible ledger and one that breaks down quite nicely.

One of the most interesting facts over those playoff games is that Central never lost a CIAC state tournament game in regulation when Clingan was in the line-up.

Clingan played in a total of five state tournament games (one as a freshman, four as a senior) and dropped just his first one as a first-year player.

That season, Central—ranked 23rd in the CIAC Division III bracket—the Rams traveled to No. 10 New Milford for an epic first round showdown back on March 5, 2019.

The Rams dropped a tough 65-61 decision in overtime as Clingan just ran out of gas—and fouls.

And the Green Wave didn't know what to do against the then 6-foot-10 Clingan as the home team bombed away from three-point territory, struggling the entire game from deep.

Clingan posted a season-high 37 points in that showdown and Damion Glasper's only shot of the game—a contested lay-up—helped tie the contest late to force overtime.

The next season, Central was 16-4 in regular season play—an eight-game improvement—and qualified for CCC Tournament play in 2020.

The Rams, as the seventh seed in the CCC Tournament, defeated No. 10 New Britain 57-50 in first round play on February 27.

Two days later, Central fell to No. 2 East Catholic—the eventual tournament winner—85-48 from the Babe Allen Fieldhouse on the campus of Bulkeley High School.

That was the last time East Catholic defeated a Donovan Clingan team and was the squad's final postseason loss with the seven-footer patrolling the paint.

Central was going to be one of the featured teams in the Division II bracket in 2020—ranked fourth overall—and was scheduled to battle No. 29 Bunnell in first round home match

But COVID stopped the tournament in its tracks, and the postseason was lost for Clingan's middle two seasons.

During the CIAC's playoff experience of 2021, Central ran through three of the top five teams in the state as the fourth seed in the CCC Tournament.

Since Central went undefeated in regular season play, the Rams made up one of the eight teams in the championship bracket.

No. 4 Central started tournament play on March 22 spinning No. 5 Windsor by a 73-59 final and then two days later, Clingan started the game against No.1 Northwest Catholic with two big three-point bombs as the squad from Bristol booted the Lions by a 71-60 final.

That set up a memorable showdown against No. 3 East Catholic on March 26 in Manchester.

Central led by as many as 21 points in regulation but the Eagles made a furious rally to force overtime.

In OT, and Central trailing by one, a missed East Catholic free throw saw the Rams storm down the court as Victor Rosa found Clingan for the game winning hoop as the squad from Bristol won 69-68—seizing its first CCC Tournament title since 2003.

Clingan scooped in 33 points and 26 rebounds over that CCC Tournament championship tilt.

Here's the bracket from the 'Playoff Experience' in 2021:

Championship Bracket

Round 1—March 22

#8 EO Smith 45, #1 NW Catholic 75
 #5 Windsor 59 at #4 Bristol Central 73
 #6 Middletown 40, #3 East Catholic 82
 #7 East Hartford 58, #2 Maloney 57

Semifinals—March 24

Bristol Central 71, Northwest Catholic 60
 East Hartford 38, East Catholic 55

Consolation—March 24

Newington 43, EO Smith 66
 Middletown 62, Maloney 70

Finals—March 26

Bristol Central 69, East Catholic 68 (OT)

***

Checking the Records

Clingan's first season in 2018-19 saw the Central program just qualify for state tournament play.

And the Rams had to scratch and claw to get there.

The team started off 0-4 and never got it back to .500 before the completion of the regular season.

But after that campaign, Central lost just five games over his sophomore, junior, and senior campaigns combined.

Here's the breakdown of Clingan's individual statistics and how the team fared:

Clingan—Freshman Year

Highlights:

*21 points and 18 rebounds per game as Central was 8-13.

*On December 14, 2018, in Clingan's very first scholastic game, Central never got a foothold in the contest against Manchester, falling 88-43.

*No other opponent scored more than 79 the rest of the way.

*After dropping the first game of the Bristol Central Holiday Tournament to Wolcott (72-63) on December 27, the team went .500 the rest of the way.

*Three of those wins were by 11 points or more while the other five victories were by six, eight, eight, one, and nine points—including a 47-39 triumph at Bristol Eastern on January 18, 2019.

*The Rams (ranked 10th in Class L) lost its CIAC Tournament opener to No. 7 New Milford, 65-61, in overtime.

Sophomore Year

*Averaged 24.8 points, 17.2 rebounds and 6.4 blocks per game.

*Central was 17-5, putting together two winning streaks of seven games.

*The Rams lost their opener at Glastonbury (57-37) on December 20 in another one of those tough shooting gyms and were 3-2 after a tough 54-36 setback to New Britain (January 3).

*Central won seven straight from there, defeating Eastern 75-36 on January 24, as the program entered the end of the month at 10-2.

*The Rams then got thumped by Eastern Catholic (70-31) on January 30 but hung around at Windsor to open play in February—falling 75-71.

*From there, Central won seven more in a row which included a 57-50 victory over New Britain in first round play of the CCC Tournament.

*On February 29, the Rams fell at East Catholic, 85-48, but the locals were battle-tested and many saw the program as a dark horse in the CIAC Division II Championships.

*Ranked No. 4 in the CIAC Division II field, the program's battle against No. 29 Bunnell (8-12) was nixed due to COVID.

Junior Year

*Averaged 27.3 points, 17.2 rebounds, 3.1 assists and 5.8 blocks in 2020-21.

*Named the Gatorade Player of the Year in Connecticut as Central was undefeated (15-0).

*Only Avon (78-76) gave Central any kind of run that season and that was due to a huge fourth quarter comeback.

*Twelve of Central's next 13 games were won by at least 13 points with Plainville (64-61 on February 27) the only exception.

*Along the way to the CCC Tournament Championship, Central defeated Windsor, Northwest and East Catholic—all squads ranked in the top-5 of the state, along with the Rams.

*Over that three-pack of CCC games, Clingan roasted those elite CCC teams for a total of 101 points and 79 rebounds.

Senior Year

*Clingan put together one of the most dominant stat-lines over a single season in state history:

*The 7-foot-2 center—again named Gatorade Player of the Year in Connecticut—averaged 30.3 points, 18.4 rebounds, 6.2 blocks and 3.1 assists (hitting 10 three-pointers for good measure) helping the program go 28-0 and brought a state championship back to Bristol Central.

*Out of the 28 games the Rams played in, three games were decided by single digits (at Springfield Central, versus Northwest Catholic in the CCC Tournament, and against No. 4 Wilton in the Division II semifinals) and Central won both overtime challenges.

*Clingan and the senior core left the program on a 43-game winning streak.

***

Clingan's Suitors

The 7-foot-2 center had his choice of NCAA Division I programs to choose from.

The first offer came a couple of days after Clingan attended "Orange Camp" up at Syracuse.

On August 26, 2019, Cuse made an offer to the Bristol Central center, and the following year, Iowa, Georgetown, Providence, UMASS, and UConn (on April 21, 2020) followed suit.

And then it was time to get serious as Clingan was looking for potential landing spots among an amazing field of programs.

UConn, Michigan, Syracuse, Ohio State, Notre Dame, Rutgers, Georgetown, and Providence made his elite eight list—turning away offers from Boston College (where Malcolm Huckaby went), Iona (playing for Rick Pitino?!?), Iowa, Maryland, Michigan State, South Carolina, UMASS, Virginia Tech, Wake Forest, and Yale.

Clingan committed to join UConn on July 2 after completing his official visit to the campus the previous day.

UConn extended a scholarship offer to Clingan in October, and he signed his National Letter of Intent on November 10, 2021.

***

Bristol's State Champions and runners-up in boys basketball

The 2021-22 Bristol Central boys basketball team was the 19th squad from the city to play in a state title game, becoming the tenth team from the Mum City to win a CIAC championship. Here's the complete list of Bristol teams that went to a state title game:

Year   Final Score

1923-24   Hillhouse 32, Bristol High School 16
1926-27   Bristol 27, Hillhouse 13
1927-28   Bristol 22, Harding 17
1928-29   Bristol 22, Hillhouse 16
1931-32   Hillhouse 24, Bristol 20
1932-33   Bristol 23, Hillhouse 21
1933-34   Bristol 35, Bridgeport Central 33
1936-37   Hillhouse 34, Bristol 24
1940-41   Windham 25, Bristol 24
1945-46   Hillhouse 34, Bristol 29
1959-60   Suffield 64, St. Anthony 62
1973-74   St. Paul 71, Hand 70
1974-75   St. Paul 59, Ansonia 38
1980-81   St. Bernard 64, Bristol Eastern 46
1985-86   Harding 54, St. Paul 51
1986-87   Harding 69, Bristol Central 49
1987-88   St. Paul 54, New London 52
1989-90   Bristol Central 66, St. Joseph 65
2021-22   Bristol Central 56, Northwest Catholic 36

***

Connecticut's Boys State Champions (2021-22)

Division I—East Catholic 50, Notre Dame-West Haven 49

Division II—Bristol Central 56, Northwest Catholic 36

Division III—Hand (Madison) 56, Kolbe-Cathedral 39

Division IV—Bloomfield 58, Granby 54

Division V—Windham 62, Sports & Medical Sciences Academy 56

The longest active winning streaks heading into 2022-23

MaxPreps put together a list of the longest winning streaks in the United States at the conclusion of the scholastic season and all of these programs will be taking those tallies into 2022-23.

 Overall, 47 teams will enter next winter with 20 straight victories—including Bristol Central.

To end the winter campaign, three programs in all of the United States have won 40-plus straight games.

Our Lady of the Sacred Heart in Coraopolis, Pennsylvania finished the 2021-22 season with the longest active high school boys basketball win streak in the nation with 68 straight victories.

Second on the list was Weddington of Matthews, North Carolina—winners of 49 straight.

Bristol Central was third.

Central jumped ahead of programs such as Bishop Gorman of Las Vegas, Centerville, Ohio and Avoca Central of Avoca, New York as all three of those programs drew losses before the completion of 2022.

But what about Connecticut's longest winning streak of all time? The Rams would have to stay perfect over the following two seasons or so to surpass the state's record.

Connecticut's longest winning streak of all time was 80 straight victories by Middletown High School from 1975-1978.

And via the MaxPreps' website, the all-time national record for consecutive wins in boys basketball is 159 by Passaic (N.J.) from 1919 to 1925.

Central needs to tally just 116 additional victories in a row to tie the national record. Boy, Coach Barrette and his staff better get right back to work!

Here's that list, courtesy of MaxPreps:

Streak   School

68   Our Lady of the Sacred Heart (Coraopolis, PA

49   Weddington (Matthews, NC)

43   **Bristol Central (Bristol, CT)**

36   Lapwai (ID)

35   Roosevelt (Sioux Falls, SD)

32   Zachary (LA)

32   Annandale (MN)

32   Hayfield (Alexandria, VA)

The Champion of Champions

During the middle of April, MaxPreps put together a list of every state's best championship team of 2022.

And for the state of Connecticut, the entity recognized Bristol Central as the best champ from the Nutmeg State.

Only teams who won a state championships this season were considered.

The best team in each state was determined by overall body of work, including wins against quality opponents, strength of schedule, postseason results and overall record.

Bristol Central was picked over other Connecticut state winners East Catholic (Division I champs), Daniel Hand (Division III), Bloomfield (Division IV), and Windham (Division V).

***

MaxPreps All-America Team

When MaxPreps released its All-American Team, Donovan Clingan made a very exclusive list from Connecticut. The MaxPreps All-America Team has recognized the top high school basketball players in the country for the past 17 years going all the way back to 2006.

658 players from all over the country have made the list since 2006—including the likes of Kevin Durant, James Harden, DeMar DeRozan, Jayson Tatum and countless others. Clingan is only the second player from Connecticut to earn a spot on the list

According to the website, 'selections are based on team success, individual production and local, regional and state honors. Potential at the college and professional level is not a primary consideration.'

Here's the list from Connecticut:

Mustapha Heron—Sacred Heart (Waterbury, 2016)

Donovan Clingan—Bristol Central (Bristol, 2022)

***

MaxPreps All-America Team (2021-22)

Clingan earned another postseason honor, nabbing a spot on MaxPreps All-America Team. Since 2006, MaxPreps put together its list which included future stars such as Zach LaVine, Karl-Anthony Towns, Trae Young, and Andrew   Wiggins.

MaxPreps made selections 'based on team success, individual production and local, regional and state honors from the recently completed season. Potential at the college and professional level is not a primary consideration. Players in post-graduate and non-scholastic programs are not eligible for inclusion.'

Clingan earned a spot on the Honorable Mention Team. Here's the website bio:

Donovan Clingan, Bristol Central (Bristol, Conn.) 7-1 | Senior | Center | CT Piled up 52 points* and 31 rebounds in a single game, averaged 30.3 points, 18.4 rebounds, 6.2 blocks and 3.1 assists to lead Central to its first state title since 1990. Clingan finished his career with 43 consecutive victories and 2,268 points.

* 51 points, one short of the city scoring record held by Mark Noon (St. Paul).

Bristol Central's Boys All-Time Leading Scorers—1,000 Point Club: In Memory of Dennis Hernandez

City Rank/Name	Years	Points	College
1. Donovan Clingan	2018-2022	2,268	UConn
3. Martin Huckaby	1985-1988	1,825	Howard
4. Malcolm Huckaby	1986-1989	1,645	Boston College/Miami Heat
9. DaQuan Brooks	2005-2008	1,313	Western Connecticut State
10. Jeff Salovski	2001-2004	1,269	UMASS/SHU
11. George Benoit	1962-1964	1,246	CCSU (1,088 points)
13. Aaron Hernandez	2004-2006	1,222*	Florida/Pats
14. Jaekwon Spencer	2014-2018	1,196	Nichols College
15. Bruce Kuczenski	1976-1979	1,093	UConn/ Nets/ Pacers/ Sixers
20. Todd Hasler	1976-1978	1,036	Marist
21. D.J. Hernandez	2001-2004	1,033	UConn
22. Deja Dennis	1981-1984	1,024**	

* = Hernandez's name is no longer in the BCHS trophy case for 1,000-point scorers.

** = Dennis played his freshmen and most of his junior seasons at Crosby. BCHS does not recognize him as a 1,000-point scorer for the program.

Bristol Central Box scores: 2021-2022

Game 1—December 18, 2021

Bristol Central Boys Basketball—2021 GHPA High School Basketball Classic

BRISTOL CENTRAL 55, SOUTHINGTON 29

from the Ferris Athletic Central, Trinity College in Hartford

Southington (0-1)   7 15 2 5—29

Bristol Central (1-0)   16 10 10 19—55

SOUTHINGTON (29): Raysean Epps 1 0 2, Ryan Hammarlund 6 0 15, Aiden Buck 1 3 6, Nathan Cofrancesco 0 0 0, Eli Whitehead 0 0 0, Carson Lentini 0 0 0, Dan McGetrick 0 0 0, Senbato Heath 0 0 0, Ian Beierle 0 0 0, Luke Penna 3 0 6. **Totals: 11 3 29.**

BRISTOL CENTRAL (55): Victor Rosa 1 1 3, Damion Glasper 5 6 16, Tre Blair 0 0 0, Steven Alseph 0 0 0, Mason Stokes 1 0 3, Aaron Brown 0 0 0, Carson Rivoira 3 3 9, Donovan Clingan 11 2 24, Julius Powell 0 0 0, Jayeson VanBeveren 0 0 0, Jonmanuel Gomez 0 0 0. **Totals: 21 12 55.**

Three-point field goals: Ryan Hammarlund (S) 3, Aiden Buck (S), Mason Stokes (BC).

Records: Bristol Central 1-0; Southington 0-1.

Game 2—December 20, 2021

Bristol Central Boys Basketball—The Day's Classic

BRISTOL CENTRAL 74, EAST CATHOLIC 59

from Mohegan Sun Arena

Bristol Central (2-0)   19 17 19 19—74

East Catholic (2-1)   14 9 17 17—59

BRISTOL CENTRAL (74): Victor Rosa 1 0 2, Damion Glasper 7 0 19, Steven Alseph 3 1 9, Mason Stokes 1 0 2, Carson Rivoira 3 3 9, Donovan Clingan 11 7 29, Julius Powell 2 0 4. **Totals 28 11 74.**

EAST CATHOLIC (59): Rob Elliot 3 0 6, Luke Reilly 3 4 10, Allyn Wright 3 2 9, Sam Reilly 4 2 11, James Jones 3 0 6, Leondre Sanchez 3 2 8, Matt Morgan 2 0 5, JJ Hay 0 2 2, Preston Fowler 1 0 2. **Totals 22 12 59.**

Three-point goals: Glasper (BC) 5, Alseph (BC) 2, Wright (EC), Morgan (EC), S. Reilly (EC). **Records**: Bristol Central 2-0 overall; East Catholic 1-1.

***

Scholastics sports were shut down right before Christmas due to upticks in COVID.

Game 3—December 28, 2021

Bristol Central Boys Basketball—Holiday Classic

BRISTOL CENTRAL 73, BRISTOL EASTERN 24

from the Charles C. Marsh Gymnasium, Bristol

Bristol Eastern (0-3)   3 7 5 9—24

Bristol Central (3-0)   22 22 22 7—73

BRISTOL EASTERN (24): Nasir Walker-Jenkins 1 0 3, Elijah Borgelin 0 0 0, Lucas Sward 1 0 2, Ben D'Amato 2 0 6, Nate Fries 0 0 0, Preston Guarda 1 0 2, Isaiah Lawrence-Bynum 2 1 5, Cheniel Serrano-Perez 0 0 0, Caleb Molinsky 1 1 3, Dante DePass 0 0 0, Naseem Walker-Jenkins 1 0 3. **Totals: 9 2 24.**

BRISTOL CENTRAL (73): Jaysun Dominquez 0 2 2, Victor Rosa 3 0 6, Mike Allen 0 1 1, Damion Glasper 4 1 10, Tre Blair 0 2 2, Steven Alseph 3 0 6, Zach Vanasse 0 0 0, Mason Stokes 2 0 5, Aaron Brown 0 0 0, Harry Ross 1 0 2, Dylan Brown 0 0 0, Carson Rivoira 1 0 2, Donovan Clingan 11 0 23, Julius Powell 4 0 8, Jayeson VanBeveren 3 0 6. **Totals: 32 9 73.**

Three-Point goals: Nasir Walker-Jenkins (BE), Ben D'Amato (BE) 2, Naseem Walker-Jenkins (BE), Damion Glasper (BC), Mason Stokes (BC), Donovan Clingan (BC).

Records: Bristol Central 3-0 overall; Bristol Eastern 0-3

Game 4—December 30, 2021

Bristol Central Boys Basketball—Holiday Classic Championship

BRISTOL CENTRAL 77, SOUTH WINDSOR 33

from the Charles C. Marsh Gymnasium, Bristol

South Windsor (3-3)   5 13 6 9—33

Bristol Central (4-0)   18 18 22 19—77

SOUTH WINDSOR (33): Hakim Montgomery 2 0 4, Ben Brochu 7 0 19, Ty Casey 0 0 0, Colby Carr 0 0 0, Emeka Okoh 1 0 2, J.P. Dargati 3 1 8, Joey Bemis 0 0 0, Jack Whitlock 0 0 0. **Totals: 13 1 33.**

BRISTOL CENTRAL (77): Victor Rosa 2 0 4, Mike Allen 1 0 2, Damion Glasper 4 1 9, Tre Blair 2 0 4, Steven Alseph 1 2 5, Mason Stokes 2 1 5, Aaron Brown 2 0 4, Dylan Brown 1 0 2, Carson Rivoira 5 0 10, Donovan Clingan 13 0 26, Julius Powell 2 0 4, Jayeson VanBeveren 0 0 0, John Manuel Gomez 1 0 2, Jaysun Dominguez 0 0 0, Zach Vanasse 0 0 0. **Totals: 35 5 77.**

Three-Point goals: Ben Brochu (SW) 5, J.P. Dargati (SW), Damion Glasper (BC), Steven Alseph (BC).

Records: Bristol Central 4-0 overall; South Windsor 3-3

Game 5—January 3, 2022

Bristol Central Boys Basketball—CCC South Game

BRISTOL CENTRAL 81, PLAINVILLE 42

from the Ivan Wood Gymnasium, Plainville

Bristol Central (5-0)   23 16 28 14—81

Plainville (1-5)   13 4 10 15—42

BRISTOL CENTRAL (81): Victor Rosa 1 0 2, Mike Allen 0 0 0, Damion Glasper 8 0 17, Tre Blair 2 0 4, Steven Alseph 2 3 7, Mason Stokes 3 0 8, Aaron Brown 3 0 7, Carson Rivoira 6 1 13, Donovan Clingan 8 0 16, Julius Powell 1 2 4, Jayeson VanBeveren 1 0 2, Jaysun Dominguez 0 0 0, Zach Vanasse 0 1 1, Jelani Walton 0 0 0, Henry Ross 0 0 0. **Totals: 35 7 81.**

PLAINVILLE (42): Roman Lee 0 0 0, George James 1 0 2, Brady Wieczorek 3 0 8, Kevin Rondini 1 0 3, Brennan Staubley 5 2 15, Dylan Brewer 3 1 8, M.J. Bakaysa 0 0 0, Cam Lamothe 2 0 4, Seve Urena 1 0 2. **Totals: 16 3 42.**

Three-point goals: Damion Glasper (BC), Mason Stokes (BC) 2, Aaron Brown (BC), Brady Wieczorek (P) 2, Kevin Rondini (P), Brennan Staubley (P) 3, Dylan Brewer (P).

Records: Bristol Central 5-0, Plainville 1-5.

Game 6—January 10, 2022

Bristol Central Boys Basketball—CCC Interdivisional Game

BRISTOL CENTRAL 69, NEWINGTON 35

from the Charles C. Marsh Gymnasium, Bristol

NEWINGTON (35): Alex Cucuta 0 0 0, Gavin Gray 3 3 9, Freddie Martine 0 2 2, Sebby Baez 0 2 2, Trey Guest 3 1 7, Nick Gagliardi 2 0 5, Adam Alexander 1 0 2, Avery Mickens 2 0 5, Sean Hurley 1 0 2, Nick Kelley 0 1 1. **Totals 12 9 35.**

BRISTOL CENTRAL (69): Jaysun Dominguez 0 2 2, Victor Rosa 2 0 4, Damion Glasper 5 0 10, Tre Blair 1 0 2, Steve Alseph 5 0 11, Mason Stokes 1 0 2, Jelani Walton 2 1 5, Carson Rivoira 0 0 0, Donovan Clingan 14 1 29, Jayeson VanBeveren 1 0 3, Jonmanuel Gomez 0 1 1. **Totals: 31 5 69.**

Three-point goals: Nick Gagliardi (N), Avery Mickens (N), Steve Alseph (BC), Jayeson VanBeveren (BC).

Records: Bristol Central 6-0 overall; Newington 3-4

Game 7—January 12, 2022

Bristol Central Boys Basketball—CCC Interdivisional Game

BRISTOL CENTRAL 70, EAST HARTFORD 47

from the Bernard C. Dandley Memorial Gymnasium, East Hartford

Bristol Central (7-0)   19 19 14 18—70

East Hartford (3-5)   13 9 9 16—47

BRISTOL CENTRAL (70): Victor Rosa 2 0 4, Damion Glasper 1 0 2, Tre Blair 0 0 0, Steven Alseph 2 0 4, Aaron Brown 2 0 4, Jelani Walton 0 0 0, Carson Rivoira 7 1 18, Donovan Clingan 18 3 40, Julius Powell 1 0 2, Jayeson VanBeveren 0 0 0, Mason Stokes 0 0 0. **Totals: 31 4 70.**

EAST HARTFORD (47): Favour Okeke 1 1 4, Eli Serrano 2 0 5, Zander Robinson 7 1 17, Chris Lomax 3 0 7, Dom Laduca 2 0 5, Jaze James 0 0 0, Azeem Indawala 1 0 2, Chris Brown 3 0 7. **Totals: 19 2 47.**

Three-Point goals: Donovan Clingan (BC), Carson Rivoira (BC) 3.

Records: Bristol Central 7-0 overall; East Hartford 3-5.

Game 8—January 14, 2022

Bristol Central Boys Basketball—2022 Hoophall Classic

BRISTOL CENTRAL 53, SPRINGFIELD CENTRAL 44

from Blake Arena at Springfield College

Bristol Central (8-0)   14 18 7 14—53

Springfield Central (4-1) 7 9 12 16—44

BRISTOL CENTRAL (53): Donovan Clingan 10 4 24, Damion Glasper 0 0 0, Victor Rosa 3 0 7, Carson Rivoira 5 0 12, Steven Alseph 3 3 9, Julius Powell 0 1 1, Jayeson VanBeveren 0 0 0, Aaron Brown 0 0 0. **Totals 21 8 53.**

SPRINGFIELD CENTRAL: Joe Griffin Jr. 7 6 20, William Watson 0 2 2, Deavin Reynolds 3 2 9, Antonio Richardson 2 1 5, Josiah Griffin 3 0 6, Jayden Bass 1 0 2. **Totals 16 11 44.**

Three-point goals: Rivoira (BC) 2, Rosa (BC), Reynolds (SC)

Records: Bristol Central 8-0 overall; Springfield Central 4-1.

Game 9—January 17, 2022

Bristol Central Boys Basketball—CCC South Game

BRISTOL CENTRAL 74, MALONEY 30

from the Charles C. Marsh Gymnasium, Bristol

Maloney (2-4) 8 6 10 6—30

Bristol Central (9-0) 21 23 20 10—74

MALONEY (30): Tylee Flowers 1 0 2, Donte Kelly 4 0 10, Tijion Johnson 2 0 4, Tomas Medina 1 0 2, Marquis Ward 2 3 7, Gavin Moorer 1 0 2, Ja'vony De'Leon 1 1 3. **Totals 12 4 30.**

BRISTOL CENTRAL (74): Victor Rosa 1 0 2, Mike Allan 0 1 1, Damion Glasper 3 2 9, Steve Alseph 4 0 9, Zach Vanasse 1 0 3, Aaron Brown 2 1 5, Jelani Walton 2 0 6, Carson Rivoira 3 1 7, Donovan Clingan 12 0 26, Julius Powell 2 0 4, Jayeson VanBeveren 1 0 2. **Totals: 31 5 74.**

Three-point goals: Donte Kelly (M) 2, Damion Glasper (BC), Steve Alseph (BC), Zach Vanasse (BC), Jelani Walton (BC) 2, Donovan Clingan (BC) 2.

Records: Bristol Central 9-0 overall; Maloney 2-4

Game 10—January 18, 2022

Bristol Central Boys Basketball—CCC Interdivisional Game

BRISTOL CENTRAL 80, MIDDLETOWN 50

from the Charles C. Marsh Gymnasium, Bristol

Middletown (3-3)   9 14 11 16—50

Bristol Central (10-0)   23 19 25 13—80

MIDDLETOWN (50): Chace Petgrave 4 0 11, Matt Steuerwald 4 2 12, Tim Vaughters 1 0 2, Omar Gutierrez 1 0 3, Eli Wilborn 2 1 5, Quadir Murphy 1 0 3, Marshall Butler 1 0 2, Addison Brown 0 1 1, Nasir McDaniel-Cade 2 0 5, Justice Freeman 1 0 2, Branden Torres 2 0 4. **Totals: 19 4 50.**

BRISTOL CENTRAL (80): Victor Rosa 3 1 7, Mike Allen 0 0 0, Damion Glasper 6 4 17, Tre Blair 0 0 0, Steven Alseph 5 0 12, Zach Vanasse 2 0 5, Mason Stokes 0 0 0, Aaron Brown 1 0 3, Carson Rivoira 4 0 11, Donovan Clingan 8 3 19, Julius Powell 2 0 4, Jayeson VanBeveren 0 0 0, Jelani Walton 1 0 2. **Totals: 32 8 80.**

Three-point goals: Chace Petgrave (M) 3, Matt Steuerwald (M) 2, Omar Gutierrez (M), Quadir Murphy (M), Nasir McDaniel-Cade (M), Damion Glasper (BC), Aaron Brown (BC), Steph Alseph (BC) 2, Zach Vanasse (BC), Carson Rivoira (BC) 3.

Records: Bristol Central 10-0 overall; Middletown 3-3

Game 11—January 25, 2022

Bristol Central Boys Basketball—CCC Interdivisional Game

BRISTOL CENTRAL 91, ENFIELD 63

from the Charles C. Marsh Gymnasium, Bristol

Enfield (3-8)   6 18 18 21—63

Bristol Central (11-0)   25 22 28 16—91

ENFIELD (63): Kaden Birkett 4 0 8, Josiah Whaley 2 0 5, Fritz-Carly Andre 2 5 9, Isaiah Plummer 4 0 11, Joel Schmidt 1 0 3, Josiah Upson 0 1 1, Justin Paoletta 2 0 5, Alex Herron 4 0 8, Tighe Thebodeau 3 2 11, Jason Mahon 0 2 2. **Totals: 22 10 63.**

BRISTOL CENTRAL (91): Victor Rosa 3 0 6, Mike Allan 1 0 2, Damion Glasper 5 6 18, Tre Blair 1 2 4, Steven Alseph 5 2 13, Zach Vanasse 0 0 0, Mason Stokes 2 0 4, Carson Rivoira 2 2 6, Donovan Clingan 11 2 25, Julius Powell 1 0 2, Jayeson VanBeveren 2 0 5, Jelani Walton 2 0 4, Harry Ross 1 0 2, Jayson Dominguez 0 0 0, Jonmanuel Gomez 0 0 0. **Totals: 36 14 91.**

Three-point goals: Josiah Whaley (E), Isaiah Plummer (E) 3, Joel Schmidt (E), Justin Paoletta (E), Tighe Thebodeau (E) 3, Damion Glasper (BC) 2, Steven Alseph (BC), Jayeson VanBeveren (BC), Donovan Clingan (BC).

Records: Bristol Central 11-0 overall; Enfield 3-8.

Game 12—January 27, 2022

Bristol Central Boys Basketball—CCC Interdivisional Game

BRISTOL CENTRAL 85, HARTFORD PUBLIC 71

from the Fieldhouse at Hartford Public

Bristol Central (12-0)   26 22 23 14—85

Hartford Public (not 12-0) 14 13 18 26—71

BRISTOL CENTRAL (85): Donovan Clingan 13 5 31, Mike Allan 0 1 1, Steve Alseph 3 2 9, Victor Rosa 3 0 6, Mason Stokes 0 0 0, Carson Rivoira 3 1 7, Julius Powell 4 0 8, Damion Glasper 6 1 14, Jelani Walton 1 0 2, Zach Vanasse 0 0 0, Aaron Brown 0 0 0, Jayeson VanBeveren 3 1 7, Jonmanuel Gomez 0 0 0. **Totals 36 11 85.**

Three-point goals: Glasper (BC), Alseph (BC).

Records: Bristol Central 12-0 overall; Hartford Public 2-7.

Game 13—January 31, 2022

Bristol Central Boys Basketball—CCC South Game

BRISTOL CENTRAL 79, PLATT 48

from the Thomas M. Monahan Gymnasium

Bristol Central (13-0)   25 22 23 9—79

Platt (9-4)   16 3 14 15—48

PLATT (48): Makhai Anderson 4 0 10, Anthony Nimani 9 3 22, Juan Dancy 3 0 7, Justin Black 2 1 7, Elijah Rodriguez 1 0 2, Deante Torres 0 0 0, Nelson Rondon 0 0 0, John Rivera 0 0 0, Josh Day 0 0 0, Kamani Johnson 0 0 0, RayQuan Bradshaw 0 0 0, Sam Quinn 0 0 0. **Totals 19 4 48.**

BRISTOL CENTRAL (79): Donovan Clingan 21 4 47, Mike Allan 0 0 0, Carmelo Thompson 0 0 0, Mikey McMahon 0 0 0, Steve Alseph 0 0 0, Victor Rosa 4 0 9, Mason Stokes 0 1 1, Carson Rivoira 2 1 5, Julius Powell 1 0 2, Damion Glasper 4 0 10, Jelani Walton 1 0 2, Zach Vanasse 1 0 2, Harry Ross 0 1 1, Aaron Brown 0 0 0, Jayeson VanBeveren 0 0 0, Jonmanuel Gomez 0 0 0. **Totals 34 7 79.**

Three-point goals: Anderson (P) 2, Black (P) 2, Dancy (P), Nimani (P),

Glasper (BC) 2, Rosa (BC), Clingan (BC).

Records: Bristol Central 13-0 overall; Platt 9-4.

Game 14—February 2, 2022

Bristol Central Boys Basketball—Sixth Annual Robert Saulsbury Invitational

BRISTOL CENTRAL 71, WILBUR CROSS 59 (OT)

from the Floyd Little Athletic Center, New Haven

Bristol Central (14-0)   15 14 20 10 12—71

Wilbur Cross (8-6)   12 23 7 17 0—59

BRISTOL CENTRAL (71): Victor Rosa 3 0 7, Damion Glasper 6 7 21, Steve Alseph 3 1 7, Carson Rivoira 3 1 7, Donovan Clingan 12 5 29, Julius Powell 0 0 0. **Totals 27 14 71.**

WILBUR CROSS (59): Jamal Lee 3 0 6, Elijah Guillaume 1 1 3, Camar'ee Williams 7 0 15, Christian McClease 7 2 17, Fredo Delgado 6 0 18. **Totals 18 3-6 59.**

Three-point goals: Delgado (WC) 6, Williams (WC), McClease (WC), Glasper (BC) 2, Rosa (BC).

Records: Bristol Central 14-0 overall; Wilbur Cross 8-6.

Game 15—February 8, 2022

Bristol Central Boys Basketball—CCC South Game

BRISTOL CENTRAL 68, LEWIS MILLS 40

from the Thunderdome on the campus of Lewis Mills, Burlington

Bristol Central (15-0)   22   18   18   10—68
Lewis Mills (6-8)   11 10 8 11—40

BRISTOL CENTRAL (68): Victor Rosa 2 0 4, Michael Allan 1 0 2, Damion Glasper 2 0 4, Steven Alseph 2 0 4, Mason Stokes 0 0 0, Aaron Brown 1 0 2, Harry Ross 0 0 0, Jelani Walton 0 0 0, Carson Rivoira 6 0 12, Donovan Clingan 15 3 34, Julius Powell 2 0 4, Jayeson VanBeveren 1 0 2, Zach Vanasse 0 0 0. **Totals: 32 3 68.**
LEWIS MILLS (40): Brice Waldron 1 0 2, Colby Cables 4 0 9, Logan Cowger 0 0 0, Ryan Mayes 0 0 0, Jon Schibi 5 0 15, Jack Stanislaw 1 0 2, Connor McAtee 1 0 3, Jacob Hall 1 0 2, Charlie Joiner 1 0 2, Connor Evans 2 0 5, Eli Pelletier 0 0 0. **Totals: 16 0 40.**

Three-point goals: Clingan (BC), Schibi (LM) 5, Cables (LM), McAtee (LM), Evans (LM).

Records: Bristol Central 15-0 overall; Lewis Mills 6-8.

Game 16—February 10, 2022

Bristol Central Boys Basketball—CCC Interdivisional Game

BRISTOL CENTRAL 83, WINDSOR 67

from the Charles C. Marsh Gymnasium, Bristol

Windsor (12-3)   17 11 16 18—67

Bristol Central (16-0) 19 23 22 17—83

WINDSOR (67): Jakeel Martin 2 0 4, Tyler Betsey 6 5 19, Rashawn Tibby 3 0 8, Prince Samuel 5 1 12, Raymond Rodriguez 3 0 7, Quintin Floyd 3 0 7, Jon Stapleton-Georges 1 2 4, Johnny Pierce 1 0 2, Anthony Williams 1 0 2, Kaiden James 1 0 2. **Totals 26 8 67.**

BRISTOL CENTRAL (83): Victor Rosa 5 0 12, Carson Rivoira 1 0 2, Julius Powell 0 0 0, Donovan Clingan 23 5 51, Damion Glasper 4 2 10, Steven Alseph 2 0 5, Jayeson VanBeveren 1 0 3, Mike Allan 0 0 0, Zach Vanasse 0 0 0, Mason Stokes 0 0 0, Aaron Brown 0 0 0, Jelani Walton 0 0 0. **Totals 36 7 83**

Three-Point goals: Tibby (W) 2, Samuel (W), Floyd (W), Betsey (W) 2, Rodriguez (W), Alseph (BC), Rosa (BC) 2, VanBeveren (BC).

Records: Bristol Central 16-0 overall; Windsor 12-3.

Game 17—February 12, 2022

Bristol Central Boys Basketball—CCC South Game

BRISTOL CENTRAL 54, BERLIN 33

from the Charles C. Marsh Gymnasium, Bristol

Berlin (11-5)   7 6 4 16—33

Bristol Central (17-0) 13 9 18 14—54

BERLIN (33): Marino Fanelli 4 0 12, Mike Ciarcia 0 0 0, Toby Lavender 0 0 0, Zach Skinner 3 2 9, Jake Smalley 3 0 8, Kyle Hyde 0 0 0, Tanner Sparks 0 0 0, River Eberhardt 1 1 4. Ryan Stec 0 0 0, Jonathan D'Amore 0 0 0. **Totals 11 3 33.**

BRISTOL CENTRAL (54): Victor Rosa 2 0 5, Carson Rivoira 6 0 12, Julius Powell 0 0 0, Donovan Clingan 13 1 27, Damion Glasper 2 0 5, Steve Alseph 0 0 0, Jayeson VanBeveren 0 0 0, Mike Allan 0 0 0, Zach Vanasse 1 0 3, Mason Stokes 0 0 0, Aaron Brown 0 0 0, Jelani Walton 0 0 0, Carmelo Thompson 1 0 2. **Totals: 25 1 54.**

Three-Point goals: Fanelli (Berlin) 4, Skinner (Berlin), Smalley (Berlin) 2, Eberhardt (Berlin), Rosa (BC), Glasper (BC), Zach Vanasse 9BC0.

Records: Bristol Central 17-0 overall; Berlin 11-5.

Game 18—February 15, 2022

Bristol Central Boys Basketball—CCC South Game

BRISTOL CENTRAL 80, MIDDLETOWN 34

from the LaBella-Sullivan Gymnasium at Middletown High School

Bristol Central (18-0)   21 25 20 14—80

Middletown (11-6)   6 10 13 5—34

BRISTOL CENTRAL (80): Victor Rosa 4 0 8, Damion Glasper 1 1 4, Steve Alseph 1 0 2, Carson Rivoira 5 3 15, Donovan Clingan 12 8 32, Zach Vanasse 2 0 6, Jaysun Dominguez 1 0 2, Mike Allan 0 0 0, Aaron Brown 2 0 4, Julius Powell 1 0 2, Jonmanuel Gomez 0 0 0, Jayeson VanBeveren 0 0 0. **Totals: 31 13 80.**

MIDDLETOWN (34): Chace Petgrave 0 0 0, Matt Steuerwald 0 1 1, Tim Vaughters 3 1 7, Omar Gutierrez 1 0 2, Marshall Butler 2 0 4, Nasir McDaniel 4 1 9, Quadir Murphy 1 0 2, Caiden Byrd 1 0 3, Adison Brown 2 0 5, Justice Freeman 0 0 0, Brandon Torres 0 1 1, Quincy Rhodes 0 0 0, Dariyon Drake 0 0 0, Teejay Jackson 0 0 0 0. Totals: 14 4 34.

Three-point goals: Rivoira (BC) 2, Vanasse (BC) 2, Glasper (BC), Byrd (M), Brown (M).

Records: Bristol Central 18-0 overall; Middletown 11-6.

Game 19—February 18, 2022

Bristol Central Boys Basketball—CCC South Game

BRISTOL CENTRAL 68, MALONEY 30

from Howie Hewitt Court at Francis T. Maloney High School

Bristol Central (19-0) 21 22 12 13—68

Maloney (6-12)   0 4 14 12—30

BRISTOL CENTRAL (68): Donovan Clingan 10 1 22, Mike Allan 0 0 0, Carmelo Thompson 0 1 1, Steve Alseph 2 0 5, Victor Rosa 2 0 5, Carson Rivoira 3 0 6, Julius Powell 2 0 4, Damion Glasper 4 0 9, Jelani Walton 3 0 7, Zach Vanasse 0 0 0, Harry Ross 0 0 0, Aaron Brown 1 0 2, Jayeson VanBeveren 1 0 2, Jonmanuel Gomez 1 0 2, Mikey McMahon 1 0 3, Jaysun Dominguez 0 0 0. **Totals 30 2 68.**

Three-point goals: Clingan (BC), Glasper (BC), Rosa (BC), McMahon (BC), Alseph (BC), Walton (BC).

Records: Bristol Central 19-0 overall; Maloney 6-12

Game 20—February 21, 2022*

Bristol Central Boys Basketball—CCC South Game

BRISTOL CENTRAL 76, BRISTOL EASTERN 50

from the Thomas M. Monahan Gymnasium, Bristol

Bristol Central (20-0)   23 21 19 13—76

Bristol Eastern (4-16)   11 5 9 25—50

BRISTOL CENTRAL (76): Victor Rosa 3 0 8, Mike Allan 0 0 0, Damion Glasper 2 0 5, Tre Steve Alseph 3 0 6, Zach Vanasse 1 0 3, Mason Stokes 0 0 0, Aaron Brown 0 0 0, Harry Ross 0 1 1, Carmelo Thompson 2 0 6, Jelani Walton 0 0 0, Carson Rivoira 1 0 2, Mikey McMahon 0 0 0, Donovan Clingan 14 3 31, Julius Powell 4 0 8, Jayeson VanBeveren 3 0 6, Jonmanuel Gomez 0 0 0. **Totals: 33 4 76.**

BRISTOL EASTERN (50): Elijah Borgelin 1 0 2, Lukas Sward 6 1 16, Brayden Dauphinais 1 4 7, Ben D'Amato 1 0 3, Nate Fries 1 1 4, Isaiah Lawrence-Bynum 3 2 8, Cheniel Serrano 0 0 0, Caleb Molinsky 0 0 0, Dante DePass 0 0 0, Jerry Tatum 2 3 7, Zaveyn Tate 0 0 0, Xavier Kalanquin 1 0 2, Jordan Chisholm 0 0 0, Brady Bell 0 1 1. **Totals: 16 12 50.**

Three-Point goals: Victor Rosa (BC) 2, Damion Glasper (BC), Zach Vanasse (BC), Carmelo Thompson (BC) 2, Lukas Sward (BE) 3, Brayden Dauphinais (BE), Ben D'Amato (BE), Nate Fries (BE).

Records: Bristol Central 20-0 overall; Bristol Eastern 4-16.

Bristol Central Boys Basketball—Central CT Conference Tournament

Game 21—February 24, 2022

2022 CCC Boys Basketball Tournament—Round One Game

No. 1 BRISTOL CENTRAL 66, No. 16 LEWIS MILLS 29

from the Charles C. Marsh Gymnasium, Bristol

Lewis Mills (11-10)   9 8 5 7—29

Bristol Central (21-0)   21 15 22 8—66

LEWIS MILLS (29): Brice Waldron 1 0 2, Colby Cables 1 0 2, Ryan Mayes 0 0 0, Jon Schibi 3 0 8, Jack Stanislaw 0 0 0, Jacob Hall 1 0 2, Charlie Joiner 1 0 2, Connor Evans 3 0 8, Eli Pelletier 1 0 3, Logan Cowger 1 0 2, Tristan Mooney 0 0 0, Gavin Daly 0 0 0, Jack Nestor 0 0 0. **Totals: 12 0 29.**

BRISTOL CENTRAL (66): Victor Rosa 0 0 0, Michael Allan 0 0 0, Damion Glasper 7 0 21, Tre Blair 0 0 0, Steve Alseph 2 0 4, Zach Vanasse 0 0 0, Mason Stokes 1 0 2, Aaron Brown 1 0 2, Harry Ross 0 0 0, Jelani Walton 0 0 0, Carson Rivoira 3 0 6, Donovan Clingan 12 1 25, Julius Powell 0 0 0, Jayeson VanBeveren 3 0 6, Carmelo Thompson 0 0 0. **Totals: 29 1 66.**

Three-point goals: Evans (LM) 2, Pelletier (LM), Schibi (LM), Glasper (BC) 7.

Records: Bristol Central 21-0 overall; Lewis Mills 11-10.

Game 22—February 26, 2022

2022 CCC Boys Basketball Tournament—Quarterfinal Round Game

No. 1 BRISTOL CENTRAL 73, No. 8 MIDDLETOWN 58

from Enfield high school

Middletown (15-7)   16 3 20 19—58

Bristol Central (22-0)   11 19 19 24—73

MIDDLETOWN (58): Chance Petgrave 4 0 9, Matt Steuerwald 7 0 15, Tim Vaughters 2 0 4, Omar Gutierrez 0 0 0, Elijah Wilborn 2 2 6, Marshall Butler 6 0 14, Nasir McDaniel 3 0 7, Dariyon Drake 1 0 3. **Totals: 25 2 58.**

BRISTOL CENTRAL (73): Victor Rosa 1 4 7, Michael Allan 0 0 0, Damion Glasper 4 6 14, Tre Blair 0 0 0, Steve Alseph 2 5 9, Mason Stokes 0 0 0, Aaron Brown 0 0 0, Jelani Walton 0 0 0, Carson Rivoira 2 0 5, Donovan Clingan 16 5 38, Julius Powell 0 0 0, Jayeson VanBeveren 0 0 0. **Totals: 25 20 73.**

Three-point goals: Petgrave (M), Steuerwald (M), Butler (M) 2, McDaniel (M), Drake (M), Rosa (BC), Rivoira (BC), Clingan (BC).

Records: Bristol Central 22-0 overall; Middletown 15-7.

Game 23—March 1, 2022

2022 CCC Boys Basketball Tournament—Semifinal Round Game

No. 1 BRISTOL CENTRAL 57, No. 4 WINDSOR 37

from Enfield high school

Windsor (18-4)   11 11 11 4—37

Bristol Central (23-0)   14 16 8 19—57

WINDSOR (37): Tyler Betsey 9 0 20, Rashawn Tibby 1 0 2, Prince Samuel 0 2 2, Raymond Rodriguez 2 0 4, Quintin Floyd 2 2 7, Johnny Pierce 1 0 2. **Totals: 15 4 37.**

BRISTOL CENTRAL (73): Victor Rosa 1 0 2, Damion Glasper 5 1 14, Steve Alseph 4 0 9, Carson Rivoira 2 0 4, Donovan Clingan 12 4 28, Julius Powell 0 0 0, Jayeson VanBeveren 0 0 0. **Totals: 24 5 57.**

Three-point goals: Betsey (W) 2, Floyd (W), Glasper (BC) 3 Alseph (BC).

Records: Bristol Central 23-0 overall; Windsor 18-4.

Game 24—March 3, 2022*

2022 CCC Boys Basketball Tournament—Championship Game

No. 1 BRISTOL CENTRAL 63, No. 2 NORTHWEST CATHOLIC 56

from Enfield high school

Northwest Catholic (22-2) 14 12 15 15—56

Bristol Central (24-0)   19 11 16 17—63

NORTHWEST CATHOLIC (56): Jehyvic Spencer 1 0 3, London Jemison 3 0 6, Gianni Mirabello 3 0 8, Matt Curtis 12 3 28, Hayden Abdullah 1 0 2, Badara Diakite 2 0 6, Tanner Ostop 1 0 3. **Totals**: 23 3 56.

BRISTOL CENTRAL (63): Victor Rosa 0 1 1, Damion Glasper 3 0 7, Steve Alseph 1 0 3, Carson Rivoira 3 0 7, Donovan Clingan 22 1 45. **Totals: 29 2 63.**

Three-point goals: Diakite (NWC) 2, Curtis (NWC), Mirabello (NWC) 2, Spencer (NWC), Ostop (NWC), Glasper (BC), Alseph (BC), Rivoira (BC).

Records: Bristol Central 24-0 overall; Northwest Catholic 22-2.

***The 2021-22 Bristol Central Boys Basketball Team won the CCC Tournament Championship for the second straight year.**

CIAC Boys Basketball Postseason—CIAC Division II Tournament

Game 25—March 10, 2022

2022 CIAC Boys Basketball Tournament—Division II, Second Round

No. 1 BRISTOL CENTRAL 65, No. 16 AMISTAD 38

from the Charles C. Marsh Gymnasium, Bristol

Amistad (14-8)   5 16 13 4—38

Bristol Central (25-0) 17 17 20 11—65

AMISTAD (38): Rodney Cook 2 0 4, Bernett Scott 0 0 0, Arion Robinson 4 2 12, Brandon Hicks 2 0 6, Aden Goffe 4 2 12, T'hmiri Reddick-Gist 0 2 2, Eveyon Pearse 1 0 2. **Totals: 13 6 38.**

BRISTOL CENTRAL (65): Victor Rosa 2 0 5, Damion Glasper 4 0 10, Steve Alseph 4 0 9, Carson Rivoira 7 0 14, Donovan Clingan 12 2 26, Julius Powell 0 0 0, Jayeson VanBeveren 0 0 0, Aaron Brown 0 1 1, Tre Blair 0 0 0, Zack Vanasse 0 0 0. **Totals: 29 3 65.**

Three-point goals: Robinson (A) 2, Hicks (A), Goffe (A) 2, Glasper (BC) 2, Rosa (BC), Alseph (BC).

Records: Bristol Central 25-0 overall; Amistad 14-8.

Game 26—March 11, 2022

2022 CIAC Boys Basketball Tournament—Division II, Quarterfinal Round

No. 1 BRISTOL CENTRAL 70, No. 8 WATERFORD 48

from the Charles C. Marsh Gymnasium, Bristol

Waterford (19-7)   14 11 8 15—48

Bristol Central (26-0) 16 15 23 16—70

WATERFORD (48): Juan Morel 4 0 8, Jordan Elci 4 0 9, Evan Piotrowski 0 1 1, Evan McCue 3 0 8, Sean O'Connell 4 4 12, Patrick Barrs 0 2 2, Logan Peabody 2 3 8. **Totals: 17 10 48.**

BRISTOL CENTRAL (70): Donovan Clingan 19 6 45, Victor Rosa 2 0 4, Carson Rivoira 4 1 9, Damion Glasper 2 0 4, Steven Alseph 3 0 8, Julius Powell 0 0 0, Jayeson VanBeveren 0 0 0, Aaron Brown 0 0 0, Tre Blair 0 0 0, Zack Vanasse 0 0 0, Jelani Walton 0 0 0. **Totals: 30 7 70.**

Three-point goals: Elci (W), McCue (W) 2, Peabody (W), Clingan (BC), Alseph (BC) 2.

Records: Bristol Central 26-0 overall, Waterford 19-7.

Game 27—March 15, 2022

2022 CIAC Boys Basketball Tournament—Division II, Semifinals

No. 1 BRISTOL CENTRAL 54, No. 4 WILTON 52 (OT)

from the Floyd Little Athletic Center, New Haven

Wilton (21-5)   8 8 9 20 7—52

Bristol Central (27-0)   8 11 14 12 9—54

WILTON (52): Zarius Eusebe 2 2 6, Tommy McKiernan 5 0 15, Parker Woodring 6 0 13, Kevin Hyzy 4 0 11, Max Andrews 1 0 2, Craig Hyzy 1 0 3, Max Silva 1 0 2. **Totals 20 2 52.**

BRISTOL CENTRAL (54): Victor Rosa 2 0 5, Damion Glasper 4 3 12, Steve Alseph 1 4 7, Donovan Clingan 7 16 30, Carson Rivoira 0 0 0, Tre Blair 0 0 0, Jayeson VanBeveren 0 0 0. **Totals 20 23 54.**

Three-point goals: McKiernan (W) 5, Woodring (W), K. Hyzy (W) 3, C. Hyzy (W), Rosa (BC), Glasper (BC), Alseph (BC).

Records: Bristol Central 27-0 overall; Wilton 21-5.

Game 28—March 19, 2022

2022 CIAC Boys Basketball Tournament—Division II Championship

No. 1 BRISTOL CENTRAL 56, No. 2 NORTHWEST CATHOLIC 36*

from Mohegan Sun Arena, Uncasville

| **Northwest Catholic (25-3)** | 10 10 07 09 - 36 |
| **Bristol Central (28-0)** | 10 12 17 17 - 56 |

NORTHWEST CATHOLIC (36): Jehyvic Spencer 1 0 2, London Jemison 2 0 5, Gianni Mirabello 1 0 3, Matt Curtis 5 5 15, Hayden Abdullah 1 0 2, Badara Diakite 3 2 8, Cavin Pollard 0 1 1. **Totals: 18 8 36.**

BRISTOL CENTRAL (56): Donovan Clingan 8 9 25, Victor Rosa 1 0 2, Carson Rivoira 2 2 6, Damion Glasper 4 6 15, Steven Alseph 3 0 6, Julius Powell 0 0 0, Jayeson VanBeveren 0 0 0, Aaron Brown 1 0 2, Tre Blair 0 0 0, Zack Vanasse 0 0 0, Jelani Walton 0 0 0. **Totals: 19 17 56.**

Three-point goals: Mirabello (NWC), Jemison (NWC), Glasper (BC).

Records: Bristol Central 28-0 overall; Northwest Catholic 25-3.